Best Wishes

D1444992

Dreams Precede Realities

A History of the People
Who Have Shaped and Influenced
the First 40 Years of
SOUTH PLAINS COLLEGE
1958-1998

by L. Terry Isaacs

Direct inquiries and/or orders to:
South Plains College Foundation
1401 S. College Ave.
Levelland, Texas 79336
www.spc.cc.tx.us

Inquiries about South Plains College may be directed to:
Office of College Relations
South Plains College
1401 S. College Ave.
Levelland, Texas 79336

South Plains College acknowledges the assistance of Donald L. Cotten who served as a consultant in publishing this volume.
Cotten Publishing Company
P.O. Box 16243
Lubbock, Texas 79490

ISBN 925854-20-4

Printed and bound in the United States of America.

Cover jacket designed by Paul Davidson.

For Nancy, Tera, Gina and Ryan

TABLE OF CONTENTS

ACKNOWLEDGMENTS

The success of South Plains College's first 40 years can be attributed to many individuals within this community. I am indebted to those who shared their thoughts, time and talents to tell SPC's story. Moreover, we, as a community, are indebted to those individuals who had the foresight to persist in their dreams for an institution of higher learning. Their vision has become what Dr. J.R. McLemore of Paris Junior College said in 1959 when he visited SPC: "evidence of one of the finest junior colleges I have ever visited."

It could not have been so without the direction and guidance of many – first, Dr. Weldon Marcom, a true educational pioneer, whose graduate thesis embodied the very idea for SPC. J.G. Stacy, a Levelland businessman, worked tirelessly for the college. Dr. Tom Spencer, SPC's first president; exhibited a commanding presence as an educational leader across the state. Dr. Marvin L. Baker, the president of SPC for 33 years, molded the institution into its premier position among community colleges in Texas. And finally, there are those early administrators and faculty members like Nathan Tubb, Earl Gerstenberger, Bob Burks, Charles Sylvester, W.L. "Hi" Walker, Harley and Anne Bulls, Henry and Myrtle Lucke, Paula Bell, Bob Beck, Sycily Lattimore and Don Stroud. They came to a small community in dusty West Texas and developed an excellent community college. To the many others who contributed to SPC and this history, I send my sincere appreciation.

Stephen John and the College Relations Office continually produce the finest in college publications. The college relations staff worked their technical "magic" in producing this volume. Stephen electronically designed the overall contents of the book. Dianne Whisenand, a 25-year SPC veteran, is one of the unsung champions of South Plains College and helped in reviewing and proofreading this volume. Charles Ehrenfeld researched the section on Texan sports and contributed to its writing. Dan English assisted with collecting and printing the many photographs which fill this book. Paul Davidson designed the book's jacket cover and coordinated the electronic scanning of the photos and art. Once again, their work is exemplary. We are privileged to call them "colleagues."

In addition, I had the honor of working on this project with John Sparks, associate professor of telecommunications. John carried his video equipment through countless airports, buildings and private homes to record our 40-year history. John's meticulous attention to detail is evident in the *Video History of South Plains College*. John's talented use of video, his knowledge of SPC and his wit contributed to a delightful research project.

In addition, I am indebted to those with whom I work each day. President Dr. Gary McDaniel, Academic Vice President Dr. James Taylor, and Arts and Sciences Dean Dr. Otto Schacht provided immeasurable advice and guidance. They, along with Social Science Department Chairperson Travis Spears, gave tremendous support to this project. I am especially indebted to Dr. Ronald Carden, Dr. Randy Rowan, Dr. Mike Felker and Lee Weldon Stephenson. They are excellent teachers, historians, writers and gentlemen who love their profession. They edited this volume, correcting my many errors. Two other men, the late David Randolph Stanley and W.A. Wise, were instrumental in making this story possible. Their wise counsel, compassionate spirits and inspirational legacy continue in the halls of SPC. May it ever be so.

Indeed, it has been delightful examining SPC's history in the *Levelland Daily Sun News*, SPC yearbooks and the Board of Regents' minutes. However, that delight cannot compare with the countless hours of fascinating interviews with those who became a part of South Plains College. Mrs. Tom Spencer provided wonderful insight into the beginning of SPC. Judy Hendrix Schlechten, the first "Miss SPC," beautifully revealed the life of a college freshman in 1959, and Wolfram Von Maszewski, SPC's first foreign student, brought a unique view of the people in Levelland who supported his education. Finally, Judy Bryant, chairperson of the Physical Education Department, and Jeanelle Permenter amazed me with their ability to identify those pictured in the many photographs we used in the book. Barbara Gilley, who served as Dr. Marvin Baker's secretary for more than a decade, was very helpful with this project. René Heard, Dr. McDaniel's secretary, and Stacia Doshier provided tremendous help in compiling the lists of former and current SPC employees which are found in the Appendix.

To these people, and many others, I say thanks for sharing your thoughts and memories for a wonderful experience.

Terry Isaacs, Associate Professor of History, December 1998

INTRODUCTION

*"One of the biggest things Hockley County
could ever do is build a junior college."*
W.A. (Tony) Hunt, Ph.D.

D r. Hunt's admonition to the Levelland Rotary Club in July 1957 came only days before Hockley County voters resoundingly endorsed the building of South Plains College.[1] Now four decades later, SPC has rewarded Levelland, Hockley County and the entire South Plains with a community college of the first order.

The quest for a junior college on the South Plains began with a small group of Levelland citizens who believed the building of a college would expand the educational and cultural horizons for the area's population, as well as provide opportunities for economic development within the county. The college's supporters spanned the social spectrum of Hockley County and the surrounding counties. Those who established the college came from many occupational fields, civic clubs and religious organizations in the area.[2] As they promoted the idea of a college during the early 1950s, they established the framework that would eventually lead to SPC. Before achieving success, however, they first had to overcome

---

[1] In March 1957, "G.C. Brown and 559 other duly qualified resident property taxpaying voters of Hockley County" petitioned the Hockley County Commissioner's Court, "praying that an election be held in and throughout Hockley County, Texas," to establish the college. The Commissioner's Court set the election for April 2, 1957, and results overwhelmingly revealed, 1,577 to 644, the desire for a college in the county. Three months later on July 13, 1957, county voters, by a margin of 856 to 404, voted in favor of $900,000 in bonds to support the new college. In that same election, voters approved a 25-cent maintenance tax to operate the college by an 840 to 418 vote margin. In fact, the college levied a 19-cent tax for bond retirement and a 25-cent tax for maintenance and equipment. Interestingly, the voting totals reported in the *Levelland Daily Sun News* varied slightly from those in the SPC Board of Regents' minutes. The newspaper reported the bond vote as 856 to 414, while the maintenance tax vote was recorded in the *News* as 840 in favor to 428 against.

[2] The Levelland Rotary Club, in large measure, can be given credit for spearheading the drive to establish South Plains College. The noon club's membership consisted of influential business leaders, Levelland public school administrators and the community's health care professionals.

1

The 1956 Chamber of Commerce Board of Directors is largely responsible for rekindling the community's desire to establish a junior college. The board appointed and commissioned the 1956 Citizens Committee to seek approval for a college from the community and the State Board of Education. Board members included (seated left to right) Chamber Director Robert Walker, Gene McDonald, Chamber Secretary Twila Kauffman, Ansil O'Neal, Chamber President J.G. Stacy, Dr. George Payne, Bob Buster, (standing left to right) Bob Shaw, Bill Dison, Bob Reid, Sam Newberry, Bill Hardin, LaVern McCann, Cecil Evans and Howard Vaughn.

ORLIN BREWER, 1956 Citizens Committee Chairman
Levelland Daily Sun News editor Orlin Brewer continually promoted the establishment of a college in his column, "A Day in the Sun." Brewer, a civic-minded and progressive newspaperman, joined with the newspaper's publisher, Forrest Weimhold, to espouse the benefits of South Plains College on the front pages of the daily newspaper. Brewer later became the editor of the *Vernon Daily Record*, in Vernon, Texas. According to former SPC Academic Dean Dr. Bud Joyner, Brewer chaired the Citizens Committee that established Vernon Regional Junior College. Joyner served seven years as dean of students and administrative services at Vernon. "He put the full force of the newspaper behind establishing the college." Joyner recalled Brewer sat at the table with the Board at the Vernon College Regents' meetings. He actively participated in Regents' discussions, something that Brewer had done earlier as editor of the *Levelland Daily Sun News*. Joyner described Brewer as a "dear friend who was the Board's conscience and had as great a love of his community as anyone I've ever seen." Brewer was first and foremost a newspaperman who could be critical, scrutinizing, and yet constructive in his daily column. Brewer, a man who led the movement for establishment of SPC, assumed a similar role at Vernon. His impact certainly played a role in the establishment of that college. When Vernon Regional Junior College was established in 1972, the vote passed by a narrow margin.

2

a major obstacle placed in their path by the State Board of Education in Austin. At a 1951 meeting with Levelland citizens E.M. Barnes, George Broome, Herman Greener, C.M. Sanders, John Potts and Davis Pounds, the board dashed their hopes with a unanimous negative vote on the establishment of a college in Hockley County. The State Board of Higher Education saw little merit in a two-year college on the South Plains of West Texas.

Early proponents initially believed that the state board would view a two-county college district (Hockley-Cochran) proposal more favorably. Although petitions were being circulated in Cochran County in support of the college, the intensity of their desire to establish the college was uncertain.[3] Thus, the original governing body, the Hockley County Junior College District Trustees, voted unanimously to establish the college district within the boundaries of the county and to name the institution South Plains College. They believed the name would reflect a college for the entire West Texas area.

Disappointed but undaunted, the members of the 1951 committee were rewarded six years later when Hockley County voters overwhelmingly endorsed the college and the taxation necessary for its support. What began in July 1957 as a fledgling Hockley County Junior College quickly became a dynamic institution.[4]

This is the story of how a college emerged and grew on the dusty plains of West Texas.[5] It is the story of the people who joined together to create a marvelous educational enterprise. It is the triumph of a determined newspaper pub-

---

[3] Bud Nairn, Jr. carried petitions in the western part of the county eliciting support for the college. In Levelland "it's been a community effort from the beginning, and by that, we don't mean just Levelland. People with vision who live far out in the county have been bucking for the college all along. They've circulated petitions, collected literally hundreds of names, and they've called just about every telephone number in the city in their voluntary get-out-the-vote campaign," according to Orlin Brewer in his daily newspaper column, "A Day in the Sun."

[4] The impact of Forrest Weimhold on Hockley County politics and his influence on the college's establishment cannot be underestimated. Weimhold published the *Levelland Daily Sun News* and owned Levelland's radio station, KLVT. Through his newspaper editor, Orlin Brewer, and radio station manager, Gil Patschke, Weimhold kept the benefits of a college on the front page and in the Hockley County airwaves.

[5] Weldon Marcom's comprehensive master's thesis detailed the need, structure and success a community college would bring to Hockley County. He and other school officials like Walter L. Reed, T.O. Petty, O.R. Watkins and Davis Pounds realized the potential benefits a community college would bring to the South Plains. Although Marcom's Levelland Independent School District Board of Trustees were initially "cool" to the idea of a college, a large majority of Hockley County residents endorsed the idea.

lisher, his editor, a chamber of commerce manager, an insurance agent, a school superintendent and numerous businessmen who persisted in their dreams to change a community. Forty years later, this two-year institution rivals many universities within Texas in student enrollment, educational programs and prestige. Those who dreamed in 1957 of a college in Levelland could not imagine the South Plains College of 1998. The original campus, composed of buildings arranged diagonally on 177 acres of land, has grown to an entity unto itself. Branch campuses at the former Reese Air Force Base, the SPC Lubbock Campus on Main Street and the Byron Martin Advanced Technology Center in Lubbock are testaments to South Plains College's progressive outlook.

J.G. STACY, Levelland Chamber President
Levelland furniture store owner J.G. Stacy supported the establishment of SPC from the early 1950s. In 1956, he served as president of the Chamber of Commerce Board of Directors and was a principal leader in building support for the creation of a junior college in Levelland. As an active member of the Levelland business community, Stacy knew the benefits a college would bring to the area. "We knew the college would expand the area's education and culture and cause this community to grow," said Stacy.

C.M. PHILLIPS, M.D., Levelland Physician
Long-time Levelland physician C.M. Phillips served as chairman of the Hockley County Development Foundation. It was to Phillips that Dr. C.C. Colvert submitted his report, "A Proposal for a South Plains Junior College to be located in Levelland, Texas." Dr. Phillips was indeed a progressive Levelland supporter. He, along with Dr. John Dupre, constructed Phillips-Dupre Hospital and worked diligently to establish South Plains College.

O.W. MARCOM, Superintendent of Levelland Schools
As superintendent of Levelland Schools from 1947-1961, O.W. Marcom was the consummate educator. His master's degree thesis, "A Survey of Secondary Education in Hockley County," in 1949 became the catalyst for the establishment of South Plains College. His thesis justified the establishment of a junior college at Levelland. Marcom, from a pioneer West Texas farm family, later joined Dr. Thomas Spencer in founding San Jacinto College in Pasadena, Texas. His doctoral dissertation, completed in May, 1961, was titled "An Evaluation of Local Financial Support of Education in Texas by Selected School Districts."

O.R. WATKINS, Levelland ISD Business Manager
O.R. Watkins advanced Hockley County education for 43 years, serving on the 1956 Citizens Committee and as business manager for the Levelland Public Schools. Watkins' expertise on the committee centered on his extensive knowledge of public school tax law. His wife, Frances Watkins, taught English at South Plains College and served as chairperson of the English Department prior to her retirement in 1979.

WALTER L. REED, Levelland High School Principal
A highly respected educator, Walter Reed believed a college in Levelland would enhance the educational opportunities for the entire South Plains' graduating students. He continually encouraged graduating seniors to further their education at South Plains College.

T.O. PETTY, Hockley County School Superintendent
T.O. Petty greatly influenced the founding of South Plains College. Petty, as an educator, actively supported the college. The SPC Board of Regents later selected him to teach government and history classes at the college, then named him college tax assessor and collector.

JOHN R. POTTS, Levelland Businessman
Levelland insurance man John Riley Potts was a 1932 Levelland High School graduate, attended community college and later became secretary to S.J. Hay, president of Great National Life Insurance Company of Dallas, Texas. With the bombing of Pearl Harbor and the United States' entry into WWII, Potts was inducted into the Army and served in the European theater. He received numerous decorations, including the Purple Heart after being wounded in January 1944 in Italy. He spent 20 months in Army hospitals recovering from his wounds. After separation from active duty in 1946, Potts returned to Levelland and the insurance business. From his membership in local civic groups, he began his undaunted efforts at establishing a college in Hockley County. Potts moved to Lockhart, Texas, in 1958 and was selected as Lockhart's Most Worthy Citizen in 1974. Potts died in 1978 at San Antonio State Chest Hospital due to injuries sustained in WWII.

ROBERT C. WALKER, Chamber of Commerce Director
R.C. "Bob" Walker was a dynamic supporter of South Plains College and the City of Levelland. According to Levelland Rotarian J.G. Stacy, Walker worked tirelessly for the college and was instrumental in attracting the owners of Levelland Vegetable Oil Mill to locate in Levelland. He was named director of the chamber in early 1956, coming to Levelland from Winters, Texas. The push to establish a junior college became his first major project as the new chamber manager.

LaVERN McCANN, Levelland Attorney-at-Law
The Levelland Chamber of Commerce Board of Directors believed the Citizens Committee needed an attorney, and LaVern McCann was appointed to fill that position.

Surviving members of the 1956 Citizens Committee, Dr. O.W. Marcom, Walter L. Reed and J.G. Stacy, met with SPC President Dr. Gary McDaniel Dec. 19, 1997, to remember the 1957 ground-breaking ceremonies for South Plains College. Members of the college's original Board of Regents, the Citizens Committee, the Chamber of Commerce and Levelland city officials gathered at the site of the new college Dec. 23, 1957, amid earth-moving equipment to pose for a photo for the *Levelland Daily Sun News*.

PETITION

THE STATE OF TEXAS   :

COUNTY OF HOCKLEY   :

THE HOCKLEY COUNTY JUNIOR COLLEGE DISTRICT OF HOCKLEY COUNTY, STATE OF TEXAS:.

    TO THE BOARD OF TRUSTEES OF THE HOCKLEY COUNTY JUNIOR COLLEGE DISTRICT

OF HOCKLEY COUNTY, STATE OF TEXAS:

    We, the undersigned, legally qualified, resident, property taxpaying voters of the The Hockley County Junior College District of Hockley County, State of Texas, who own taxable property in said District and who have duly rendered the same for taxation, respectfully pray your Honorable Body to order an election in said District for the purpose of submitting the following propositions to the resident, qualified electors who own taxable property in said District and who have duly rendered the same for taxation for their action thereupon:

PROPOSITION NO. L

A   "Shall the Board of Trustees of The Hockley County Junior College District of Hockley County, State of Texas, be authorized to issue the bonds of said Junior College District in the amount of $900,000.00 to become due and payable serially as follows:

```
$25,000.00- 1958
 30,000.00- 1959 to 1961 both incl.
 35,000.00- 1962 to 1964  "      "
 40,000.00- 1965 to 1967, "      "
 45,000.00- 1968 and 1969 "
 50,000.00- 1970 and 1971
 55,000.00- 1972 and 1973
 60,000.00- 1974
 65,000.00- 1975 and 1976
 70,000.00- 1977
```

bearing interest at a rate not to exceed Five (5%) per cent per annum for the purpose of the construction and equipment of school buildings and the acquisition of sites therefor within the limits of the District, and whether there shall be annually levied and collected on all of the taxable property in said Junior College District for the current year and annually thereafter while said bonds or any of them or interest thereon, are outstanding, an ad valorem tax sufficient to pay the current interest on said bonds and to pay the principal thereof as the same becomes due, provided that the bond tax for any one year shall not exceed the limit prescribed by Chapter 70, Acts 1947, 50th Legislature, Regular Session."

PROPOSITION NO. 2

    "Shall the Board of Trustees of the Hockley County Junior College District of Hockley County, State of Texas, be authorized to levy an annual ad valorem tax on all of the taxable property in said Junior College District, at a rate not to exceed Twenty Five Cents (25¢) on the One Hundred Dollars ($100.00) Valuation of taxable property for the maintenance of schools in said Junior College District."

In June 1957, Levelland and Hockley County residents petitioned the Hockley County Commissioners to call for a vote on the question of an ad valorem tax to fund the "Hockley County Junior College." An earlier petition in March 1957 "of G.C. Brown and 559 other duly qualified resident property taxpaying voters of Hockley County" had been submitted to establish the district. The list of the petitioners *(found on the following page)* contained the names of many prominent Levelland citizens.

DATED this the 21st day of June, 1957.

G. E. WHISINHUNT	MRS. PERCY WADE, JR.	HAROLD B. COMBS	MRS.E. W. BALSIGER
MRS. HAROLD B. COMBS	MRS. CHOICE CASTLE	J. C. DEERE	MRS. HASKELL D. ROBERTS
R. M. RAILSBACK	MRS. RAY WILEY	JOHN C. HARPER	MRS. NETTIE ALSHROOKS
MRS. JOHN C. HARPER	MRS. GRADY TERRILL	MORRIS E. HUDSON	MRS. IVAN TIPPS
L. E. MABE	JACK MCCUTCHIN	CYRUS HUMPHREYS	MRS. JACK MCCUTCHIN
T. L. CAUSSEAUZ	MRS. H. A. FULKS	MRS. H.D.HILL,JR	J. M.. HICKMAN
GEO. E. HOWARD	MRS. J.M.HICKMAN	MRS. FRANK KISER,JR	MRS. DANO W.SMITH
MRS. FRANK BARTLEY	MRS. E.E. STAGNER,JR	MRS. R.L.SONNENBURG	MRS. VIC SHEA
T. E. LORAN, JR	GRADY TERRILL	LYNN MASSENGALE	MRS. J. W. HOOD
L. L. TATHAM	MRS. G. R. MORRIS	MRS. L. L. TATHAM	MRS. TOM STEELE
MRS. GENE KNIGHT	TOM STEELE	KATHRYN HARDER	MRS.LAWRENCE MIZE
MRS. E. C. PAYNE, JR	E. C. PAYNE, JR	MRS. ED WILLIAMS	ED WILLIAMS
R. H. KENNEDY	BILLY B. KENNEDY	J. C. PEELER	FLOYD SHOEMAKAR
GORDON SMITH	ROBERT WALKER	MRS. ROBERT KAUFFMAN	B.H.CHADWICK,SR
T. O. PETTY	C. C. PETTY	ORLIN F. BREWER	MRS.T.A.BRUNER
MRS. J. C. HOWELL	JOE WARD	H. W. FERGUSON	C.C.WOODSON,JR
MRS. ORLIN BREWER	I. F. LEA	LILLIAN BRASHER	MARY L. LEA
EDITH G. DENNEY	T. E. LORAN	HAYES DENNEY	MRS.D.A.PICKENS
GRANVILLE V. HOLDER	BUNNA ROBERTS	JESSE W. DEARMOND	MOSETTA ROBERTS
VERNA L. DARMAND	MRS.GERNIE COOPER	B. J. ROGERS	GERNIE COOPER
BERT EADS	C. A. LUCK	MRS. MUARINE EADS	MRS.C.A.LUCK
DR. J. C. WILLMON	MRS. HARRIET BEACH	MRS.J.C.WILLMON	MRS.FRANK SHIELD
MRS. EDGAR E. RUSSELL	FRANK F. SHIELD,JR	A. F. MATHIS	MRS.J.M.BLACKWELL
MRS. A. F. MATHIS	MRS. DAN COOPER	DAVIS POUNDS	DAN COOPER
MRS. DAVIS POUNDS	MRS. W.A.NANCE,JR	MRS.O.L.WATSON	MRS.DAN L.ALLRED
BERT WADE	ROHLIN SULLINDER	FLORENCE SULLINDER	JEFF HARDIN
CARRIE WADE	ELIZABETH HARDIN	MRS. R. C. HARRAL	HARVIE D. POOL
MR.&MRS.F.D.NELSON	MR.&MRS.H.W.DURHAM	MR&MRS.ROY W.COCHRAN	JEWELL W. POOL
J. G. STACY	MRS. ME. G. MORRIS	MRS. W. W. SHOEMAKER	E. W. BOEDEKER
MRS. ANSIL O'NEAL	ED HOFACKET	MRS. J. M. BOWMAN	LAVERN I. MCCANN
MRS. G. S. BEASLEY	JAME T. HATCH	MRS. C. V. SMITH	U. I. BRIDGES
MRS. MORRIS HUDSON	MRS. D. A. RAYMOND	MRS. E.W.BOEDEKER	D. A. RAYMOND
C. C. SUDDERTH	MRS. EDDIE PAXTON	F. P. ALLEN	MRS.BERTELL JACKSON
MRS. J. J. GEORGE	MRS. JOHN DUPRE	MRS. LYNWOOD PIRTLE	MRS. JOHN A.ELLIS
LYNWOOD PIRTLE	JOHN A ELLIS	MRS. J. W. WEBB	HELLEN S. BURGETT
P. J. MARCOM	MRS.R. H. GRELL	M. G. WYATT	MRS. J. BURTNER
MRS. HOWARD BROWN	MR R. HAWS	HOWARD BROWN	W. D. TYLER
MRS. O. F. DOLASEK	FERN HAWS	MRS. E.L.FLATT	EDGAR E. RUSSELL
SHELBY HALL	HOWARD HENSLEY	MRS. N.L.WITT	MARGARET STONCH
MARVIN BROCK	WILBURN SHELL	J. C. HOWELL	MRS.W.T.BAIRD
MRS. MAURICE MILLER	MRS. LUCILLE STUBBLEFIELD	JOHN D. MORTON	BERTELL JACKSON
FORREST WEIMHOLD	MRS. GENEVA BLAIR		DR.G.W.PAYNE

LEE MACKLIN	E. J. KENNEY	MRES. E. J. KENNEY	ERNEST STEWART	
J. N. MURRAH	HOMER JOHNSON	PAULINE SHRUM	J. E. MORRIS	
WILMA PETERSON	BISHOP B.KEELING	LETA DURHAM	GENE MCDONALD	
VIRGIL CORFEE	EUGENE YEAGER	GIL PATSCECKE	ELSIE MAE JENKINS	
EUEL PALMER	MRS. T. B. MITCHELL	MRS. C. H. MIDDLETON	D. B. CLARY	
C. L. CASH	JAMES LATKAM	H. J. PIERCE	GANO TUBB	
L. LUNA	JOYCE CASH	MRS. T. H. DOBBS	OSCAR J. BROWN	
MRS. J. L. BLACK	MRS. C. L. AWBREY	REX HUDSON	B. R. LEWIS	
MRS. A. L. CHRISTOPHER	UDELL B.LEWIS	E. J. HEATH	WILLIAM W.SHOEMAKER	
JASPER SOMS	CARL W. MCINROE	JOHNNIE WATERS	JAMES W. HARTLINE	
J. J. MCDERMITT	MRS. WILLIS MORROW	RUBY RAGIN	HAROLD ROBERTS	
J.W.S. WILDER	MRS. LEMOND N.WORLEY	H. H. MORIN	MRS. J.W.S.WILDER	
JAMES HARDER	FLOYD CORSEY	J. D. LEWIS	MRS. WILSON COX	
MRS. J. L. BIRTCIEL	C. E. CORDER	CECIL SHARBUTT	WILSON S. COX	
W. D. CRUMP	MARY FARMER	DALE SELF	J. H. FARMER	
JACK DANIEL	IMOGENE DAVIS	MRS. JACK DANIEL	T. I. ROBINSON	
H. L. CHAMBERLAIN,JR.	DAN L. ALLRED	PERCY BAILEY	MRS. MASON POLK	
E. A. WRIGHT	JAMES C. DORSETT	R. B. TAYLOR	WILLIAM H. CULBIRTH	
MRS. AL SANDERS	W. J. O'CONNOR	AL SANDERS	MRS. COY WINN	
CAROL ROBINSON	BILL ROBINSON	BILL THOMMAN	L. W. WATERS	
ELDON BOULTER	MRS. L. W. WATERS	W. H. HORNE	MRS. J.M.MAYFIELD, JR	
ROBERT R. ROBINS	H. G. ATWOOD	MRS. BOB ROBBINS	WILLIS MERROW	
MRS. H. G. ATWOOD	V. L. WARD	MAURICE MILLER	MRS. JIM PEELER	
MRS. J. B. RICHARDSON	COY CHELA	GEORGE LEAVELLE	H. W. BAILEY	
MILES WILLIAMS	MRS.CLINTON WILLIAMS	LELA CAUSY	G. CAUSY	
MARY JANE BLAKLEY	MRS. J.M.HAYES	B. D. CARTER	MRS. LAMAR WEST	
ROY JONES	SPENCER TIPTON	MRS. BILL CARTER	MRS. HERBERT RAY	
HERBERT RAY	IVAN TIPPS	MRS. R. E. TIPPS	MRS. H. T. HARRELL	
E. M. ERWIN	MRS. E. M. ERWIN	MRS. C.E.DANNER	JAMES G. RENEGAR, MD	
WOODSON D.FIELDS	MRS. O.H.DAVIS	OSCAR H. DAVIS	A. L. WALSH, MD	
DOUGLAS R. MCSWANE	DALE D. CAMPBELL	JIMMIE CAMPBELL	MRS. J.C.LEWALLEN	
J. C. LEWALLEN	MRS. R. R. PARSONS	R. R. PARSONS	SAM NEWBERRY	
MRS. SAM NEWBERRY	CLINTON WILLIAMS	MRS. H.L.CHAMBERLAIN	MRS. J. G. RENEGAR	
MRS. LEE M. JACKSON	J.L.SISK	MRS.J.O.MCDONALD	AT C. CRAIG	
MRS. W. L. BRESHEARS	W.L.BRESHEARS	JENNETT CRAIG	H. M. BREEZE	
MRS. W. L. REED	FRANK BURNETT	MRS. BELL HORNE	W. L. REED	
VELDA BURNETT	ROY CUNNINGHAM	MRS. L. L.COX	L. L. COX	
CHARLIE SPPED	MRS. L.F.RAWSON	L. F. RAWSON	J. G. NIPPER	
RUTH BELLE NIPPER	ORENA SPEED	GERALDINE SPENCER	ROBERT S. BURKS	
DEANE R. BURKS	G. S. BEASLEY	EDITH A. BEASLEY	ERNEST RAILSBACK	
BERNICE RAILSBACK	MRS. G.W.PAYNE	MRS. W. J. O'CONNOR	W. J. O'CONNOR	

CHAPTER 1

The Founding Years, 1957-1961

Thomas Spencer, Ph.D., loved a challenge. The establishment of a new two-year college in Texas, the first in more than a decade, qualified as a challenge to the Blinn College president. Spencer was the natural choice to oversee a new college on the South Plains, according to the "dean of Texas community colleges," Dr. C.C. Colvert at the University of Texas.[1] Hockley County's civic leaders accepted Colvert's advice and named Spencer the first president of Levelland's college. Spencer's educational experience at Blinn College and in the public schools made him pre-eminent among Texas community college leaders.

Spencer arrived early, even prior to the Hockley County vote endorsing the college, to speak to the civic clubs, women's study clubs and any group that expressed an interest in building a college. Few Levelland residents were surprised when Spencer was named South Plains College's first president. Despite photographs of the tall and imposing Spencer which depict him as a stern, serious educator, he possessed a keen sense of humor. In midsummer 1957, when he and his family arrived in Levelland, he focused his complete attention on the creation of a college. Interestingly, Spencer would leave Levelland only for an even greater challenge, establishing San Jacinto College in Pasadena, Texas, four years later. His wife, Rachel, recalled that she pleaded with her husband not to leave Levelland

---

[1] In December 1956, Dr. C.C. Colvert launched an intensive three-day study of the feasibility of a junior college in Levelland. As the survey was completed, members of the original steering committee telephoned community leaders in the surrounding counties to invite them to hear the Colvert study report. One hundred twenty leaders from across the six-county area turned out to hear the results which Colvert labeled a "preliminary" report.

for the Houston area. Nevertheless, Spencer left his educational mark on two greatly diverse areas of Texas – Levelland and Pasadena. His legacy remains in the institutions he founded.[2]

Spencer arrived in Levelland to a maize field and little else. "When I came to Levelland, we didn't have a waste basket or a pencil sharpener," said Spencer in 1961. Initially, Spencer established an office at the First National Bank but later moved to the San Andres Hotel.[3] The San Andres subsequently became the Carlo Inn and housed numerous SPC students during the next three decades.

Spencer's instructions from the SPC Board of Regents were quite simple. He was given a budget of $1,086,920.01 and instructed to open a college the fall semester of 1958.[4] Within months after Spencer's arrival, public support for the South Plains College District appeared evident within the community.[5] Simulta-

---

[2] The founding of SPC could be viewed as the beginning of a second phase of community college education in Texas. After the founding of SPC in 1957, Midland College, Western Texas College, Tarrant County Junior College, the Dallas County colleges, Grayson County College and San Jacinto College were founded. In a sense, men like Weldon Marcom, Forrest Weimhold, Orlin Brewer, John Potts, J.G. Stacy, O.R. Watkins, T.O. Petty, Walter Reed, Davis Pounds and Dr. Tom Spencer were responsible for the renewed educational trend that benefited thousands of students across the Lone Star State.

[3] According to Tom Spencer Jr., his father moved his SPC office to the San Andres Hotel after a bank officer read a study that indicated most bank robberies occurred in banks with a back door. Dr. Spencer used the bank's back door for access to his office. The bank bricked up the entry way.

[4] "$1 Million Budget Set for First Year," *Levelland Daily Sun News,* Sept. 1, 1957.

[5] Two days after Hockley County voters endorsed the establishment of a college, the Sundown Independent School Board, in a regular meeting, sought an agreement with the junior college trustees. "Whereas the Sundown Board of Education, in recognition of the current economic stress, earnestly wishes to cooperate to the fullest extent by proposing to save several hundred thousand dollars for the taxpayers of Hockley County if the Junior College Trustees should see fit to consumate an agreement with the Board of Education of Sundown." The Sundown trustees proposed that the Sundown "High School Building, which was erected in 1949, could be made available for use by the Junior College District." A decline in the Sundown school enrollment had occurred after oil companies operating in Sundown decided to eliminate lease houses previously made available for their employees. The decrease in student population resulted in empty school classrooms. Apparently, the Sundown trustees believed the new college could provide an economic resurgence for the community. Dewey Waggoner, Sundown postmaster, and H.K. Boswell, an employee with Pan-American Oil Company, met with the Sundown trustees and discussed "the possibilities of getting the Hockley County Junior College located at Sundown. Sundown ISD board member Cy Foster moved and Elmer McInturff seconded the motion to contact the new college's board." The Sundown ISD trustees held additional discussions in a called meeting April 29, 1957. The discussions were unproductive. President Spencer wanted to build an entirely new college.

neously, the wheels for annexation of the Whiteface Independent School District were set in motion at the February 1958 Board of Regents' meeting. In April 1958, the Whiteface Independent School District, "not heretofore a part of the Hockley County Junior College District," was annexed into the SPC taxing district. The reasons for the annexation were clear to anyone traveling across the area. Numerous oil wells, a taxable commodity that would ease the farmers' burden, tapped the abundant oil reserves in the Whiteface District. Probable oil exploration and production would yield valuable tax revenues for the college. To this end, the college published two "question and answer" brochures for residents of the Whiteface school district in the successful annexation proposal. The profession-ally-printed brochures touted the educational benefits a college would bring to Whiteface High graduates.

THOMAS SPENCER, Ph.D.
Dr. Spencer was hired June 1957 as the first president of the newly created South Plains College. He and his family came to Levelland from Blinn College in Brenham, Texas, where he had served as president.

In addition, Nathan Tubb, the well-respected Whiteface superintendent of schools, supported annexation into the college district and his influence within the farming community proved invaluable. With the college board's unanimous annexation vote, Spencer continued his tireless work of building a college.

Spencer's initial challenge involved supervising the construction of the five original buildings on land acquired from the Post-Montgomery estate. The land, known as the Double U Ranch, was part of the vast holdings of the C.W. Post ranching empire. During a visit to Levelland, heirs to the estate met with the college's supporters and authorized ranch manager Monta Moore to sell 177 acres, one Labor of land, to the Hockley County Junior College Regents at an appraised valued of $667.80 per acre or $118,267.38 for the entire tract.[6] Within weeks

---

[6]   A "Labor" is a Spanish land grant term and is about 177 acres.

When the Hockley County Junior College District Committee (1956 Citizens Committee) initially met, they believed all portions of the county should be represented on the proposed college's governing body. Thus, highly respected individuals from across the county were encouraged to run for the first Board of Regents. When the college opened for classes in September 1958, board members included *(seated from left)* E.M. Barnes, Lamar West, (standing from left) C.M. Sanders, L.C. Kearney Jr., John V. Morton and Verne Beebe. Not pictured is Emmett Kerr. West was selected as the first chairman of the South Plains College Board of Regents, E.M. Barnes was selected as vice chairman, while L.C. Kearney was named secretary.

bulldozers cleared the initial construction site, the northwest quarter of the property, for the five proposed buildings. The initial payment for the original 44 acres was $29,566.85.

Frequent summer rainstorms delayed the prime contractor and undoubtedly caused Spencer some sleepless nights. Contractor Harry E. Miller agreed to complete construction by Sept. 10, 1958. The initial construction project on the original site included the Administration Building, Gymnasium-Student Center, Library-Fine Arts Building, Agricultural Shop Building and the Auditorium. In addition, the college president's home was constructed on the original site.[7]

Heirs to the Post-Montgomery estate agreed to a progressive sale of the remaining three-quarters of the site. Regents agreed to a 3 percent per annum note. The first annual installment payment was due on Nov. 1, 1958, two weeks

---

[7] Years later, in 1984, the original president's home was transformed into the SPC Visitors Center and offices for the College Relations Office.

Levelland businessman E.M. Barnes worked tirelessly to convince area residents of the need for a community college in Levelland. Barnes, the local Gulf Oil distributor, spent much of his work day explaining the benefits of a college while delivering fuel and visiting with the farmers and ranchers of Hockley County. Barnes' son, E.D. Barnes, M.D., followed in his father's footsteps and served on the SPC Board of Regents from 1963 to 1977.

SPC President Dr. Tom Spencer *(center)*, Dean Clyde Prestwood *(left)* and Tax Assessor-Collector T.O. Petty *(seated)* worked continually to ensure the college's facilities were ready for the first classes on Sept. 15, 1958.

Construction on the original South Plains College buildings began at a hurried pace in anticipation of the first registration. Students began classes on Sept. 15, 1958, in the five original buildings of South Plains College. They are, clockwise from right, the Administration Building, the Auditorium, the Agricultural-Shop Building, the Gymnasium-Student Union Building and the Library.

after the first semester began.[8] The district would then pay for the "remaining land over a five-year period, with clear title to a portion equal to that paid released to the college each year." The final payment to the Post-Montgomery estate took place on Nov. 1, 1962.

A New College

South Plains College's administration and faculty eagerly awaited the construction of the original five buildings and the upcoming fall semester of 1958.[9] One of the first instructors hired by President Spencer was Earl Gerstenberger, a former Blinn College agriculture and science instructor. He arrived in midsummer 1958 to find the college facilities uncompleted as the college's first registration neared. Classes were scheduled to begin on Sept. 15, 1958. Consequently, Gerstenberger worked as a finish carpenter, hanging chalkboards in the newly completed classrooms only to use the same chalkboards days later in his agriculture and science classes.

The first registration at South Plains College was an astounding success with 576 students enrolling in day and evening classes.[10] The faculty worked until midnight processing the registration forms for the 60 classes scheduled to meet the next day. Apparently, the few nay-sayers who still questioned the new college's location in close proximity to Texas Technological College had fallen silent. South Plains College's initial footsteps into higher education were disrupted only momentarily when, midway through the day's registration, an unwelcome inhabitant took up residence in the front doorway of the Administration Building. A skunk had wandered in from the nearby farm and temporarily hampered the flow

---

[8] South Plains College Board of Regents minutes noted that the remaining three-quarters of the 177 acres were to be rented to Joe Tarbert on a year-to-year basis "as long as he farms the property in a farmerlike manner" until expansion of the college requires additional space.

[9] Spencer awaited the students' arrival before planning the concrete walkways in the quadrangle area. According to Sycily Lattimore, Spencer said, "Let's wait and see where the students walk, then put the sidewalks there." Few street lights existed on College Avenue and no campus driveway or parking lot lighting existed the first years of the college's existence. Thus, evening college faculty, like Lattimore, walked across campus with their flashlights.

[10] Enrollment figures from Jack Wardlow in the SPC Office of Institutional Research indicate 536 students enrolled that first semester. The variance can be attributed to the final state auditor's count of the 12th day class roll.

of prospective students. This interruption in enrolling students allowed the faculty to catch up with mounds of paperwork that characterized every fall registration.

The job of "grounds supervisor" and improving the campus appearance was assigned to Gerstenberger. In fact, President Spencer and Gerstenberger doted over the architectural drawings, street maps and aerial photographs to plan the SPC campus. In addition to Gerstenberger's agriculture classes, he sponsored the Rodeo Club and Agriculture Club, managed the college farm and taught biology classes. Gerstenberger's science background and his ability to envision the entire Labor of land led to a beautiful campus. From his arrival in 1958, Gerstenberger began planting trees, sowing grass, placing underground sprinklers, planning sidewalks and arranging the flower beds that transformed the maize field into a campus. Gerstenberger believed a variety of trees and shrubs should dominate the landscape. Thus, he planted live and red oaks, honey locusts, hackberry trees

South Plains College's first agriculture instructor and grounds supervisor was Earl Gerstenberger. He planted numerous trees and shrubs across the 177-acre campus, including the honey locust, *Gleditsia triacanthos*, for its filtered shade, the live oak and the mimosa. Gerstenberger coordinated his tree planting efforts with Levelland's Progressive Garden Club. In this Jan. 27, 1959, photograph commemorating Arbor Day, Gerstenberger and club members planted six mimosa trees on the campus. He was assisted by (from left) Mrs. J.L. Warren, Mrs. Grady Henry, Mrs. Fern Maddera, Mrs. Ted Darwin, Mrs. J.W. Webb and Mrs. W.B. Goates, chairwoman of the project. Fern Maddera was president of the Garden Club and her four-year-old daughter, Sharon Maddera, assisted in the foreground. Sixteen years later, Sharon graduated from SPC.

SPC's agriculture instructor, Earl Gerstenberger, in addition to supervising the grounds beautification of the campus, sponsored the Agriculture Club. This 1959 photograph pictured the following club members: Glen Edwards, club president; Bobby Birdsong, vice president; Milton Holloway, reporter; Merle Todd, secretary; and members Louis Glass, Dewey Hakin, Harry Miller, Leonard Groves, Billy Magee, Stanley Boutler, Charles Ward, Stanley Nicholson, Joel Cookston, Don Ewing, Stevie Bryant, Cecil Johnson, Don Bowman, Dave Swinford and Kenneth Ellerd. The Agriculture Club Sweetheart was Nancy Mueller from Sundown, Texas.

and a host of shrubs.[11] "The Board of Regents wanted a developed landscape plan that would be both attractive and appealing to the eye," said Gerstenberger. Later, Director of Maintenance L.C. O'Bannon took some of the landscape responsibilities from Gerstenberger, and only with the arrival of horticulturist Danny Doak in 1984, did Gerstenberger relinquish his landscape duties. A trip through the SPC campus reveals three decades of Gerstenberger's desire for an attractive South Plains College.[12]

According to Tom Spencer Jr., now president of Garland County Community College, Hot Springs, Ark., his father encountered a myriad of tasks and difficulties in establishing SPC. Spencer wrote the college catalog, supervised construction of the buildings, hired the administration and faculty, spoke to the area's

---

[11] In the Nov. 26, 1958, edition of *The Plainsman,* a short news report indicated that Gerstenberger involved his horticulture class in the planting of shrubs on the SPC campus. After he gave students a shovel, they received a "hands-on experience."

[12] Gerstenberger was the first recipient of the Excellence in Teaching Award in 1965. The award was originated by the First National Bank to recognize an excellent SPC teacher.

civic clubs and gave numerous commencement addresses at high school gradua-
tions in May 1958.[13] Those graduating students could within three months be
walking the newly constructed halls of South Plains College. Often, President
Spencer took his son to those graduation ceremonies. According to the younger
Spencer, "Dad had three speeches that he gave at commencements, and I knew
the punch lines to most of them." Spencer usually stressed one key theme as he
warned, "You make the three hardest and most important decisions in your life
as a young person when you don't want any advice and you don't know anything
about what you're deciding. You choose your education, your career and who
you'll marry without seeking advice." President Spencer's speech in reality struck
harmonious chords with the parents. They quickly realized the new college
president's wisdom, and whatever reservations they might have had about the
new college in Levelland began to disappear. Spencer's leadership, calm demeanor
and keen sense of humor garnered support among residents of the South Plains.

The new college's administration represented a variety of educational backgrounds. Nathan Tubb, former superintendent of Whiteface schools, became the

---

[13] Thomas Spencer Jr. interview with author; Regents' minutes indicated the initial SPC catalog
cost 38 cents per copy. Later, 2,000 additional catalogs at 15 cents each were printed. The 1998
college catalog of 200 pages cost 80 cents per copy. The college contracted for 28,000 catalogs for
the 1998 - 1999 academic year.

**R. F. Miller *(left)* and Jesse Perez *(partially obscured)* planted one of the many mimosa trees on
the SPC campus. In the ensuing years, the mimosa trees were unsuccessful and were replaced
with honey locusts, live oak, red oak, hackberry and mulberry trees across the college campus.
The Jeep and trailer, made from the undercarriage of an aircraft, were United States Air Force
surplus equipment purchased by the college.**

South Plains College's first registrar was Nathan Tubb, former superintendent of schools at Whiteface. Tubb later became academic dean and vice president. After his retirement, he served eight years on the SPC Board of Regents. Tubb came from a family of West Texas educators. His brothers Gano, Harvey, Francis and Floyd all had distinguished educational careers. Levelland High School's gymnasium is named after Gano Tubb, the long-time Levelland Lobo basketball coach.

college registrar and Clyde Prestwood, principal at Navasota High School, accepted the position of administrative dean. Bob Burks, a Levelland public school administrator, served as dean of the evening school, and T.O. Petty, former Hockley County school superintendent, originally hired to teach American history, was named tax assessor and collector.[14]

According to Tubb, "We had to be in his (Spencer's) office constantly. He was the only one of us (the administrators) with college experience. I didn't know any more about the college environment than a saddle horse." Tubb learned quickly, however, and his sage advice became highly valued. Before his retirement, Tubb served as SPC academic vice president and was later elected to the SPC Board of Regents. He described Spencer "as one of the strongest leaders I ever worked with. Although an imposing presence, he let everyone throw out their ideas during our meetings, but if anything was done, he gave us credit without seeking the recognition for himself. We would all jump in there and get the job done."

According to Evening School Director Bob Burks, after the administrators met to chart the evening school's direction, Spencer informed Burks that the evening school would be "bound only by your imagination and capacity for hard work." Just as the regular day classes were filled with students, the evening school also proved a success. While Spencer traveled the

---

[14] In the months prior to the construction of the college buildings, Spencer, Bob Burks and T.O. Petty, along with the Board of Regents, met frequently in the homes of the college's administrators. Deane Burks-Espensen recalled the meetings at their home, 518 Double U Drive, where "Dr. Spencer would always sit in the smallest rocking chair we had." Laughingly, Burks-Espensen said, "Dr. Spencer liked that small rocker, and he was a big man, so several times we had to reglue the spindles."

speaking circuit by day, Burks, familiar with the community and oil field personnel, talked with industry representatives by night. A burgeoning West Texas oil industry welcomed Burks' presentations about SPC.[15]

Dr. Spencer believed transportation to SPC from the outlying towns of Brownfield, Littlefield, Plains, Denver City, Smyer, Ropesville, Sundown and Anton would encourage students to enroll. In fact, the bus transportation system Spencer instituted at SPC imitated the system that had worked effectively at Blinn College.[16] The Board of Regents directed Spencer to purchase five buses to make the daily trips to Levelland. The college hired student drivers to pick up other students along the way. Dean Prestwood chose Danny McClellan, an entering freshman, as one of the bus drivers. He left Plains, Texas, each day at 6:00 a.m., picked up 10 students and arrived at SPC by 8:00 a.m. McClellan parked the bus due east of the original Gymnasium, and at the conclusion of classes, he reversed the route. For their services, the drivers received college tuition. In addition to their regular routes, the drivers also drove

Billie Robnett, a freshman from the Springlake-Earth community, drove an SPC bus to Levelland each day. Robnett drove the bus from the fall semester of 1958 until May 1960. He and the other student-drivers received tuition and fee waivers as compensation for their bus driving duties. After completing his education, Robnett joined the U.S. Department of Agriculture and retired in 1993. *(Photo courtesy of Mrs. Billie Robnett)*

the basketball team to their games. The longest bus route required Billie Robnett to bring in his bus from Earth, Texas, some 60 miles one-way, to SPC each day.

[15] Dr. Tom Spencer Jr. said of Nathan Tubb, "He (Tubb) and my father were kindred spirits in education." Both were lifelong educators who centered their attention on the student.

[16] In February 1958, Regents purchased two Ford buses from Grady Terrill Motor Company and two Chevrolet buses from Bob Reid Chevrolet Company. Regents later purchased another bus when the college opened.

On Nov. 2, 1958, Texas Governor Price Daniel joined an estimated 2,500 Hockley County and area well-wishers at the formal dedication ceremonies of South Plains College and open house that followed. Gov. Daniel *(center in hat)* is greeted by SPC President Dr. Thomas Spencer and Student Body President Mack Hicks, while Sue Copeland pins a boutonniere on Board Chairman Lamar West. Gov. Daniel's dedication address was held that afternoon in the College Auditorium which could accommodate only about 300 people. Speakers were positioned in the hallways of adjacent buildings. Other guests listened on their car radios to the address which was broadcast by KLVT radio.

A flag raising ceremony in the freshly graded quadrangle marked the opening of the dedication ceremonies. Members of the Hockley County Sheriff's Posse presented the flag, while members of the American Legion and Veterans of Foreign Wars raised the flag. State Senator Preston Smith, Governor Price Daniel, College President Tom Spencer and Board of Regents Chairman Lamar G. West watched as a new educational era began on the South Plains.

College President Dr. Tom Spencer *(above)* and other college officials escorted Governor Daniel on a tour through the new SPC facilities which included the Administration Building which served as a primary classroom building. The Governor, along with Spencer and Dean Clyde Prestwood, examined some of the SPC Library's holdings. The College's Board of Regents authorized $35,000 for the initial acquisition of books for the Library. At a noon luncheon *(right)*, State Senator Preston Smith introduced Governor Daniel to an audience of Levelland's elite at the San Andres Hotel. Smith helped champion the need for a community college in the South Plains area.

The bus transportation system continued for several years, but the number of students taking advantage of the free transportation declined with the arrival of the 1960s. The last student bus service provided by the college to the Pep community ended in 1969. Gery Franklin had driven what he affectionately called the "Gray Goose," a GMC Suburban-type vehicle that had seven seats. "I picked up about 17 people everyday and played lots of spades in the SUB waiting for everyone to get back on the bus to go back home," said Franklin. "Clarence Albus had driven the bus the year before I did it, but because there were fewer Pep students that year, he drove a station wagon," added Franklin. Few students wanted to utilize the bus service in the fall semester of 1969 so the last college bus route was cancelled.

The bus service posi-tively affected SPC's early enrollment. It enabled students from the neigh-boring towns to attend SPC with no transporta-tion costs. The buses clearly provided an added bonus when Spencer and his Board of Regents spoke to the various com-munities about SPC. Spencer's underlying idea

Student parking problems at South Plains College during the early years were minimal. The college's five buses transported students from Denver City, Plains, Sundown, Ropesville, Anton, Pep and Whiteface.

that the community college should serve the broadest possible group of students was exemplified by the bus system. As times changed, the South Plains became more prosperous, students became increasingly more mobile, and SPC adapted to the college students' changing needs. The yellow SPC buses that fanned across the South Plains each weekday were phased out and the college entered a new era.[17] Construction of the first three dormitories transformed the SPC students' education into a college experience.

---

[17] Apparently, even with bus transportation, automobile parking problems existed on campus. Dean Clyde Prestwood, in the February 1959 edition of *The Plainsman,* implored SPC students to park their cars in front of the Auditorium rather than in the Administration Building parking lot. Further, in February 1963, student journalist Ray Luper suggested "parking stickers" to alleviate the parking congestion in front of the Administration Building and Library. It seems students and instructors could not arrive to class on time. Similar problems have beset the SPC student population throughout the college's 40-year history.

A New Faculty

President Spencer not only recruited students but worked diligently to hire outstanding faculty. His optimism was clearly revealed in his communications to prospective instructors. Quite often his letters included, "The buildings are coming along nicely, prospects for enrollment are good, and looking forward to working with you as a member of our staff." That same optimism was reflected by those joining the faculty. Charles Sylvester, math instructor and later college registrar, wrote, "I consider it an honor to be selected as a member of the faculty and look forward to a very pleasant and challenging school year." Spencer and Sylvester's optimism proved correct on Sept. 15, 1958, as Spencer and his newly hired faculty greeted more than 500 day and evening class students enrolled at South Plains College.[18]

In preparation for that first semester in the Science and Physical Education Departments, Spencer hired Henry and Myrtle Lucke to join the team of SPC instructors. The Luckes had known Spencer at Blinn College. Lucke headed the Science Department, while Mrs. Lucke taught women's physical education and served as dean of women. The Luckes formed the nucleus of the original faculty who steered a college in academics, athletics and in student conduct. Their noteworthy arrival in mid-April 1958 coincided with a West Texas sandstorm.

President Spencer invited the Luckes to come to Levelland from Brenham to examine the city, community and people. Spencer wrote, "The Board feels, however, that it will be better for you to make a visit to Levelland to determine the housing facilities available and observe other factors which make satisfactory living in a community." Those other factors were plainly evident to the teaching couple when they passed through San Angelo on their way to view Levelland. A severe sandstorm (frequent during the 1950s and 1960s) limited visibility for their trip into Levelland. Mrs. Lucke said, "It was a terrible dust storm and we couldn't see very much at all; it was a terrible drive." Henry Lucke said, "She (Mrs. Lucke) had a white jacket, the sand came in through the windows and by

---

[18] An examination of SPC records indicated that few of the original faculty members had employment contracts in their personnel files. In most cases, a simple typed document with the faculty member's name and yearly salary is the only document indicating a faculty member's employment. According to Nathan Tubb and Earl Gerstenberger, Dr. Spencer "hired us on a handshake;" no contract was necessary.

SOUTH PLAINS COLLEGE
HOCKLEY COUNTY JUNIOR COLLEGE DISTRICT
LEVELLAND, TEXAS

January 14, 1958

THOMAS M. SPENCER
PRESIDENT

Mr. Earl Gerstenberger
Blinn College
Breham, Texas

Dear Earl:

Thank you for your letter of inquiry under date of January 13th.

I should be very happy to have you make application for our agriculture job. In fact, I had thought of writing to you about it, but had decided that you and June probably would not be interested in moving this far from home.

Enclosed is a copy of our salary schedule and an application form. The salary is shown for nine months and the Agricultural job will be for twelve months. You may project your salary for the total amount. In returning the application form, please enclose an official copy of your transcript.

May I suggest if you are seriously interested in moving to this part of the country that you and June should make a trip out here at the earliest possible date to look the situation over and determine whether or not you would enjoy living here. Personally, our family enjoys it, but it is different in every respect from the section to which you are accustomed.

Looking forward to hearing from you again, I am,

Very truly yours,

Thomas M. Spencer, President

TMS/lw

encl- application form
      salary schedule

MASTER DEGREE INSTRUCTIONS

NUMBER YEARS EXPERIENCE	SALARY SCALE FOR SOUTH PLAINS COLLEGE
0	$ 4,184.
1	4,238
2	4,292
3	4,346
4	4,400
5	4,500
6	4,600
7	4,700
8	4,800
9	4,900
10	5,000
11	5,100
12	5,200
13	5,300
14	5,400
15	5,500
16	5,600
17	5,700
18	5,800
19	5,850
20	5,900
21	5,950
22	6,000
23	6,050
24	6,100
25	6,150
26	6,200

When the instructor obtains the Doctors Degree with a major

in his teaching field, allow an additional $400 per year

for the degree and a maximum salary of $6,600.

When Earl Gerstenberger accepted his teaching position as agriculture instructor at SPC, President Thomas Spencer sent Gerstenberger a copy of the faculty salary schedule. Traditionally, the SPC faculty have been at the approximate average salary level for community college faculty across Texas. *(Chart courtesy of Earl Gerstenberger.)*

Opposite page: President Thomas Spencer assumed the reins of South Plains College in the summer of 1957 and began to assemble an instructional staff of former colleagues and educators from across the state. Spencer, having previously been president of Blinn College in Brenham, had experienced the vastly different climate of West Texas. Often President Spencer's communication with prospective employees urged them to visit the South Plains before agreeing to move to the area. Although Spencer did not mention the biting north winds, pleasant fall evenings and blinding sandstorms, he insightfully gave those interested in SPC employment a hint of what West Texas weather might be like. During the spring sandstorms, which were particularly wicked in the late 1950s and early 1960s, Spencer often said, "The real estate is moving today." In January 1958, while he officed in the First National Bank building, Spencer did not have a secretary to type his letters. As the summer of 1958 arrived, Spencer moved his office to the San Andres Hotel.

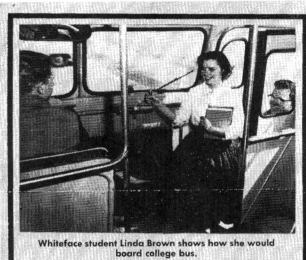

Whiteface student Linda Brown shows how she would board college bus.

College District
MEMBERSHIP:
WHAT IT WILL MEAN

Questions and Answers
for Residents
of the
Whiteface School District

Live at home,

yet attend

college

Free bus service will be one of several distinct and important advantages for Whiteface students if the March 22 election to join the South Plains College District is approved by Whiteface Voters.

Linda gets helping hand from fellow-student Charles Newton as she and Kenneth Welch leave bus as they would on arriving at college campus.

Two different brochures were printed to answer questions about the annexation of the Whiteface Independent School District. The brochures were widely distributed and estimated the college district costs for Whiteface taxpayers. The average farmer with a 200-acre farm would pay about $6.10 a year in college taxes. An average homeowner would pay about $3.09 per year. Two elections were required to make Whiteface ISD a part of the college district. The first was held March 22, 1958, where qualified voters expressed their approval to join the college district.

the time we got to Levelland, that jacket was red with sand." In spite of the sandstorm, they arrived at the San Andres Hotel for an interview with Spencer in surroundings quite different from the humidity and rolling hills of Brenham.[19]

The Luckes were greeted by Spencer and Board Chairman Lamar West. During the interview, West commented, "If you stay in this weather, you'll be a West Texan."[20]

Nevertheless, the Luckes became West Texans and molded the academic and athletic programs at SPC. Mrs. Lucke remembered, "We didn't participate in women's intercollegiate sports for the first several years. The gym wasn't ready anyway, so we did archery outdoors in the freezing cold. We did whatever we could do outside until we finally got in the gym during the spring. I ordered equipment as we needed it." In addition to her women's physical education classes, Mrs. Lucke taught geography, educational psychology and a section of biology in the spring semester of 1959. "I was committed to getting women into intercollegiate competition, so we began with the individual sports like tennis, badminton and

The First Faculty Handbook

The original SPC Faculty Handbook, 25 pages in length and written by President Spencer, was given to the new college's instructors in September 1959, one year after classes began. In the handbook's foreword, Spencer stated his goal in writing the document: "for clarifying and strengthening our organization." Long known as a strict disciplinarian, Spencer detailed the instructor's role in maintaining proper classroom conduct. "Each faculty member is his own disciplinarian in class and is authorized to correct any infraction of accepted decorum for ladylike and gentlemanly conduct anywhere on school property at any time." Spencer held regular faculty meetings "for discussion and decision." He scheduled the meetings for the Wednesday following the second Tuesday of each month at 4:00 p.m. Faculty members on nine-month contracts were required to turn in their building keys at the end of each school year. Each faculty member sponsored a campus organization and the handbook specified that "all college personnel will be expected to serve as officials in Interscholastic League Events sponsored by the college when requested to do so. Assignments will be made by the Dean." (See Appendix for list of organizations and sponsors.)

---

[19] Within months of the completed construction of the original five buildings, the West Texas wind wreaked havoc on the new construction. A wind and sandstorm on Feb. 9, 1959, blew the window casements loose in the Library. Lumber props were nailed to the floor and connected to the window casements to prevent the windows from being completely blown into the Library.

[20] West's participation in the Lucke interviews was coincidental. According to Nathan Tubb, West had complete confidence in Spencer's hiring decisions and apparently only happened into Spencer's office as the Luckes arrived.

those kinds of competition. The second year I started with volleyball, because it was not frowned upon as much as basketball by some of our administrators and the athletic director." During the 1950s, adult volleyball leagues held tournaments in the SPC gym. "It gave my team a chance to compete before we began competition against Texas Tech and Lubbock Christian College," said Mrs. Lucke.

Mrs. Lucke's remembrance of the different attitudes toward women's sports is understandable in view of the traditionalism of the 1950s. Vocal in her support of women's athletics, Mrs. Lucke pressed SPC's athletic director and first basketball coach, Bill Powell, a University of Texas graduate, to endorse the women's program. Initially, Powell provided little encouragement for women's intercollegiate play. Other influences in the early 1960s would change the provincial gender attitudes held by many West Texans.

Mrs. Lucke's work assignments demanded even more of her attention. President Spencer wanted a drill team, later known as the Tex-Anns, patterned after the Kilgore Rangerettes and the Tyler Apache Belles, to perform at all college functions. The drill team, separate from the cheerleaders, began under the tutelage of Rose Marie Pilcher, a former Apache Belle and Business Department faculty member. After Miss Pilcher's departure, Mrs. Lucke, despite having almost no training in drill team activities, accepted the position of Tex-Ann sponsor. Describing the growth of the program she recalled, "Later, Dr. (Marvin) Baker really promoted the drill team, and he sent us to summer camps to learn drill

Since the college's first registration four decades ago, prospective students continue to endure long lines in the registration process. In this early 1960s registration photograph, students signed up for SPC classes in the Women's Gymnasium, the same location used by the college for current registrations.

When South Plains College began classes on Sept. 15, 1958, the Gymnasium was not completed. Women's physical education instructor Myrtle Lucke taught archery on a barren field until the gym was constructed. These unidentified young ladies became proficient at the sport as the indoor facilities were not completed until midwinter.

team work. A newly formed professional football team in Dallas, the future Cowboys, asked us to come perform for the Cowboy games, and we (Dr. Baker and Lucke) decided against doing that because the girls would have to be out (of class) and it would involve lots of time." Of the Tex-Anns name, "it just seemed a natural thing since we were Texans."[21]

---

[21] Spencer knew the benefits of a drill team in promoting the college. After he departed SPC in 1961 and founded San Jacinto College, he replicated the Tex-Anns at his new college. There they were called the San-Jans.

Little Old Ladies with Briefcases

When the college opened its doors in 1958, 30 women, not having an earlier opportunity to attend college, enrolled amidst the 18-year-old freshman class. The women, having raised their children, took advantage of SPC's day and evening class schedules to complete their education. One Levelland housewife, Mrs. Hazel Blakeley, recalled, "I had always wanted to be a teacher. When my daughter went to college and got married, I went back to school. I went to SPC and then Tech and completed my education." Mrs. Blakeley, and most of her briefcase-carrying colleagues, became public school teachers. "We carried those briefcases because we didn't want our stuff scattered about," said Mrs. Blakeley, a 26-year veteran of the teaching profession. Although Mrs. Blakeley and her classmates were not the standard college freshmen in 1958-1959, their studious approach toward education produced exemplary results. They graduated and achieved a goal that had eluded them for so many years.

The First Graduates

At the conclusion of SPC's first academic year, President Spencer and Registrar Tubb wanted to certify a graduating class. Thus, Billie (Pete) Alexander, a Levelland veteran returning to college, and Betty Rowell, a Levelland High School graduate, enrolled at SPC. Both had attended Texas Tech the previous year and, with the required semester hours, qualified for the first SPC diplomas. The graduation ceremony was held in the SPC Auditorium and it "was filled to capacity; everyone in town wanted to be there," said Rowell.[22]

Alexander epitomized the SPC student. He worked at the Levelland Gasoline Plant during the day and attended evening classes. Upon graduation, Alexander attended Baylor Law School and began his private practice in 1962. Alexander said, "When I was young, Brownfield, Levelland and Littlefield were all about comparable towns, and when the college came in there, Levelland became the bright star. That college has made the difference in that town." Since 1962, Alexander has practiced law in many of the county courtrooms in West Texas.[23]

Betty Rowell contacted Registrar Nathan Tubb about evening school business classes. Tubb encouraged Rowell to enroll in a course of study that would result in the associate of science degree. Rowell, then the mother of two small children, agreed, and at the conclusion of the academic year joined Alexander "at the front of the graduation line."[24]

"I got a lot of encouragement from Mr. Dawson, Mr. Gerstenberger and Michael Knowles, who talked me into taking the second half of shorthand," said Rowell. "He told me I wouldn't make an 'A' in the class because I had to learn two semesters of shorthand in one semester. It almost killed me, but I did it and made an 'A.'" Her dedication to hard work paid dividends. After her SPC graduation, Rowell attended Texas Tech, completed her bachelor's degree and taught in the Levelland and Lamesa public schools for 22 years.

---

[22] Betty Rowell's daughter, Sally Rowell Snow, a 1971 SPC graduate, was named a Distinguished Alumna in 1995. Snow is trauma coordinator at Cook Children's Hospital, Fort Worth, Texas. Betty Rowell is retired and living at Lake Graham, Texas.

[23] Alexander's office is in Odessa, Texas.

[24] To pay her tuition and fees, Betty Rowell worked part-time in Nathan Tubb's office. With the student loans she received and the encouragement of Registrar Tubb, Rowell completed her degrees. Her husband, Joe Bob Rowell, enrolled in the first SPC welding class taught by instructor John Christmas.

South Plains College's first commencement exercises on May 25, 1959, produced two graduates: Levelland students Betty Moore Rowell, now a resident of Graham, Texas, and Billie G. Alexander, now living in Odessa, Texas. One year later, during spring graduation 1960, 43 graduates walked across the SPC stage. Forty years later, in the spring of 1998, 707 students graduated from South Plains College.

Levelland native James Earl Van Stavern was South Plains College's first evening school graduate. When he received his associate of business administration degree in May 1961, Van Stavern was the oldest student at age 44 to graduate from SPC.

CANDIDATES FOR GRADUATION
& HIGH SCHOOL REPRESENTED

Adams, Argus Daine	Levelland
Barton, Marilyn Sue	Levelland
Bell, Jackie David	Sundown
Brown, Carolyn	Levelland
Burnett, Evie Anita	Whitharral
Butler, Barbara Lynn	Lubbock
Cogburn, Thelma	Whiteface
Diersing, James	Pep
Edwards, Barbara Allen	Levelland
Epperson, Robert Joe	Ropesville
Glass, Louis S.	Levelland
Grant, Gary Lyndell	Ropesville
Hannaford, Mindon Garland	Roby
Hicks, Mack	Levelland
Holloway, Milton L.	Levelland
Johnson, Cecil	Littlefield
Macon, Alton Dwayne	Levelland
Melton, Doris June	Pettit
Miller, Harry	Littlefield
Myatt, Jerry William	Levelland
McClure, Syble Eugenia	Levelland
McClure, Wanda Joyce	Levelland
Newton, Charles Edwin	Whiteface
Oliver, Vance E.	Cotton Center
Oliver, Virginia Lucy	Cotton Center
Peacock, Billye Jean	Levelland
Petty, Robert Duane	Brownfield
Porter, Jackie Lee	Plains
Ragland, Howard E.	Levelland
Rhodes, David Ronald	Spade
Setser, Joy Foster	Brady
Simnacher, Elaine W.	Pep
Sims, Mary Beth	Smyer
Smith, Charles Edkar, III	Whiteface
Stanley, David R.	Pettit
Stark, Carol Ed	Levelland
Taylor, Thomas Perry	Levelland
Todd, Merle Lee	Plains
Vernon, Shirley Ann	Levelland
Vinyard, Judy	Sundown
Vinyard, Mike	Levelland
Ward, Charles R.	Seagraves
Wood, Violet M.	El Campo

South Plains College's first graduates, Billie Alexander and Betty Rowell, walked across the SPC graduation stage in 1959. One year later, on May 26, 1960, the college's second graduating class numbered 43. Interestingly, Dr. O.R. Douglas, superintendent of the Brownfield Public Schools, gave the commencement address. Douglas must have given that speech with mixed emotions. He had led the efforts of a small group of Brownfield citizens only five years earlier to locate a community college in Brownfield. Former Brownfield Mayor Herb Chessir, interviewed by the author just before his death in 1997, said, "We sat on our backsides while Levelland worked and got the college."

Saying Good Night on the Front Porch

Foremost in Mrs. Lucke's daily tasks was her role as dean of women. Maintaining a strict moral code, enforcing discipline and encouraging "ladylike conduct" became synonymous with the name Dean Lucke. Her disciplinary duties multiplied with the construction of Sue Spencer Hall in 1960. Forty years later, the restrictions placed upon students by Dean Lucke are still the topic of discussion among veteran college faculty members and former students.

Excerpt from "Tips for Tex-Anns"

"Dresses are always the proper attire for young ladies. Dresses are worn in all academic buildings, except when special permission is given. Slacks, pedal pushers, Bermudas and Jamaicas may be worn when traveling with young ladies or with your family or to the Student Union building in the afternoon. YOU ARE YOUR LOVELIEST IN A DRESS.

Sunday is a special day at South Plains College, and clothes should be in keeping with the day; dress up properly for church and dinner."

Initially, Dean Lucke wrote and published a "Tips for Tex-Anns" brochure. The brochure spelled out the "dos and don'ts" of college life for the young ladies attending SPC. Further illumination on a young lady's conduct was found in the student handbook. The guidelines and directives of Dean Lucke are a mirror of the 1950s. Simply put, Dean Lucke's directives culminated in Article V, rule 16, "Any girl who is too ill to go to class is too ill to go on a date."

Former SPC faculty and students remember a more rigorous "informal" dress code imposed by the dean of women. Bright red dresses or designs, such as polka-dots, were thought to be provocative and were unacceptable. Apparently SPC's young men must have been easily distracted from their studies. Blue jeans were not allowed "except at rodeo events," and women's patent leather shoes, which may have been reflective, were banned as was any type clothing deemed by the Dean to be immodest.

Student conduct across the SPC campus drew the attention of Dean Lucke and Administrative Dean Clyde Prestwood. College administrators instituted a demerit system to encourage proper student behavior. Social probation was swift and sure for the SPC student who violated the college's student conduct rules. After three demerits, a student was "campused." Campusing required the offending students to be in their dorm rooms from 8:00 p.m. Friday until 8:00 a.m. Monday. "During the hours of campus, said individual may not receive any visitors or phone calls unless a case of emergency arises." The college's student code of conduct remained in place through the 1960s. As late as 1968, dorm policy still required women to sign out when they departed for home or to stay with family in Levelland. "The Constitution of Women's Residence Halls" indicated tardiness was the most frequent offense committed by SPC students. "Late minutes will be given for girls coming in after the time set forth by the college. After 15 late minutes, a weekend campus beginning at 8:00 p.m. Friday ending at 8:00 a.m. Monday will be installed."

Probably the most frequent student infractions in the dorm rooms included "blinds raised at night and obvious displays of affection (ODA) while saying 'good night' on the front porch. Demerits will also be given for ODAs in cars in front of the residence hall during the daytime. After three campuses have been given, a trip to the Dean of Women for supervision will be necessary."

Former SPC students Lyndon and wife Judy (Roberts) Hardin recalled their brush with Lucke discipline. Dean Lucke witnessed "hand holding in the parking lot," and Judy Roberts, then a resident of Gillespie Hall, 1966-67, was given a demerit. Hardin, who attended SPC in 1965-67 and lived in Stroud Hall, was a member of the men's basketball and tennis teams. Since 1983, he has been SPC women's basketball coach.

Registrars and Directors of Admissions

Nathan Tubb, Registrar, 1958-1967

Charles Sylvester, Registrar, 1967-1973

Jerry Barton, Director of Admissions and Registrar, 1973-1981

Bobby James, Director of Admissions and Registrar, 1981-1992[25]

Andrea Rangel, Registrar, 1992-1998[26]

Deans of Women

Myrtle Lucke, 1958-1967

Carole Long, 1967-1998[27]

Henry and Myrtle Lucke joined with the other 41 original faculty members to "share the excitement of a new adventure. The administration and everybody was so upbeat, we never doubted our success," said Mrs. Lucke. Finally, the Lucke era ended in the summer of 1967 when Henry and Myrtle Lucke moved to Beeville

[25] James became dean of admissions and records in 1992.

[26] It seems that all SPC registrars have served in the Financial Aid Office at one time or another. Rangel served in the Financial Aid Office on the Lubbock Campus before being named registrar.

[27] In 1994, the dean of women's position was renamed associate dean of student life.

S.P.C. Administration and Faculty 1958

Thomas Spencer · Nathan Tubb · Clyde Prestwood · Bob Burks · J.O. Petty

Don Appling · Anne Bulls · Deane Burks · John Christmas · Arthur Dawson · Earl Gerstenberger

Inez Grant · Shirley Kennedy · L.A. Kendrick · Henry Lucke · Myrtle Lucke · Bill Powell

Roger Mae Smith · Charles Sylvester · Wilburn Wheeler

The college's full-time administration and faculty numbered 20 educators on the college's opening day in September 1958. A number of part-time faculty members were hired to help teach the unexpected number of students who registered that fall. By the following year, the number of faculty members had more than doubled to 41 instructors. In 1998, the college employed 211 full-time and 121 part-time faculty. Administrative support staff totalled 188. This collage of photos of the original faculty was produced by Photocraft Studios in Levelland and has hung in the SPC Library since the college's first year of operation.

and assumed faculty positions at the newly constructed Bee County College. The demerit system disappeared from disciplinary proceedings. A restrictive dress code and "obvious displays of affection" became things of the past. Those social guidelines gave way to the miniskirts, bell bottoms and a vastly different college climate.[28]

Dr. Spencer left his indelible mark on the institution during four short years. He would, albeit reluctantly and over the objections of his wife, leave SPC for the challenge of San Jacinto College in Pasadena, Texas. There, Spencer faced a variety of new challenges which he accepted with the same determination that characterized his tenure in Levelland. When Spencer assumed the presidency at San Jacinto College in 1961, all but one of Tom Spencer's family moved from Hockley County. Tragically, one of Spencer's twin daughters, 15-year-old Vera Sue, died Aug. 6, 1958, and was buried in Levelland City Cemetery.[29] Tom Spencer's educational career excelled as he led the Texas Public Community/Junior College Association as its president for 25 years before his retirement in 1983.

Dr. Spencer died in 1985 and was buried in the plot adjacent to his daughter, Vera Sue. Each year at the college's graduation ceremonies, a deserving coed is presented the Vera Sue Spencer Award, and in 1998, South Plains College officials instituted the Thomas Spencer Sr. Award to honor an outstanding young man. Two women's dormitories share the Sue Spencer name to continue the SPC Spencer legacy. And interestingly, within 50 feet of the headstone on Tom Spencer's grave in Levelland Cemetery are buried a quorum of the men who formed the original SPC Board of Regents. Their foresight, guidance and judgment coupled with Dr. Spencer's expertise established the solid framework for South Plains College.[30]

---

[28] In the "Constitution of Women's Residence Halls, 1968-1969," a dress code for SPC coeds was still in effect. "Levis are not to be worn to class or the Library. If weather is 29 degrees or below, slacks may be worn to classes and Texan Hall for meals."

[29] Vera Sue Spencer died five weeks prior to the opening of South Plains College.

[30] Spencer stressed the need for a Faculty Women's Club and the importance of the college's "image in the community," said Deane Burks-Espensen, a member of the faculty. "Spencer emphasized the importance of our dress, speech and actions in the community."

Three dormitories were constructed on the South Plains College campus during the administration of Dr. Tom Spencer. In 1960, Frazier, Stroud and Sue Spencer Halls joined the five original buildings on the Levelland campus. Later, South Sue Spencer, Lamar, Gillespie and Magee Halls and the Smallwood complex completed student housing on campus. The construction of residence halls enabled the college to enter a period of growth in the years after Dr. Marvin Baker became president in 1961. The city of Levelland *(background)* had an approximate population of 10,700 when the college opened its doors in September 1958. The college athletic track *(foreground)* was slated for major renovations in 1998.

When Marvin Baker, Ph.D., arrived at SPC in 1961, he was the youngest college president in Texas at age 36. Baker, shown with wife, Mildred (Storey), daughter, Barbara, and son, Tommy, retired as SPC president in 1994 and was named president emeritus by the Board of Regents. According to Nathan Tubb, registrar, academic dean and later academic vice president, there was no college president "more student-oriented than Doc Baker."

38

CHAPTER 2

The Early Growth Years

The Board of Regents named Marvin L. Baker, Ph.D., president of South Plains College in June 1961, bringing a new administrative team to SPC. Baker, having served two years in the U.S. Navy, earned a degree at East Texas State Teachers College and taught mathematics at Southwest Texas Junior College in Uvalde, Texas, in 1949. Two years later, Baker became the evening school director at Howard County Junior College in Big Spring, Texas. In 1953, Baker entered the Community College Leadership Program at the University of Texas and studied with Dr. C.C. Colvert. After completing his study, Baker returned to Howard College as assistant to President Dr. W.A. Hunt until August 1960 when he joined Florida State University in Tallahassee as professor and consultant in junior college administration.

From that position Baker, then called "Doc" by all who knew him, was the unanimous choice of the Board of Regents to become president of South Plains College when Dr. Spencer departed in 1961.[1] At age 36, he was the youngest community college president in the state when he took the reins of SPC. His management style, innovative educational attitudes and ability to work with the Board of Regents would transform SPC from a fledgling college to a comprehensive community college with an enrollment that approached 6,000 students.

Baker realized the integral role Nathan Tubb had played in the establishment of the college. Tubb's knowledge of West Texas, the students and the taxpayers

---

[1] Don Appling taught at SPC from 1958 until 1967 and worked for Presidents Spencer and Baker. When asked about their administrative talents, he said, "Dr. Spencer was more the organizer but both were excellent leaders and directors," and they both wanted you "to pick up the ball and run with it."

who supported SPC was plainly evident. Baker promoted Tubb to academic dean and delegated to him the day-to-day tasks of running the college. Simultaneously, Baker began doing what he knew best, "charting the course of a community college." His 33-year tenure and legacy can be found in the buildings, programs and reputation of SPC.

When Baker arrived in 1961, he assembled a new administrative staff to oversee the varied entities and divisions on campus. For the first year, Baker and his administrative team worked from 8:00 a.m. until noon on Saturdays to meet the challenges of a growing college. With Tubb as academic dean, Baker named William L. "Hi" Walker as administrative dean. Walker, a dirigible pilot during WWII, held degrees from Central Missouri State and West Texas State College and had previously worked with Baker at Howard College. Walker inherited what may

South Plains College's second president, Marvin "Doc" Baker, Ph.D., *(with back to camera)* had observed the founding of South Plains College while serving as assistant to the president at nearby Howard College in Big Spring. Board of Regents members who hired and worked with Dr. Baker included *(clockwise from left)* C.M. Sanders, Clarence "Hank" Mathews, E.D. Barnes, Board Chairman Lamar G. West, Verne Beebe and John V. Morton. Regents resided in all portions of the county. Several farmers served on the board. Like Spencer, Baker enjoyed the quips of his Regents as they performed the tasks of establishing and governing SPC. Sanders, in particular, was noted for his homespun humor during meetings. While discussing the frequent tornadoes that dot the South Plains in the spring, Sanders was asked what he would do in case a storm developed in the area. Sanders replied, "I'd go lay down in the black-eyed pea patch." When asked why, Sanders, having experienced the Great Depression in West Texas, said, "Those black-eyed peas saved my life before; they'll save it again."

have been the most difficult of all the Baker administrative jobs. He supervised the college buildings and vehicles, was director of student activities and served as disciplinarian of the student body. In addition, all maintenance of college facilities came under the watchful eyes of Dean Walker. Dean Walker's initial difficulties emerged within days of his arrival in late July 1961. The construction of Forrest Hall, a men's dorm, had been delayed due to inclement weather and when the fall semester began, Walker was faced with finding accommodations for the residents of the yet-to-be completed dorm. He arranged for the young men to stay in the Carlo Inn, formerly the San Andres Hotel, for several weeks until the construction was completed. In any event, Walker fondly recalled his 20-year career with SPC: "We had a sock hop in the gym or a dance in Texan Hall after every basketball game to provide social events for the students." Walker's no-

William "Hi" Walker joined SPC President Dr. Marvin Baker as part of the SPC administrative team. Walker served as administrative dean for two decades before retiring in August 1981. He directed the administrative functions of the college in a matter-of-fact, business-like manner. "As a faculty member or employee of the college, you always knew where you stood with Dean Walker," said Robert Pearce, long-time Math Department Chairman. Although Walker appeared quite "military" in his demeanor, his compassion and concern for students and faculty were well-known.

Dean J. Frank Hunt joined the South Plains College faculty in 1961 when Dr. Marvin Baker became the college's president. Initially, Hunt served as evening school administrator and taught American history. In 1965, Hunt became dean of the Technical, Vocational and Occupational Division, retiring in 1997. Interestingly, Hunt's father, Dr. Anthony Hunt, president of Howard College, Big Spring, Texas, frequently spoke to Levelland's civic clubs during the late 1950s, promoting the establishment of South Plains College.

nonsense approach to discipline is renowned among long-time faculty members. As dean of men, Walker demanded male students wear a tie to the Sunday noon meal in Texan Hall.

Frank Hunt, another University of Texas graduate, became evening school director, taught United States history and government classes and served as SPC's track and field coach.[2] In 1967, Hunt, also a graduate of Southwest Texas State, was named dean of the Technical, Vocational and Occupational Division. During the middle 1960s, technical, vocational and occupational (TVO) education emerged as the focus of many educational institutions in America. South Plains College had since its inception taught vocational short courses and evening seminars. The vocational nursing program, welding and drafting courses prompted keen interest within the Levelland community. These programs were the nucleus of what would grow into the hub for TVO education on the South Plains after SPC was named an "Area Vocational-Technical School" in 1967. Federal matching

---

[2] Hunt's father, Dr. Anthony Hunt, was president of Howard College in Big Spring, Texas, and an early supporter of SPC.

In 1962, John Dickson *(right)* joined the SPC administrative staff as tax assessor-collector. In 1983, Dickson became the college's business manager. Jean Bowman *(left)* worked as secretary to Presidents Tom Spencer and Marvin Baker and prior to her retirement in 1988 served as the college bursar.

funds legislation enabled the construction of the Technical Arts Center in 1968. At that time, TVO programs occupied only the second floor of the building. Many arts and sciences courses were taught in the first-floor classrooms. The TVO program contributed to increased enrollment and a bustling college campus as numerous buildings were erected and programs implemented during the coming years. By the fall of 1968, SPC offered 12 technical, vocational and occupational programs.

Finally, a year after Hunt's arrival, Baker completed his administrative team with the addition of John Dickson as tax assessor-collector. Dickson, then with the Levelland Public Schools, joined the SPC administration in 1962. Dickson remained as the school's "tax man" until 1982 when he became business manager. President Baker had overseen the business aspects of the college's operation since his arrival in 1961. However, with the expanded growth Baker hired Dickson

Dr. Mavin Baker (center) visits with then State Senator Preston Smith (left) of Lubbock and State Representative Olen Ray Petty (right) during the 1960 growth years of the college. During his tenure, Dr. Baker earned a reputation for being a shrewd lobbyist for the junior college cause in Texas. Working with the Texas Public Community/Junior College Association, Dr. Baker and C.A. Robinson, business manager and later chancellor for the Tarrant County Junior College District in Fort Worth, helped develop and push through the Texas Legislature a piece of landmark legislation which established contact-hour rate funding for community colleges. That legislation was the work of the Public Junior College Formula Study Committee and is credited with providing an appropriate level of state funds which fueled the growth of the community college movement in Texas in the 1970s and early 1980s.

with an extensive financial management background to direct the college's fiduciary operation. Dickson remained as SPC business manager until his retirement in 1993.[3]

Amazingly, while other community colleges and senior colleges in the state have experienced financial crises, South Plains College has remained financially sound. "We never had a serious financial strain while I was at the college," said Dickson. Although the college briefly flirted with an unbalanced checkbook that first semester of 1958 and experienced a "tightening of its financial belt" when the price of oil fell drastically in 1985, the college's presidents have judiciously managed the college's funds. The administration's insistence on maintaining a strategic financial reserve has protected the institution during the past 40 years.

The Academic Deans

Nathan Tubb, 1965-1981

Luther Bud Joyner, Ed.D., 1981-1982

Orlo Sundre, Ph.D., 1983-1989

Otto Schacht, Ph.D., 1989-1998[4]

Finally, South Plains College's administrators wisely avoided the pitfalls experienced by several other colleges across the state and nation. Several colleges invested in mortgage derivatives during the early 1990s, but what appeared to some financial strategists across the state as a budgetary windfall failed to attract the local college's administration. Their reluctance to participate in the derivative market rewarded the institution with an enhanced financial statement. Since the college's founding, a local accounting firm has conducted a yearly financial audit of the college records.[5] Local accountant Jeff Pate and the Texas State Auditor's Office examine enrollment, student residency status, tuition collection, class size, TASP compliance and accounting practices to ensure compliance with Texas law.

By 1968, South Plains College's enrollment had grown from 574 students to 1,641 students studying in more than 42 programs. A burgeoning student population from around the world changed the student body as numerous foreign

---

[3] Long-time employee Jean Bowman retired as the college bursar. Bowman began her career in 1959 as secretary to the president. She became financial bursar in 1963 and retired in 1988.

[4] Schacht joined the SPC faculty teaching agribusiness technology in August 1983, became chairman of the Science Department in August 1986, and was named the Dean of Arts and Sciences.

[5] Since the early 1980s, the firm of Pate and Parmer, and subsequently Pate and Downs, has audited the college's financial records.

During the 1962 dedication of Forrest Hall, long-time *Levelland Daily Sun News* publisher Forrest Weimhold was honored. Weimhold *(photo on left)* worked tirelessly for the establishment of the college and directed his newspaper staff to keep the junior college campaign alive on the pages of the paper. Pictured at the dedication ceremony are *(from left)* President Marvin Baker, Mrs. Mary Weimhold of Vega, Texas, mother of Forrest Weimhold, Mrs. Forrest (Ruth) Weimhold, and James Allison, a newspaper publisher and friend of the Weimhold family from Midland, Texas.

In 1965, Lamar Hall was constructed and named for Lamar G. West, former Levelland Mayor and original member of the Levelland Board of Development. West, the owner of West Lumber Company, worked closely with the Chamber of Commerce to establish South Plains College. He served as chairman of the Board of Regents from the establishment of the college until two days before his death, June 15, 1963. Lamar Hall, completed in 1965, was a $310,000 project. The dorm houses 88 students in 44 rooms.

students studied at SPC. The college celebrated its 10-year milestone with an anniversary edition of the *Levelland Daily Sun News*. The new publisher of the paper, Al Gardner, just as his predecessor Forrest Weimhold, supported SPC in all its endeavors. As the college prepared to enter the 1970s, residents of Levelland, Hockley County, the South Plains and Eastern New Mexico realized South Plains College was on the educational map.

Don't Rock the Jukebox

Presidents Spencer and Baker believed student activities enhanced the SPC students' educational experience. Thus, from that first semester in 1958, a variety of social events took place in the college's facilities. While some religious groups within the community cast a negative eye toward dancing on the campus, the age of jitterbugging, Elvis and rock and roll proved an irresistible force.

As the decade of the 1960s dawned, SPC students found much of their entertainment on campus. Student activities during the day centered around the Student Union Building jukebox, and frequent dances chaperoned by SPC faculty highlighted the school's social events. Levelland High School then allowed only one dance per year, the senior class prom. Upon arriving at SPC, those same Levelland High grads were "amazed that we could put a nickel in the jukebox and dance during the day," said former SPC student (1959-1960) and now retired Dean of Students Jerry Barton. The SUB's jukebox blared out, sometimes to the faculty's chagrin, the students' favorites.[6] Initially the college leased a jukebox from an entertainment company but because the jukebox was so profitable, "we bought our own, just as we later purchased the pool tables," remembered former Dean of Students Earl Gerstenberger.[7]

Interestingly, during the first few years "in the SUB, students played lots of dominoes, cards and ping pong," said Barton. During the early years, at any moment during the day or early evening, students gathered in the SUB to play hearts, spades or gin rummy. Although gambling of any type was strictly forbidden by

---

[6] During the 1960s, the Beach Boys and Beatles selections dominated the jukebox play. For a number of years, the country-western favorite *Pop a Top, Again,* played endlessly on the SUB jukebox. With the SUB renovations in 1981-1982, the jukebox was placed in the game room and did not fill the entire SUB with music.

[7] Later, in the early 1970s, the jukebox became a center of controversy between Hispanic and Anglo students over which recordings would be on the play list. The dean of students quickly resolved the issue by placing some popular Tejano hits in the jukebox and the issue disappeared.

Four Miss Caprock Beauties were selected by a panel of judges in 1961-1962. The honored ladies were *(from left)* Betty Holt of Bula, Claudine Campbell of Anton, Linda Wilks of Post, and Donna Williams of Matador. Claudine Campbell Oliver joined the SPC faculty in 1981 at the Lubbock Campus and later became director of guidance and counseling on the Levelland Campus.

the student handbook, penny-ante poker flourished during the 1960s in the college dorms, especially Magee Hall, according to Joe Tubb, then attending SPC on a golf team scholarship.[8] Billiards tables were not placed in the SUB until years later.

While the jukebox dominated the SUB's daily musical scene, local dance bands like *The Sparkles* from Seagraves, Texas, *The Gents* from Levelland, and *The Emeralds* from Brownfield, Texas, provided rock and roll for dances in Texan Hall.[9] Danny McClellan, a former member of the *Sparkles*, said each band member received $25 for the night's work. For a more formal event, Bob LaMont's Orchestra performed for the "dress up" dances in the Gymnasium during the early 1960s. Apparently, controversy developed when Levelland High School students attended the dances on campus until the administration restricted admission to college students. On special occasions, other students were allowed entry.

Harold "Lucky" Floyd, one of *The Sparkles* recalled the band performed once a month in Texan Hall. "At the time we had two No. 1 hit records in Lubbock and the Southwest, 'The Hip' and 'Jack and the Beanstalk.' Dr. Baker thought it would promote the college to have members of *The Sparkles* attending class, so he gave me a full scholarship," explained Floyd. As a member of the SPC Jazz Band and

---

[8] The author and fellow Brownfield High School graduates, David Brown and David Lester, and "the Seminole, Texas, crowd" staged nightly poker games in Frazier Hall during the late 1960s.

[9] *The Sparkles* original members included Guy Ballew, Jesse Ballew, Stan Smith, Bob Huckeby, Bobby Donnell, Gary Blakely and Johnny Waller. After several members of the band were called into military service, new members such as "Lucky" Floyd formed the band and used the *Sparkles* name.

Choir, Floyd was named "Mr. Music" while studying at the college. Floyd completed his degree at West Texas State University and has been a public school band director for the past 24 years.[10]

SPC athletic director and former student Joe Tubb recalled, "Oh, it was fun, it was a good time. We (Levelland) had the Spade Drive-in and the Wallace Theater so there were always things to do," said Tubb.[11] Still the SUB dominated the student activity scene. Former student Lynn O'Connor, 1964-66, recalled the first day of classes in the spring of 1966 when Brownfield native Gary P. Nunn, now of the Lost Gonzo Band, Austin, Texas, sat in the SUB playing his guitar. His impromptu performance in the SUB proved a precursor to a successful music career. Music in the late 1970s and 1980s would vault SPC into national prominence.

---

[10] Floyd is band director at Cary Middle School in Dallas.

[11] The Spade Drive-in Theater was located on the northeast corner of Hwy 114 and Alamo Road. It was torn down in the early 1980s. R & K Autoplex is located where the old theater once stood.

South Plains College student Betty Holt from Bula was selected as the Circle K Sweetheart and Claudine Campbell from Anton was named attendant in 1962. Both were featured in a parade through Levelland. Robert Chadwick of Levelland, Circle K president, was the driver of the Cadillac and Lubbock native Robert Kruse was the parade escort. Although the spirited students who prepared the convertible for the parade were well intentioned, apparently they had not yet enrolled in English class with SPC instructors Frances Watkins, Gertrude Creel, Eleanor Bond or Inez Grant. Traditionally, any comma splice or misspelled word resulted in a grade of "F" on any freshman English theme.

Two very active social clubs, Circle K and Koshare, the largest clubs on campus, sponsored the formal dances. Both clubs mimicked the Kiwanis Club in their social and service activities. A smaller but similarly active Rodeo Club also contributed to the social events and held rodeos at the college agriculture farm throughout the academic year.

Goat Ropers and Cat Daddies

Rodeo competition at SPC began with the college's founding. The college agriculture farm was the scene of numerous rodeo events through the fall and spring semesters. The college maintained an array of rodeo livestock for competition in the National Intercollegiate Rodeo Association (NIRA) Southwestern Region. Rodeo team scholarships were awarded by team sponsor Earl Gerstenberger and in 1961 by Tommy Buckner to outstanding competitors from across the South Plains and Eastern New Mexico. Jim Jenkins became rodeo team sponsor in 1968. Numerous SPC rodeo competitors qualified for the National College Rodeo Finals in Bozeman, Mont., and became NIRA champions in their events. Among them were Pow Carter of Fort Sumner, N.M., Wade Lewis of Hereford, Eddie Puckett of Sweetwater, Marvin Schulte of Nazareth, and Bowie Wesley of Happy.

Rodeo physical education classes were held at the SPC rodeo arena with other events conducted at the Hockley County Sheriff's Posse Rodeo Arena. The college renovated the SPC arena in 1971 with a new arena, feedlot and a new 30-stall horse barn and livestock judging building. To be sure, some friendly rivalry occurred on campus between "cowboys and city slickers." Those who in an earlier era would have been called "drug store cowboys" were labeled "cat daddies." Conversely, they referred to the young men in cowboy hats and boots as "goat ropers." During each year's "Spring Fling," a popular social event sponsored by the Student Activities Office, the "Cat Daddy Rodeo" generated a great deal of excitement. Students unfamiliar with rodeo sports and some SPC faculty participated in the event. Throughout the 1960s and the early 1970s, "the bucking barrel" was placed behind Frazier Hall for the rodeo students' practice.[12]

---

[12] The bucking barrel was suspended between four metal poles. Students sat astraddle the barrel while other students pulled on the spring-mounted wires supporting the barrel. A sand pit beneath the barrel cushioned the rider's inevitable fall.

Intercollegiate rodeo competition continued into the early 1980s when budgetary considerations forced cancellation of several SPC athletic programs.[13] Nevertheless, the college's competitors made their mark on the professional rodeo world. Pow Carter received the honor of being named "Rookie of the Year" in 1970 in the professional ranks and enjoyed a successful professional rodeo career. As the 1980s progressed, rodeo competition among community colleges declined. Still, many SPC students arrive each fall semester in pickup trucks with a horse trailer in tow. Rodeo physical education classes are offered and roping livestock is maintained by the college for interested students.

South Plains College's Student Activities Office has directed a variety of social events for students during the past four decades. Although Dean Clyde Prestwood and Dean W.L. Walker directed the social events in the early years of the college's existence, in the mid-1960s a director of student activities was employed by the college. Popular *Sparkles* band member Donnie Roberts served as the first director, coordinating dances and annual special events such as Western

---

[13] With the increase of community colleges in the Southwest, recruitment of rodeo athletes became highly competitive. Vernon Regional Junior College and other newly established institutions that did not maintain complete athletic programs entered rodeo competition.

South Plains College rodeos were popular among students and faculty. Each year the "Cat Daddy" rodeo brought numerous fans to the college's agriculture farm to watch the event. The "Cat Daddy" event featured young men and women who were unfamiliar with rodeo events.

Days, movies, the Halloween Carnival and awards ceremonies. Roberts was followed by Tom Selman, who also taught government. After Selman's departure, the director's position was occupied by Ken Hare who was assisted by Judy Bryant. Later directors included Bob Fallon, tennis coach Karen Knight, Harold Nolte, Jeff Anderson, Jennifer McCasland, David Jones and Thad Anglin. The student activities director coordinated a wide variety of student clubs, student government activities and meetings held in the Student Union Building (SUB).

Particularly troublesome for the student activities director was the four-lane bowling alley constructed in the SUB. In 1967, the college purchased the used equipment from the Brunswick Company. The Physical Education Department planned a bowling course within the department for the fall semester of 1968. Delays in completing the bowling alley required women's physical education instructor

Carole Long has served since 1967 as the college's dean of women. Long, an English teacher from Spur, Texas, taught in the Olton and Brownfield, Texas, public schools before joining the SPC administration. As the second dean of women, Long provided discipline and direction to the young ladies attending SPC. As the situation demanded, Long could be the stern disciplinarian while forging lasting friendships with SPC students. Pictured with Long in the Student Union Building is Doug Chance, a popular student from Post, Texas, in 1971. Chance provided the cartoon artwork for a student brochure, *When Do We Eat: A Brief Description of Resident Hall Living at South Plains College*. The clever brochure was printed by the student services staff.

Judy Bryant to use mimetic techniques to teach bowling for the first weeks of the semester until the lanes were operational. Mechanically, the bowling alley's pin setting machines consistently malfunctioned and provided numerous problems. First Donnie Roberts, then Tom Selman and Ken Hare developed considerable skill at repairing the bowling equipment. Later, Student Activities Director Bob Fallon hired student Eddie Anaya to maintain the equipment. After the SUB was renovated in the early 1980s, the bowling alley was removed and sold.

In 1981, SPC hired Baylor University graduate Harold Nolte as student activities director. "We had a great administration and ample funding for activities," said Nolte, now vice president for student development and athletic director at Kilgore College.[14] The SUB game room continues to provide a meeting place, refreshments and a gathering point for college students.

Sock-it-to-me

A popular event during the late 1960s was "Sock-it-to-Me Days," developed by Dean of Men Earl Gerstenberger and Dean of Women Carole Long. The events centered around dormitory competition and a tug-of-war which took place over a mud pit about four feet deep. As expected, the deans were usually included in the contests staged in the spring semester. As a result of vigorous coercion, Dean Long landed in the pit, temporarily "went out of sight, stood up neck deep in mud, and panicked," said Gerstenberger. The dean of men followed, but "I took three students with me." The Sock-it-to-Me Days later became the Spring Fling.

While allowing these student events, President Baker's administration, through Dean Walker, ensured proper supervision of all college activities. Walker sent each faculty member a list of the semester's social events with the assigned faculty sponsors. Walker, stern but fair, meted out discipline to those young men who were unfortunate enough to find themselves in his office.[15] Initially, during his tenure at SPC, few student problems arose to demand Walker's attention. Some limited hazing of freshmen did occur. Generally, SPC displayed a calm campus during the 1960s. As the American society changed in the late 1960s, so did the SPC students' attitudes and conduct. Walker found the day-to-day administrative duties of running a college with a greater enrollment and expanded curriculum more demanding.

---

[14] Nolte resigned his position at SPC, completed his doctorate at Mississippi State University and has done post-doctoral studies at Harvard University.

[15] No history of SPC would be complete without mentioning what became an infamous student watering hole, the "Bloated Goat." Actually, Jack's Liquor Store was just across the state line in New Mexico. Almost as a rite of passage, parched SPC freshmen were obliged to make the 45-mile trip to "the goat" for alcoholic beverages. Prior to Dec. 11, 1960, when alcoholic beverages were sold in Lubbock and well into the 1970s, "the goat" was well known to many SPC students.

CHAPTER 3

Agriculture, Science and Social Science

Agriculture

An agricultural curriculum was one of the first academic programs established by South Plains College. Earl Gerstenberger taught the agricultural science courses until Tommy Buckner joined the staff in 1965. Buckner taught the livestock and animal science classes, while Gerstenberger taught horticulture, agriculture economics and soil science. When enrollment in the department reached nearly 200 agriculture students, David Mayo joined the department in 1967. Gerstenberger, as chairman of the department, also assumed duties as the dean of men.

Within the Agriculture Department, James Carroll taught agriculture technology and B.P. "Robbie" Robinson taught courses in irrigation technology. With further growth in the program, Jim Jenkins and Bobby Robinson were added to the faculty. Mayo chaired the department in 1973 when Dan Yates was hired to replace Bobby Robinson. Agriculture student enrollment stabilized in the mid-1970s, and it was not until 1983 and upon the retirement of James Carroll that Otto Schacht, Ph.D., joined the agriculture faculty to teach agribusiness technology. Six years later, Schacht became dean of arts and sciences, and Ron Presley Jr. joined the faculty as instructor of agribusiness technology. Enrollment increases in the late 1980s prompted the hiring of Dave Cleavinger in 1991. Although agriculture students remain numerous on the SPC campus, a consolidation of the Agriculture and Science Departments occurred in 1983.

Agriculture instructor James Carroll's agriculture technology class evaluated a grain sorghum sample for moisture in the agriculture class laboratory. Pictured from left in this 1969 photograph are Tommy Robertson, Gregory Polmeier, Wayne Turman and instructor Carroll. After extensive teaching experience in public schools, Carroll joined the SPC faculty in 1968. Carroll, a veteran of WWII, served with the 69th Division and was in the American troop contingent that linked with the Soviet Army at the Elbe River at war's end.

Agriculture technology instructor James Carroll used the available educational resources of the area in his classroom instruction. Carroll *(left)*, W.L. Goble of the Levelland Vegetable Oil Mill and students Dan Bowman of Levelland and Mitchell Hale of Afton, Texas, toured the oil mill as part of the agriculture program's curriculum.

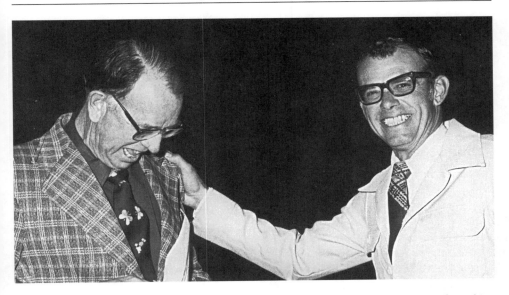

Fellow instructors James Carroll and Jim Jenkins *(at right)* shared many years of teaching agriculture to SPC students. At Carroll's retirement reception in 1983, Jenkins recalled a humorous moment between the two SPC veterans. In his retirement, Carroll has worked at restoring antique tractors and farm implements.

The agribusiness technology classes learned surveying techniques by accomplishing a differential levelling circuit across the SPC campus. In this 1978 photograph, the agriculture students are working their computations in front of the Natatorium. During the 1980s and 1990s, two new buildings were added in the area surveyed by the students. The Law Enforcement-Petroleum Technology Building was constructed in 1982 and the Math-Engineering Building was added in 1992.

The SPC Livestock Judging Team

Intercollegiate competition for SPC students involved the academic as well as the athletic. SPC entered livestock judging competition in 1970. Jim Jenkins and Dave Cleavinger have coached the college's livestock judging teams which have experienced a success unknown to most community colleges. National livestock judging competition attracts more than 35 collegiate teams from 15 states. The contests measure a student's knowledge of livestock as well as public speaking skills in orally justifying the ranking of livestock. The SPC livestock judging team first achieved success by being named Grand Champion Judging Team in overall competition at the Houston Livestock Show in 1970. Second-year SPC instructor Jim Jenkins coached Lilly Cox of Happy, Texas, Jerry Townsend of Earth, Texas, and Dewayne Gannon of Post, Texas, to the first of many SPC contest victories. Each year the judging teams competed in the premier livestock contests at Denver, San Francisco, Houston, the Arizona National in Phoenix and Kansas City.[1] After 25 years and numerous championships, Jenkins retired as coach of the judging team in 1992. He was succeeded by Cleavinger, a 1984 judging team member.

A Championship Legacy

The SPC Livestock Judging Team has established a championship reputation in its 25 years of competition. The team is the only college team in Texas to have won either the grand or reserve championship at all major contests in the nation. Here is a list of their trophy honors.

Houston Livestock Show
Grand Champions, 1970, 1985, 1992
Reserve Champions, 1971

Southwestern Livestock Exposition (Fort Worth)
Grand Champions, 1980, 1991
Reserve Champions, 1974

Arizona National Livestock Judging Contest (Phoenix)
Grand Champions, 1980, 1984, 1985
Reserve Champions, 1977, 1978, 1979, 1990

Denver National Western Exposition
Reserve Champions, 1971, 1976

San Francisco Cow Palace
Reserve Champions, 1992

---

[1] Jenkins and Cleavinger are well-known across campus for their students' manners. Team members are chosen on the basis of academics, citizenship and knowledge of livestock. Jenkins frequently sought reports from all academic instructors on his students' classroom performance. When asked about his inquiries, Jenkins said, "If they (his students) can't do the work for you (other instructors), they can't do the work for me." The list of judging team championships reflects the program's quality.

The 1974 Reserve Champion Livestock Judging Team at Fort Worth placed third overall in the Denver and Houston contests during that year's competition. The team was composed of *(from left)* Gary Moore, Eddie Wood, Billy Drennan, L.D. Hamm, Kent Lewis and team coach Jim Jenkins.

SPC agriculture instructor Jim Jenkins began coaching the college livestock judging teams in 1968. The success of his teams has made the SPC judging program among the best in the country. The 1991 Livestock Judging Team earned recognition as the winningest junior college team in the nation. Members included *(from left)* Jenkins, Skipper Carlisle from Ralls, Texas, Wesley Fraze from Portales, N.M., Troy Dodd from Melrose, N.M., Jeff Chisum from Earth, Texas, Kim Forry from Tucumcari, N.M., and Les Mayes from Roswell, N.M.

The Sciences

SPC's first Science Department chairman, Henry Lucke, charted the course of the science curriculum. Later, Bob Beck, Jim Leggitt, J.B. Balch, Polly Parmer, Gail Burrier, Glenna Cooper, Jim Wyatt, Homer McLean, Scott Couch, Duane Bowen, Jack Head and Jim Blassingame would join the department as it expanded to meet the increasing numbers of students enrolling at SPC. Moreover, SPC's first art instructor, Don Stroud, who also held a degree in science, taught geology in the Science Department during the college's early years.

Science Department Chairpersons

Henry Lucke, 1958-1967

Bob Beck, 1967-1982

Jim Blassingame, 1982-1984

Dennis Dunlay, 1984-1987

Otto Schacht, Ph.D., 1987-1989

Sam Wages, Ph.D., Biology Department, 1989-1998

Ed King, Ph.D., Science Department, 1989-1998

In 1963, SPC's Regents approved the construction of a 16,875 square feet Science Building.[2] The new facility, constructed as part of a $690,000 bond issue, cost $314,937 and was the first instructional building approved to be built after the original five campus structures.[3] Later in 1968, a Biological Sciences Building was built where biology classes were taught. Chemistry, physics and mathematics classes remained in an older building which was named the Physical Sciences Building. The expansion of the nursing program required additional anatomy and physiology classes and a further expansion of faculty and teaching areas. In 1983, the two science buildings were joined by new construction to form one complex to accommodate all science programs. Math classes were taught in the expanded building prior to that department's temporary relo-

---

[2] President Baker enjoyed the architectural planning of the SPC buildings and campus. Science classes, previously taught in the west wing of the Administration Building, were moved into the new Science Building in 1964. President Baker and science instructors Bob Beck and Homer McLean designed the inside arrangement of the science labs and lecture rooms.

[3] The bond issue entailed a five-cent tax increase for local property owners. A college district resident with a home valued at $12,400 saw an increase in his college taxes of $1.24 per year as a result of the bond issue. Proceeds from the bonds were used to expand the lounge area of the Student Union Building, build a new Agriculture Building, renovate the Gymnasium and the Administration Building and improve parking and sidewalks on campus.

cation to the Communications Building. In 1992, the college built a science annex which included three new classrooms and five faculty offices and was connected by a breezeway to the Science Building.

In 1989, the science programs were organized into two departments. Dr. Edward King assumed the role of chairman of the Science Department and Dr. Sam Wages accepted the chairmanship of the Biology Department. After King's retirement in 1998, Bill Wheeler, assistant professor of geology, was named chairman. SPC science students benefited educationally from the facilities expansion of the early 1970s. The first college greenhouse was constructed in connection with a new Agriculture Building in 1963. A Science Department greenhouse was built in 1970, and a second department greenhouse was added later.[4]

As the need for science classes grew during the late 1980s and early 1990s, Chairman Wages and Jim Young joined the Biology Department. Becky Tilton, David Etheredge, Phil Ricker, Joel McKinney, Leanna Smith, Rebecca Zamora, Iris Keeling, Jackie Wright, Ph.D., and Jacqueline Homan, Ph.D., were invited to become members of the Biology Department. Young, awarded the Excellence in Teaching Award in 1991, along with Wages, Tilton, McKinney, Wright and Homan have taught anatomy and physiology, while Ricker and Zamora have focused their students' attention on microbiology. Ricker, educated at the University of Texas, has specialized in virology, while SPC and Texas Tech University graduate Iris Keeling has taught botany and horticulture to students each semester. The Science and Biology Departments have continued to update their computer technology, utilizing video images to explain their respective fields. Ricker and Zamora have incorporated the new BIOLOG bacteria identification system in their classes to instruct students about bacteriology.

Each member of the Science Department has maintained a special field of interest within a scientific discipline. Chairman Wages' has studied parasitology, while professor Leanna Smith, who joined the college after her education at Emporia State in Kansas, has found ornithology fascinating. Smith's undergradu-

---

[4] According to former Science Department Chairman Bob Beck, at first "Earl Gerstenberger didn't want the Science Department greenhouse located next to the Science Building," adjacent to College Avenue. Gerstenberger's objections centered around the greenhouse's appearance to those driving down Levelland's main thoroughfare. Beck suggested a fence and landscaping and a compromise was worked out. The Science Department got the greenhouse, located with proper sun angle, and expanded its botanical holdings. Gerstenberger further landscaped the campus.

ate studies centered on the field of ecology but later she became an ornithologist. Smith has traveled frequently across the country, studying the bird populations of North America and has been involved in bird census studies on the Texas South Plains. Smith, an active member of the local chapter of the Audubon Society, has participated in the society's Christmas bird count on the South Plains, in Kansas and Oklahoma and the society's breeding bird survey each spring.

Meanwhile, colleague Joel McKinney, a West Texas State University graduate who teaches general zoology, has focused his study on reptiles and amphibians. As a herpetologist, he has completed additional graduate study at Texas Tech Univer-

Counseling and student advisement are an important aspect of the college's educational mission. Instructors explain their subject matter and assist students in scheduling and degree planning. Long-time botany instructor Jim Blassingame instructs two students on pteridology – the study of ferns – his favorite field of botanical study. Blassingame came to SPC in 1967 and retired in 1996. He received the Excellence in Teaching Award in 1980.

sity. Since 1990, McKinney, fellow instructor David Etheredge and Smith have sponsored the spring semester wildlife tour as part of the Introduction to Wildlife class. The faculty and approximately 25 students have toured different parts of the Southwest each year.

Spent-a-Week Trapping, Grabbing and Catching

Three SPC Science Department faculty members began to establish a wildlife specimen collection in 1969, when President Marvin Baker financed Scott Couch to collect animals, Jim Blassingame to gather plant specimens and J.B. Balch to

Science professor J.B. Balch was the sixth recipient of the Excellence in Teaching Award presented by Levelland's First National Bank. Bank President W.K. "Bill" Barnett made the $1,500 award presentation. Balch taught at Seymour High School and Levelland High School before joining the SPC faculty in 1966. Balch attended Decatur Baptist College, received his B.A. from Baylor University, and his master's degree from Oklahoma A&M in 1957. The popular instructor was one of the original 100 students selected to receive the first National Science Foundation scholarships. Approximately 50 of the honorees attended Oklahoma A&M (later Oklahoma State University) while other selectees went to Michigan State University. Balch, an avid HAM radio operator since 1939, retired from the SPC Science Department in 1982. He and his wife Wanda, a retired elementary music teacher, sent their four children to SPC. Three became medical doctors: Jim, SPC Class of 1966; Mike, 1968; and Bill, 1973. Their daughter, Candace Figg, graduated from SPC in 1970 and is a Ph.D. student at the University of Texas. During his SPC teaching career, Balch taught physical and historical geology, comparative anatomy, anatomy and physiology, nursing chemistry and freshman chemistry.

In 1973, Polly Parmer was selected by her colleagues to receive the Excellence in Teaching Award. Parmer taught botany in the Science Department for 26 years prior to her retirement in 1994. She was presented the award by First National Bank President Bill Barnett.

obtain rock samples from the Southwestern United States.[5] "Initially we thought we could collect everything in about a week," said Couch. "Dr. Baker called the trip spent-a-week, and it took almost all summer," added the veteran science teacher. The three instructors actually made three different trips that summer, one into East Texas, then South Texas, and a final excursion to the far western areas of the state.

Couch and Blassingame obtained their state scientific collecting permits in Austin, while Couch was granted the federal migratory bird permits at Albuquerque, N.M. The three SPC scientists encountered no state or federal officials during their spent-a-week expedition and were not required to display their permits. However, they did experience difficulties with the SPC vehicles. An International Travel-All van, previously used to transport Pep community students to the college, was driven by the instructors on their specimen gathering journeys. The Travel-All took the scientists several thousand miles until things went awry in the wilds of New Mexico.

"We were stopping by a rock shop in downtown Magdalena, N.M., when the engine quit and we took the air cleaner off and tried to start the engine. It coughed, and we had fire everywhere and no fire extinguisher, so it was hand fulls of sand into the carburetor. We got the fire out and spent the rest of the day at the local mechanic's shop operated by the Magdalena High School auto mechanics teacher. We decided to spend the night at Hueco Tanks State Park only to arrive and find

[5] Science Department Chairman Bob Beck accompanied the three instructors to Dr. Baker's office to request funding for the excursion. "We knew when Doc said, 'What are we gonna call this trip?' that he had approved the idea," said Beck.

that it was a day park, so we had to spend the night at a truck pull-over some-where west of Sierra Blanca," said Blassingame.

Blassingame added that after they cleaned the carburetor and resumed their journey, the engine broke down again east of El Paso near Hueco Tanks. He added, "J.B. Balch caught the parts that fell out of the distributor in his hands, put the distributor back together and we got back on the road." In addition, numerous flat tires plagued the trip in the Trans-Pecos.[6] Nevertheless, a road weary science crew returned with the nucleus of a scientific specimen collection for the department.

---

[6] Couch, Blassingame, and Balch purchased their army surplus camping cots for the trip at Helton's Hardware in Levelland. Blassingame, a botanist, Couch, a zoologist, and Balch, a geologist, probably should have taken an entomologist during their trip to the Texas coast. Blassingame maintains the Gulf Coast mosquitoes could penetrate the ducking on the underside of their army surplus cots.

In the spent-a-week program, veteran science instructor Scott Couch caught and displayed hundreds of wildlife species for the science laboratory. Couch and student Brenda Kuehler are pictured viewing a Harris's hawk, barn owl, great horned owl, short-eared owl, sand hill crane, rough legged hawk, cackling Canada goose, spoon billed duck and a meadowlark. Couch collected each species from its natural habitat on the South Plains and became a self-taught taxidermist. Kuehler, from Pep, Texas, worked in the science laboratory for Jim Blassingame. In the spent-a-week program, Couch, Blassingame and J.B. Balch traveled throughout Texas and New Mexico gathering zoological, botanical and geological specimens for the Science Department. The three instructors retired from the department and all have been recipients of the Excellence in Teaching Award.

Chemistry professor Bob Beck was the second member of the Science Department hired by Dr. Spencer. Spencer contacted Southwest Texas State College's placement service attempting to find a chemistry instructor. Beck met and interviewed with Spencer at the Driskill Hotel in Austin. Spencer was adamant that Beck, a native of the Junction, Texas, hill country, and wife, Jean, visit Levelland before accepting the faculty position. Several weeks later, in a 1951 Ford, Bob and Jean Beck traveled to Levelland. Bob interviewed with Spencer, Registrar Nathan Tubb and Dean Clyde Prestwood, and at the interview's conclusion, Beck was offered the job. Beck, however, expressed his desire to ponder his South Plains future. An insistent Spencer, known for his zeal in getting what he wanted, asked that Beck and his wife discuss the job offer on the way back to Junction and telegraph Spencer with a decision the next morning. Beck accepted the chemistry position, served as Science Department chairman from 1967 to 1982 and retired in 1996. Mrs. Beck served as Nathan Tubb's secretary from 1960 to 1964, then worked in the SPC Bookstore from 1975 until 1996. In this early 1960 photograph, Beck *(left)* explains the analytical balance to chemistry student Sandy Israel of Levelland.

Years later, Etheredge, McKinney and Biology Department faculty continue to collect and preserve wildlife specimens. Although the collection began with 200 specimens collected by Couch, Blassingame and Balch, the specimens of flora and fauna displayed and stored in the department now number in the thousands. In a cooperative effort, members of the department trade and lend specimens to other colleges and universities in the Southwest. From the original spent-a-week excursion to the current spring semester wildlife tour, the instructors' goal has been to enhance the students' zoological and botanical knowledge.

Finally, in February 1998, Etheredge and other Science Department faculty entered into a one-year wildlife baseline survey of mammals, reptiles and amphibians with the Texas Parks and Wildlife Commission. The study involves 19 trap sites in the Matador Wildlife Management Area, a 44-square-mile area in Cottle County. The project will culminate in a report to the commission. South Plains College is the only community college selected to participate in the program.

Down the Science Department hallway, students have for the past four decades weighed, balanced and experimented with chemical solutions on their way toward medical, engineering and scientific careers. Bob Beck and Jim Leggitt served through three different decades, training the pre-medical, pre-pharmacy and chemical engineers in the chemistry labs. Indeed, for more than 20 years a hand-in-glove relationship existed between the SPC chemistry program and Texas Tech University, Texas A & M and Southwestern Oklahoma State University Pharmacy School in Weatherford, Okla.

"Our relationship with Southwestern began when they sent a representative down here to encourage our students to attend Southwestern. Several of our students had gone up there and were at the top of their graduating class and they (Southwestern) wanted our students," said Beck, who chaired the Science Department for 15 years.

Beck, the second Science Department instructor hired at SPC, began his teaching career in 1959. "I was nervous when I went into that first class, but I don't think the students knew it," remembered Beck. "After Dr. Spencer hired me, he said, 'Don't go in there and tell any jokes,' because I looked younger than some of the students." Beck, a precise scientist who measured his words just as he did his chemicals for 37 years, was not given to using the classroom for levity. "I was all business," said Beck. Undoubtedly, his "business approach" toward teaching chemistry proved highly successful. Of the more than 5,000 students Beck taught, a large number are successful chemists, medical doctors and pharmacists.[7]

Marla (Maule) Swaringen, a 1974 graduate of Lamesa High School, remembered well her chemistry classes.[8] She completed her pre-pharmacy studies and graduated from SPC in 1976. Swaringen felt a bit intimidated at first but found the laboratory experiences enjoyable and "the instructors (Beck and Leggitt) were easy people to be around. I never felt overwhelmed," said Swaringen. She was named to Phi Theta Kappa at SPC and graduated from Southwestern in 1979. "South Plains College had a high reputation at Southwestern, and I experienced a smooth transition to pharmacy school. They had such good results from the SPC graduates," said Swaringen. "Three pre-pharmacy students completed the

[7] During the late 1960s, Beck, after discussion with President Baker, purchased an instrument on the cutting edge of science education, an NMR spectrophotometer. At $5,000, the instrument weighed heavily on the Science Department's budget. To offset the cost of an integral part of chemistry instruction, Beck wrote a National Science Foundation grant request and obtained one-half the funding through an NSF grant. Said Beck, "We got a lot of equipment through NSF grants in those days." At the time SPC acquired the spectrophotometer, it was the only one of its kind at a community college in Texas.

[8] Swaringen graduated sixth in her high school class and described chemistry as "her favorite subject."

prerequisites at SPC in 1976 and entered pharmacy school later that year." She added, "They (the chemistry instructors) loved their students, their subject and they taught it very well." In the same class of 1976, Matt Cearley, a Levelland High School graduate, pursued a similar pharmacy career. "When I got to Weatherford, I was prepared with a chemistry background as good or better than any student in the class," said Cearley. A pharmacist in Slaton since 1980, Cearley had strong ties to SPC. J.B. Cearley, one of the early SPC faculty members who sponsored the *Plainsman Press,* and Royce Waltrip, long-time history professor at SPC, are uncles to Matt Cearley.

Veteran SPC faculty member Ann Thompson, Ph.D., first joined the faculty in 1972 after graduating from Texas Christian University and Texas Tech University. Since her initial employment, Thompson has taught nutrition in the Science Department. Thompson was the first Ph.D. graduate in nutrition at Texas Tech in the hotel and restaurant management program. Thompson and another veteran SPC instructor, Jim Jenkins, were joined by chemistry instructors Jesse Yeh, Ph.D., Dave Millsap, Mara Winders and Timothy Werenko. The department added agriculture teachers Ron Presley in 1989 and Dave Cleavinger in 1991 to the program.[9]

The Social Sciences

The year the college opened, Arthur Dawson joined the faculty as the social sciences instructor. In addition, Dawson became the college's first baseball coach. As a veteran educator, Dawson arrived in Levelland to a rather bleak, windy West Texas.[10] Dawson taught at SPC for two years before moving into school administration in South Texas. Dawson was followed in the History Department by two Levelland school teachers, Royce Waltrip, who also became baseball coach, and Don Appling, a teaching associate of Dr. Spencer's wife, Rachel.

In like manner, Dr. Spencer found time to enter the classroom and teach government classes during those initial SPC years. Spencer, keenly aware of the Texas Legislature's watchful funding eye on community colleges, used the classroom to foster communication with his legislators. Spencer hired Olen Petty to

---

[9] Both Cleavinger and Presley are SPC graduates.

[10] Mrs. Dawson remembered her neighbor calling to warn her of an impending sandstorm, something the young mother of two had never seen. She was aghast at the storm and the need to rewash the laundry she could not retrieve from the clothesline before the storm.

teach government at SPC when the Legislature was not in session. Petty was the floor leader for junior college legislation during the legislative session. With a state legislator on his faculty, Spencer would have ample opportunity to lobby for the community colleges in Texas.[11] Petty's successor in the Legislature was Brownfield native Jesse T. George, who, at the behest of SPC's second president, Marvin Baker, also joined the SPC social science faculty. George taught history and state government at SPC when the Legislature was not in session.[12] The SPC presidents understood the necessity of maintaining contacts in Austin.[13]

Social Science Department Chairpersons

Don Appling, 1958-1967

Joe R. Baulch, 1967-1974

Travis Spears, 1974-1998

Appling, in addition to teaching history, coached the SPC tennis team, sponsored the Student Council and worked with Inez Grant sponsoring Phi Theta Kappa.[14] Appling, who remained at SPC until 1967, fondly recalled the early faculty. "We were beginning something new, had a pioneering spirit and were inspired by Dr. Spencer."[15]

After Appling's departure to attend law school, Joe R. Baulch became social science chairman until Travis Spears became chair in 1974. Five years into the college's history, Robert Van Burkleo taught sociology and psychology. During the 1960s, Dave Stanley, Bernadyne Turpin, Bill Billingsley, Gary and Gwen Wynn,

---

[11] Petty had previously served on Congressman George Mahon and Speaker Sam Rayburn's staff in Washington prior to Petty's election victory in the 1960 Democratic primary for District 90 in the State Legislature. Petty served in the 1961 and 1963 sessions of the Legislature. Petty's father, T.O. Petty, was the college's first tax assessor-collector.

[12] George represented District 90 in the 59th Texas Legislature in 1965 and the 60th Legislature in 1967. George served on four committees during that session, one of which was the Education Committee.

[13] After President Spencer left Levelland to take the helm of San Jacinto College, he continued his friendship with the Brownfield legislator. George resigned after the 60th legislative session, moved to Washington and joined President Johnson's administration. After Johnson's decision not to run for re-election in 1968, George joined the Hubert Humphrey presidential campaign.

[14] SPC's first tennis team consisted of two young men, Vaughn Culwell and Danny McClellan, both of Plains, Texas.

[15] Appling, like many SPC employees in each of the college's four decades, "took a pay cut to come to SPC. I signed on for $4,800.00 a year." Appling was the second recipient of the Excellence in Teaching Award in 1965.

Bill Pohl and Ron Carden, Ph.D., joined the Social Science Department.[16] The enrollment increases of the 1970s required additional behavioral sciences class offerings. Gary Wynn became chairman when the Behavioral Science Department was created in 1991. After his retirement in 1996, Peggy Skinner, Ph.D., who joined the faculty in 1978, became chairperson. Bob Leahy, Ph.D., Susan Dubberly, Jacqueline Specter, Virginia Mahan, Ed.D., Bill Ritchie, Ph.D., Wanda Clark, Ph.D., and Sharon Scott have taught in the department. Both Social and Behavioral Science Department faculty have been a mainstay, teaching extension courses for the Division of Continuing Education.

Behavioral Science Department Chairpersons

Gary Wynn, 1991-1996

Peggy Skinner, Ph.D., 1996-1998

With added enrollment and a reorganization of instructional departments, the Social Science Department has grown to 13 members. Rudy McCallister, an economics instructor in the Business Department since 1976, moved to the Social Science Department in 1989 following a program realignment. During the 1980s, Terry Isaacs, Larry Norris and Randy Rowan, Ph.D., were hired. Daniel Bunye, Jimmie McGee, Laura Graves, Ph.D., and Bob Bilodeau joined the department during the 1990s. Sharon Bogener, Ph.D., replaced veteran Bill Billingsley when he retired in 1997.[17]

---

[16] Student Activities director Tom Selman taught government in the Social Science Department.

[17] Isaacs and Bogener are SPC graduates.

Social Science Department instructor Travis Spears joined the SPC faculty in 1967 and followed Joe R. Baulch as chairman in 1974. The first social science chairman was Don Appling who held the position for 10 years. Spears, after attending Hardin-Simmons University in Abilene, completed his bachelor's and master's degrees at Eastern New Mexico University in 1967.

Barbed Wire, the Railroad and the Democratic Party

Social Science Department faculty members Royce Waltrip, Bill Billingsley and David Stanley brought their love of the Old West, the frontier and politics into the SPC classrooms. Waltrip, a life-long barbed wire aficionado, displayed a variety of barbed wire samples to his history students during his 21-year teaching career. Waltrip retired in 1981. Billingsley, a published scholar on the history of the Fort Worth and Denver City Railroad, taught at SPC for 29 years and retired from the Social Science Department in 1997. David R. Stanley served as Hockley County Democratic Party chairman while teaching government, geography and American history during his 22-year SPC career.

Royce Waltrip taught United States history and coached the Texan baseball team. Waltrip, who served on the SPC faculty for 20 years, was an admirer of the western frontier era. He began collecting barbed wire during the early 1960s and developed an extensive wire collection which was the subject of numerous history lectures to his students. Waltrip retired from SPC in 1981. Waltrip's long-time Social Science Department colleague, Bill Billingsley, held a fascination for the history of America's railroads. Billingsley, noted for his research and knowledge of the Fort Worth and Denver Railroad, retired from the department in 1997.

Gary Wynn, former chairman of the Behavioral Science Department, joined the SPC faculty in 1966. During his 30-year career, Wynn taught American history, sociology and anthropology. Wynn served as Magee Hall dorm supervisor from 1969-74.

Government instructor Travis Spears, since joining the faculty in 1967, has periodically taken interested government students to Austin during the legislative session. Classroom guest lecturers have included State Senators Max Sherman, Horace J. "Doc" Blanchard, Kent Hance, John Montford and State Representatives E.L. Short, Jim Rudd and Gary Walker. During Congressional recesses, George Mahon also returned to the classroom and answered students' questions about government. Pictured above is Spears' 1975 class on the Capitol steps with State Senator Max Sherman. As the college's enrollment and social science faculty increased, government instructors Larry Norris and Daniel Bunye have sponsored student trips to the State Capitol.

South Plains College's Social Science Department instructors, under Chairmen Joe R. Baulch and later Travis Spears, frequently invited state politicians into their SPC classrooms. Former State Senator Horace J. "Doc" Blanchard *(shown at right)*, his successor Kent Hance, State Representative Jim Rudd and District 80 Representative Gary Walker have been guest lecturers in the college's government classes. Blanchard and Hance campaigned across the South Plains and spoke at SPC in their heated 1974 campaign. Both candidates courted the college student vote, which Hance won, to take the seat from incumbent Blanchard. Hance was a former business law instructor at Texas Tech University and later became Congressman from the 19th District.

Terrible Tex
mascot, 1995

CHAPTER 4

Chaparrals, Conquistadors or Texans

While the college's new faculty members conducted classes and sponsored the various social clubs on campus, students undertook the task of naming the college's mascot. Former cheerleader, drill team member and college newspaper staffer Barbara Edwards (George) recalled that the newspaper staged a contest to name the SPC mascot. Suggestions such as "Comancheros, Chaparrals and Conquistadors were proposed for the students' consideration. Clearly the college president favored "Texans." According to George, "of all the schools in Texas, not a one used Texans" as their mascot at the time.[1] Some discussion was held and possibly a vote was taken among staffers of *The Plainsman*, the college newspaper, during the selection process. Apparently, Chaparrals and Texans were the favorites, and students eventually agreed with Dr. Spencer and selected Texans as the official name.[2]

One of the first SPC students with strong family ties to the college was Gary Grant. Grant, now professor of English at Howard College, not only wrote for the college newspaper and played on the first basketball team, but he drew the first mascots, "Ol' Tex" and "Tex-Ann." According to Grant, whose father was an origi-

---

[1] John Tarleton College, although now known as "Texans," did not adopt that mascot name until 1961 when the Stephenville, Texas, college "Plowboys" wanted to attract more students from urban areas of Texas. Thus, three years after SPC became Texans, Tarleton adopted the same mascot name.

[2] No mention is made of the official selection of the name "Texans" in the college newspaper. However, the first notation of "Texans" in the newspaper was in the Oct. 31, 1958, edition of *The Plainsman*, in a sports story headlined, TEX TALKS, "Terrible Texans looking better after workouts."

The original "Ol Tex" mascot *(above)* was drawn by student Gary Grant in 1958. Grant created a wooden cut-out version which was hung in Texan Gym by the Circle K Club in 1959 *(below)*.

In the fall of 1966, Richard Whittenburg *(above)*, at the behest of the Student Government, became the college's first real life "Ol' Tex." Whittenburg posed for this silhouette photograph for the yearbook. An agriculture major from Graham, Texas, he was a member of the SPC Rodeo Team and his buddies nominated him for the mascot role. He later completed his bachelor's degree at Texas Tech and was a rodeo bullrider for 16 years. While attending SPC during the summer of 1967, Whittenburg worked for Earl Gerstenberger, installing the first underground sprinkler system on the college campus.

SPC's new mascot, "Terrible Tex," *(at left)* was introduced at the All-Sports Pep Rally, Nov. 3, 1980. The administration desired a "more interactive" mascot and "Tex" became a part of the college traditions. Student Activities Director Harold Nolte travelled to Hollywood and met with Disneyland designer Rousseau who fashioned "Tex" for the college. "Tex" made a rather dramatic entry into the pep rally when the motorized maintenance cart upon which the mascot rode crashed into the door facing in the Women's Gym. The student driving the cart, Don Weems, said the steering unit in the cart malfunctioned, and he could not turn the cart to avoid the wall. SPC's athletic director and track coach, Clint Ramsey, was almost a casualty of the mishap. Ramsey was pinned between the wall and cart and suffered minor bruises. Another popular event among students at the Texan pep rallies was the "money scramble." Levelland State Bank donated $300 for a lucky student, selected by drawing, to "scramble for 30 seconds" and pick up the money scattered about the gym floor.

The SPC mascot's character has evolved during the past four decades. A desire for a "leaner and meaner" mascot led to the most recent version of "Terrible Tex" *(at right)* which was unveiled during the 1991 season. SPC's first mascot, Richard Whittenburg, returned to the campus in the fall of 1995 to help introduce "Tex's" companion and sidekick, a horse named "Tumbleweed." When Whittenburg was the mascot, his costume was nothing more than a sweater he purchased which closely resembled that worn by the Texan Cheerleaders. He wore his own boots and hat. "Tex had a cigarette dangling from his mouth, and I didn't smoke," said Whittenburg. "I would put an unlit cigarette in my mouth when we took pictures. It was lots of fun." Whittenburg resides in Comanche, Texas.

nal SPC Regent and mother, Inez Grant, was an English professor, he used a 4-foot by 8-foot piece of plywood as his canvas and blue and white paint to draw the mascots.[3] The Circle K Club sponsored Grant's "Ol Tex" and "Tex-Ann" caricatures. Both painted plywood cutouts were displayed in the Gymnasium. Later, on the west wall of the Women's Gym, the caricatures were painted on the wall until recent renovations forced their removal.[4]

During the 1960s, the student body selected a popular student to serve as "Ol Tex" for the academic year. In 1967, Robert (Bob) Brown, president of the SPC Agriculture Club and a member of the Rodeo Team, was chosen to wear the traditional SPC western wear. Brown, from Dalhart, Texas, carried the lasso and wore the SPC chaps at all college events. Brown fondly recalled his SPC classmates and instructors. "There was a tremendous amount of success in those classes during those years." Economics instructor Mitchell Masters and agriculture instructors Tommy Buckner and Earl Gerstenberger exerted a lasting impression on Brown. "Masters impressed me more than anyone in my life. He was one of the most vibrant instructors I'd ever been around. He gave you ideas and ambition instead of just a piece of paper to get a grade on. He left something with me," said Brown. The Dalhart resident, who maintains contact with more than a dozen of his 1967 SPC classmates, graduated from West Texas State University in 1969 with a degree in agribusiness.

**Faculty Sponsors
of the Texan Cheerleaders**

Myrtle Lucke, 1958-1964

Kathy Powell, 1964-1965

Nancy Morris, 1965-1967

Jeanelle Spears, 1967-1968

Judy Bryant, 1968-1974

Jeanelle Permenter, 1974-1989

Karla Payne, 1989-1990

Kelli Smith, 1990-1994

Tina George[5], 1994-1996

Rebecca Brinley, 1996-1998

---

[3] Grant drew "Ol Tex" with a cigarette dangling from his mouth. During the late 1960s and early 1970s, Grant's caricature, although reproduced in many college publications, was altered to remove the cigarette. College administrators were sensitive to the implications of a cigarette hanging from the mouth of "Ol Tex" in the drug culture of the era.

[4] Grant drew "Ol Tex" freehand and did not use a silhouette, although a picture, greatly resembling the mascot drawn by Grant, was found by the author in the SPC photograph archives. Apparently in 1966 Richard Whittenburg, an agriculture student from Graham, Texas, was nominated by fellow students to pose as "Ol Tex" for the silhouette. Art and photography instructor Don Stroud probably took the photograph of Whittenburg.

[5] Payne, Smith and George graduated from SPC.

The South Plains College Tex-Anns, the college drill team, was initiated by the first college president Dr. Thomas Spencer. After Dr. Marvin Baker became president in 1961, the team continued to perform at athletic and social events across the South Plains. Members of the 1966-67 squad included *(front row)* Olga Bowers, Jo Ann Moreland, Beverly Arnwine, *(second row)* Debbie Mathis, Jackie Parish, Vickie Williams, Jo Lynn Flowers, Karen Cannon, *(third row)* Libby Tubb, Connie Dennis, Doyleen Davis, Janice Ramsey, Carlene Benson, Carolyn Flatt, Betty Sharbutt, Gaylene Weed, Connie Reed, *(fourth row)* Judy Roberts, Donna Schoenrock, Becky Reid, Barbara Garrett, Jan Martin, Judy Reaves, Gayle Price, Pat Harper and Donna Colvin. In the late 1970s, the Tex-Anns were combined with the Texan Cheerleaders into one spirit-dance organization under the direction of Jeanelle Permenter.

Dr. Marvin Baker, long a college sports, music and student activities enthusiast, worked to cultivate positive student-administration communications. His 33-year tenure as president is testimony to his success. Conversely, Baker was not as successful at learning the latest Tex-Ann dance step as drill team instructor Myrtle Lucke explains the movement to the Tex-Anns. In this 1967 photograph, "Doc," with his favorite cigar in hand, was out of step with most of the team.

During the 1970s, the college discontinued the tradition of naming a student "Ol Tex." Nevertheless, those who were honored with being named "Ol Tex" vividly recalled their education at SPC during the 1960s.

In all likelihood, the college president chose the school colors, blue and white. Several years later, at the insistence of the college's second president, Dr. Marvin Baker, and Athletic Director Bill Powell, burnt orange was added to the blue and white. At the time in 1963, five schools in the Western Junior College Athletic Conference used blue as their primary color. President Baker called for a meeting of the college's Student Council members and faculty to consider adding orange to the colors. A committee comprised of Dr. Baker, Coach Powell, Charles Sylvester, Wilburn Wheeler, Frank Hunt, Myrtle Lucke and Dean W.L. Walker suggested the color orange. Two weeks later, according to an October 1963 report in *The Plainsman Press,* the Student Council approved the addition of orange to blue and white. Both Baker and Powell were University of Texas graduates and both held strong feelings toward burnt orange, not unlike a similar maroon malady held by other SPC administrators and faculty who graduated from Texas A & M University.

Faculty Sponsors
of the Flaming Spurs

Royce Waltrip, 1964-1968

Travis Spears, 1968-1969

Travis Spears, David Durham, 1969-1970

Travis Spears, 1970-1972

Travis Spears, Kieth Mixon, 1972-1974

The Flaming Spurs were a group of "rowdy boys" who spurred crowd participation during Texan basketball games. The group was organized in 1967, and members wore royal blue vests with the club name embroidered on the back. Students had to put down a $20 deposit to secure the vests, a lot of money for an 18-year-old college student at the time. Cameron Choban from Ontario, Canada, was a member of the first Flaming Spurs. In 1993, Choban made a sentimental journey back to SPC to ceremoniously return his Flaming Spur vest after 25 years. Choban *(at right)* presents the vest to Athletic Director Joe Tubb. The only remaining vest is displayed in the T-Club of Texan Dome.

No college environment would be complete without the enthusiastic cheerleaders traveling with the athletic teams. The Texan Cheerleaders began as a small group and have evolved during the past four decades into an exciting dance, cheer and gymnastics group who perform at all SPC events. Although Myrtle Lucke provided faculty sponsorship for the first group, apparently speech instructor Lilbern Kendrick was the SPC students' favorite to lead cheers in the college gym. Kendrick, an energetic instructor, captured students' attention when he led a cheer at each pre-game pep rally. The Texan Cheerleaders remained separate from the Tex-Anns until Jeanelle Permenter transformed both groups into an athletic dance group which, according to Athletic Director Joe Tubb, "never loses a halftime performance to any cheerleaders."

In the mid-1960s, an additional spirit organization, The Flaming Spurs, was started by Ron Kitten, Mike Kitten and Fred Blount. The Spurs in their bright blue vests patrolled the out of bounds stripes in both the old Gymnasium and Texan Dome during each Texan basketball game. The spirit organization remained as an active group into the early 1970s when they disbanded.

In 1980, the college's administration changed the Texan mascot "Ol Tex" to "Terrible Tex." The new mascot patterned his antics after those exhibited by some major league baseball teams' mascots. "He's the Philadelphia Phanatic and the San Diego Chicken all rolled into one," said Dean of College Relations Eddie Trice when the new mascot was unveiled. Since then, the "Terrible Tex" mascot has undergone several fashion updates as the times changed.

During the 1960s, a bonfire capped the Homecoming pep rally. The bonfires were held east of the college track near the baseball field. Pictured here are 1967 Texan cheerleaders Linda Collins (left) of Brownfield and Cheryl Martin of Post. Other cheerleaders that year were Paula Broadwell of Plainview, Mickie Horn of Levelland and Teresa Leonard of Lubbock.

The 1985 Texan Cheerleaders were *(from left)* Regina Powell, Melanie Cowan, Jamie Drachenberg, LaShay Box, Stacy Key, Rayla Simpkins, Eva Batto, Mary Garza, Karla Hill and Irma Gallegos. Performing as "Terrible Tex" was Jill Taylor. Jeanelle Permenter was sponsor of the Texan Cheerleaders from 1979 to 1990. *(Photo courtesy of Jeanelle Permenter)*

A School Song

The SPC alma mater first appeared in the college's newspaper in December 1960. The college faculty requested a school song in the spring of 1960 and student Thomas Taylor, having been named "Mr. Music at SPC," presented his original composition, "The Texan's Song," the following November. Taylor was a member of the SPC Band and Chorale and at the time of the song's selection was a junior music major at North Texas State University. It seems the song fell out of favor and has been altered throughout the college's history. In January 1966, the SPC student body voted on two songs, one of which became the official alma mater. A music student, Ella Faye Young from Pep, Texas, had submitted the music four years earlier.[6] Music professor Harley Bulls made several corrections and wrote the lyrics. Several years later, the song was replaced by a fight song written by band director Wilburn Wheeler and President Marvin Baker. Subsequently, to observe the 30th graduation ceremony, the fight song was rewritten by Lynda Reid to become the school's alma mater. Words to the composition were penned by English professor Lee Weldon Stephenson.[7]

---

[6] The 1966 college news release attributed the song to Ella Faye Young, "a resident of the area." Her husband was a member of the Pettit and Smyer school faculties.

[7] According to Stephenson, Director of College Relations Stephen John is to be credited with the current school song. John asked Stephenson to rewrite the lyrics in anticipation of the college's 30th anniversary in the fall of 1987. "The SPC Alma Mater," in faster tempo, is the school's fight song.

The Plainsman

The Plainsman, the college student newspaper, also experienced changes during the college's history. The first edition of the paper, Oct. 15, 1958, was published inside the *Levelland Daily Sun News* by publisher and early college supporter Forrest Weimhold. Mary Nell Copeland and Michael J. Knowles served as faculty sponsors for *The Plainsman's* initial six editions. In February 1959, Deane Burks joined Knowles as the sponsor of the student newspaper. The number of student reporters varied from seven to 17 during the early publication years.

With little fanfare, the original name *The Plainsman* was changed in December 1960 at the suggestion of *Levelland Daily Sun News* editor Orlin Brewer. Sponsor Burks said Brewer believed *The Plainsman Press* name was more "professional." Burks was the wife of the night school director, Bob Burks. The former Levelland public school English teacher possessed little experience in newspaper

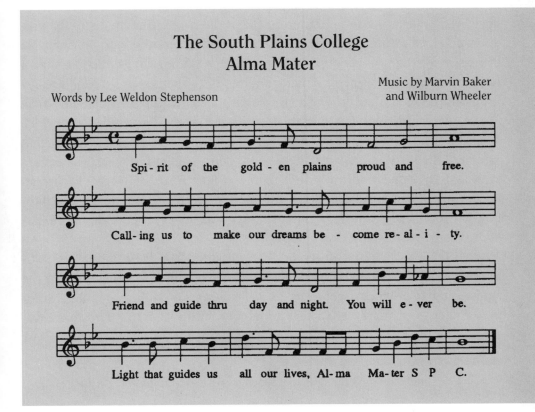

journalism and relied on the expertise of editor Brewer. In the fall semester of 1959, the Burks and Brewer team taught the journalism class, and according to Burks, "Mr. Brewer really enjoyed teaching the class.

"Dr. Spencer wanted a newspaper because he believed it brought the student body and the community along with what we were trying to do," said Burks. During the academic year, two editions of *The Plainsman Press* were mailed out to the high schools across Texas and Eastern New Mexico.

Numerous faculty members served as advisors to the college's newspaper during the next four decades. J.B. Cearly was advisor during the mid-1960s, and for a while, English Department faculty member Jim Cooper, Ph.D., advised and sponsored *The Plainsman Press*. Jon McCarroll acted as advisor in the middle 1970s, and in the 1980s, journalism instructor John Sparks advised the paper. At that time, Brazos Printing in Slaton, Texas, and Chaparral Printing in Lubbock printed the paper while the journalism lab students produced their college newspaper stories on eight electric typewriters.[8]

With the computer age, Sparks, after visits to neighboring colleges, introduced the SPC journalism program to electronic typesetting. In 1986, the program obtained a Compugraphic typesetter which interfaced with an Apple IIe computer for the production of the paper. Betty Stanley, long-time journalism teacher, became newspaper instructor and yearbook sponsor in 1983 followed by Billy Smith when Stanley joined the English Department in 1988. Often *The Press'* advisors found themselves at odds with the overzealous student reporters. According to Smith, a student wrote an editorial in the school newspaper that criticized the Board of Regents' decision to increase college tuition. The college president expressed his dismay while moments later Board of Regents Chairman and former SPC student Gary Stacy told advisor Smith it was a "wonderful editorial; tell your students it was fabulous." Such was the experience of one *Plainsman Press* sponsor.

In 1990, Carolyn Dale Husen became advisor to *The Plainsman Press*. Numerous innovations in desktop publishing and computer graphics enabled the student staff to produce the bi-monthly paper. Seven PowerMac computers, scanners and color printers were added to the journalism laboratory providing students with the latest in publishing equipment. Since 1990, *The Plainsman Press*

---

[8] During the late 1960s, the journalism program in connection with student activities published *The Plainsman Press* weekly.

Over the Wall, 1968

Several rogue journalism students briefly published *Over the Wall* during the fall semester of 1968. They distributed the anti-Nixon, anti-war, anti-George Wallace, photocopied paper across campus and stirred the ire of college administrators. Apparently, the students who initiated the paper wanted to foment interest in the upcoming national elections. However, they did include a tongue-in-cheek commentary on college students circling the Dairy Queen on Avenue H and hindering the elderly from entering the popular drive-in. As a preface to the first edition, the editors included the following: "This paper will attempt to present a somewhat biased and perverted view of the news as seen through the eyes of a liberal-conservative. Special attention will be focused on national politics and the upcoming elections. The paper will not attempt to give equal coverage to anyone, and it reserves the right to state its point of view openly on any issue it deems necessary. We in no way wish to slander the great institution of South Plains College, otherwise known as Columbia of the prairie. Therefore, any similarities in personalities or names mentioned is probably coincidental."

Although the entire *Wall* was an editorial commentary, probably most interesting was the article titled "The Goat Adds a Hawk," and a political cartoon lampooning the Mia Farrow and John Cassavettes film, *Rosemary's Baby.* The article and cartoon are found below as they appeared in the publication.

THE GOAT ADDS A HAWK

"General Curtis Lemay, retired, was recently vaulted (or stumbled) into the national spotlight, when George Wallace, with all the pomp and ceremony due a postal clerk, announced LeMay as his choice for running mate, just a heartbeat away. The surprise was not so much Lemay's acceptance, but even more surprising, is that a pert blonde named Ja-Neen Welch was not even given honorable mention as being in the running for the number two spot. But Wallace may be priming her as his successor if he is unable to change the constitution to succeed himself after the second term.

LeMay adds much in the way of prestige to the ticket. It was a superb political stroke, as George continues to surprise even himself. LeMay relinquished his high post in the U.S.A.F. for a 'peaceful' retirement. Now he finds himself on the second spot of the American Party. It is hard to say which position is more enviable, the number two spot, or retirement.

The general has distinguished himself time after time in battle and disappointed no one as he fit the good fight with the dangerous reporters of Pittsburg. He immediately got himself embroiled in an argument over the possible use of nuclear weapons. It seems impossible, but the General has, in one press conference, outdistanced the whole Goldwater campaign of '64 for ultra-conservatism."

staffers carry camera ready pages to Hereford, Texas, where the paper is printed by North Plains Printing. In addition, *The Plainsman Press* can now be found on the Internet via the SPC web site. In the fall of 1997, the college newspaper staff numbered 30, a considerable change from the first staff of seven reporters, columnists and writers. In 1994, *The Plainsman Press* staff garnered 13 awards for journalistic reporting. Eight of the honors came from the Rocky Mountain College Media Association, a group that has member colleges from 14 western states.

College administrators decided to eliminate the *Caprock*, the college yearbook, in 1990. By then, college yearbooks had fallen out of vogue for most SPC students and printing expenses had continued to escalate. Although numerous individuals decried the end of the *Caprock* which was first published in 1959, financial considerations prevailed. SPC joined a host of other community colleges and universities that ceased publishing a yearbook.

SPC-TV 13

SPC's entry into a curriculum of radio and television broadcasting took place in 1978. Since that time, graduates of the program have worked in radio and television markets across the United States. Each of the Lubbock network affiliates employs no fewer than five SPC telecom students.

The first use of television began with social science professor Gary Wynn, who received a $3,800 matching grant in 1976. Wynn initially viewed television as a teaching tool to improve the quality of education. By 1978, funds became available to purchase equipment for a small studio located on the second floor of the SPC Library. The studio had no control room; however, it represented the beginning of a popular instructional course of study.

The administration moved the studio to a larger room on the first floor of the Library in 1979, and in the fall semester, the studio was used for the first course in broadcasting taught by Pat McCutchin. The four semester hour television production course emphasized studio production activities. When McCutchin resigned at the end of the fall semester to enter private business, journalism instructor John Sparks assumed direction of the program. Sparks, in his first year of advising *The Plainsman Press* and *Caprock*, also taught the print journalism courses. However, the electronic media was Sparks' real passion. By December 1980, the telecom class moved toward broadcast journalism when it aired the first student-produced newscast on the local cable system. The first student news team included Robin Grevelle of Lubbock, Tim Torres of Lubbock and Melanie Ainsworth of Levelland. The first show included a feature about government professor David R. Stanley, local news events and the reaction of students to the death of musician John Lennon. In order to have the show broadcast on the cable system, Sparks and his students took the video tape to the cable system's broadcast control center located northwest of Levelland.

Enrollment in the telecom program grew rapidly as the Texas Higher Education Coordinating Board approved a full transfer curriculum for SPC's broadcast course in 1982. The next year the old Welding Shop Building, which years earlier had been the first auto-mechanics shop, was converted to the Mass Communications Building. It housed the SPC-TV program and *The Plainsman Press* staff. For the first time in the college's broadcast program history, the students utilized a full feature studio, control room and editing facility. Betty Stanley served as director of the print media, and Sparks turned his attention to the telecom program which had expanded to six different courses.

Landmark Cable Television installed a microwave transmission system during the winter of 1983 and SPC-TV became a full-time cable channel on the Levelland cable television system. The following year, SPC entered into an agreement with *The Learning Channel* that allowed the college to provide top quality educational shows while retaining the rights to air student-produced programming.

One student-produced program was an immediate hit with Levelland's youngsters. "Fun with Mary Freckleberry," hosted by theater major Becky Boyd, featured Levelland elementary school children in a talent show format. One local resident remembered that the front yards would be empty while the show was being aired.

In 1998, SPC telecom students produced more than 150 live news updates and telecast 10 live Texan basketball games during the academic year. Feature length documentaries and programs with public service announcements are produced and aired on the local cable system. Each year, telecom students have competed in statewide broadcast competitions with state and private universities. One measure of the telecom program's success has been the awards received by SPC students. Although it began in a small room on the second floor of the SPC Library, it has blossomed into a training ground for the area's on-and-off-camera news and journalistic talent on the South Plains.

The W. D. "Dub" Rogers Broadcast Collection

In 1992, television pioneer W. D. "Dub" Rogers, Jr. donated his extensive collection of television memorabilia to the South Plains College telecommunications program. Rogers was the founder of KDUB-TV, Channel 13 in Lubbock, which began operations in 1952 as the first television station in West Texas. The collection chronicles the growth and development of the television industry and includes rare films, audio tapes, photographs, scripts and business records.

The gift of the collection to the college resulted from the efforts of John Sparks, who first met Rogers in 1990. Sparks initially wanted to video tape an interview with the television pioneer for use in his television classes. During the following two years, the two met on several occasions to discuss the early days of television. Along the way, Rogers learned about the SPC telecom program and became convinced that South Plains College should become the permanent home of the collection. The collection is housed in the Communication Building, where it is an important resource for students who wish to learn first-hand about the early days of the television industry on the South Plains.

On Nov. 13, 1992, South Plains College honored television pioneer W.D. "Dub" Rogers, Jr. for his contributions to the telecommunications industry on the South Plains. During special ceremonies, the SPC-TV studio was named the W.D. "Dub" Rogers Studio. Pictured at the dedication ceremonies are *(from left)* John Sparks, sponsor of SPC-TV and telecommunications professor; Dub Rogers; and Dr. Otto Schacht, dean of arts and sciences. The event coincided with the 40th anniversary of the day Roger's station, KDUB-TV, Channel 13, signed on the air. KDUB-TV later became KLBK-TV.

CHAPTER 5

Dormitory and Student Life

When South Plains College's doors opened in 1958, many students sought housing in the city of Levelland. Students attending SPC from great distances found accommodations in the homes of Levelland residents. College officials cooperated with the city's residents who wanted to rent individual rooms to students. At the beginning of each semester, the dean of women published a list of prospective rental properties and landlords within the city.

South Plains College's first international student, Wolfram Von Maszewski, fondly recalled his two years, 1958-1960, at 110 Linda Lane. The Hamburg, Germany, native arrived intending to study engineering at Texas Tech. With his language skills improving and still learning about the Southwestern United States, Von Maszewski was directed to South Plains College by an advisor at Texas Tech. Von Maszewski found Levelland residents Mr. and Mrs. Clyde Younger and made lifelong friends. The Youngers offered him a room in their home and assisted Von Maszewski in finding a part-time job in Levelland. "They told me to come and go just as if it were my home. We became dear friends," said Von Maszewski.[1] Through the first 10 years of SPC's existence, numerous students found housing arrangements within the city.

As the college's enrollment grew, dormitories were added to accommodate the student housing needs. Under Dr. Tom Spencer's direction, the first three

---

[1] Von Maszewski met his future wife Betty Spencer, the President's daughter, while studying in the SPC Library.

dormitories, Frazier Hall, Stroud Hall and North Sue Spencer were constructed, and were dedicated by Congressman George Mahon in November 1960. The Board of Regents and the SPC administration named a later addition to the women's dorm South Sue Spencer Hall in 1962. Frazier Hall was named for early Hockley County pioneer Walter Frazier, while Stroud Hall was named in honor of Jim Stroud, first sheriff of Hockley County. The Sue Spencer dorm complex was named in honor of Tom Spencer's deceased daughter. In 1961, the college dedicated Forrest Hall to honor the publisher of the *Levelland Daily Sun News,* Forrest Weimhold. In addition, the Board of Regents recognized the contributions of the board's first chairman, Lamar West, by constructing Lamar Hall in 1965. At that time, the last dormitories erected on campus, Magee Hall and Gillespie Hall, were completed. Magee Hall was named in honor of Hockley County Judge D.E. Magee. Gillespie Hall was named to honor one of the first contributors to SPC scholarships, Mary Gillespie. Mrs. Gillespie moved to Levelland in 1929 from New York City, where she had been a public

"We love that pop"

In November 1962, a soft drink vending machine was placed in each of the four SPC dormitories. Each machine held 130 bottled drinks and was "sold out" each day. SPC students consumed an average of two soft drinks a day, not counting the soft drinks sold in the SUB. Another vending machine was placed in the women's dorm to provide an additional 260 soft drinks. Only weeks later, Dean "Hi" Walker implored students to return their empty bottles to the dorm. "Each bottle costs the college four cents." The student council endorsed a "Help Keep the SPC Campus Clean" campaign.

school teacher. Although Mrs. Gillespie had no children, she enjoyed the company and friendship of many SPC students and demonstrated an active interest in all the activities held on campus.

Finally in 1976, three women's dormitories, North Sue Spencer, South Sue Spencer and Gillespie Hall, were interconnected with a spacious lobby area. The new area was named the "Baker Center" to honor SPC's second president, Dr. Marvin L. Baker.

A shortage of women's housing continued until 1981 when the Smallwood Apartment Complex, on the south end of the campus, was completed and named to recognize John L. and Vergie Belle Smallwood's generous contributions to South Plains College. In addition, the Smallwood Apartments are used for housing students who desire on-campus residence during the two summer sessions held each year.

South Plains College's dormitories house 278 men in five complexes and 288 women in four dorms. In addition, numerous apartment complexes surround the college campus as Levelland entrepreneurs discovered the financial benefits of a college in the community.

In 1967, Dr. Baker named Earl Gerstenberger as dean of men and he handled student discipline. Predominant among problems the dean faced were those associated with the dormitories. "If we hadn't had the dorms we wouldn't have needed a dean of men or dean of women," said Gerstenberger. Restless young men bowled coke bottles down the dorm hallways, encouraged late-night noise making, and on occasion engaged in Texan Hall food fights.[2] Additionally, a Volkswagen could mysteriously appear inside the dorm lobby if the dorm matron failed to lock the door at curfew. In any event, during the first three years of SPC's existence with enrollment at less than 800 students, SPC remained a quiet community college in West Texas.

Racial relations during the college's first decade appeared to have been harmonious despite the tensions throughout other sections of the Southwestern United States. Davie Mac Costin, the first Mr. SPC in 1959, recalled racial harmony among all students on campus. "When we began classes we were apprehensive, but everyone socialized and I don't recall a single problem with any racial group." Costin found his SPC social life revolved around the "Circle K" club and intramural athletic events. In 1959, Costin became international vice president of Circle K.[3] According to Mildred Moore Loudder, the first black student to enroll at SPC, "I really enjoyed my years at the college." Loudder graduated in May 1964 with an associate of arts degree from SPC and completed her bachelor's degree in teacher education at West Texas State University in Canyon.[4]

The tumultuous atmosphere of the late 1960s brought numerous changes to SPC. The college's students, predominantly high school graduates from the surrounding area towns, reflected to a lesser degree the attitudes of college students across the United States. The racial tensions besetting the nation's college cam-

---

[2] Brussel sprouts, not a culinary delight of the Texan students, seemed to be a favorite for "sending messages" across Texan Hall.

[3] Costin graduated from SPC and completed his education at North Texas State University in Denton. He currently is in the insurance business in Gainesville, Texas.

[4] Like many SPC students, Mildred Loudder began her studies at SPC by enrolling in the evening college. She completed typewriting and shorthand courses her first semester.

puses failed to materialize on the SPC campus, as the Levelland college remained above the divisive fray elsewhere in America.

Another black student and a respected leader at SPC during the late 1960s was Frederick Jackson from Union, Texas. Jackson, an honor student at SPC, was elected as the first black student body president of SPC in 1971, his sophomore year. According to Jackson, "Parker McCollough and I integrated the dorm rooms. Black students had been housed in the dorms for years but a black student and white student had never roomed together. It was a bigger hubbub for the Dean than it was for Parker and I," said Jackson. According to Jackson, the Dean talked

Mr. Caprock

English instructor David Durham nudged Dean of Men Earl Gerstenberger for the title in the first "Mr. Caprock" contest in 1970. The SPC Kadettes Club sponsored the event in the Auditorium. Durham and Gerstenberger competed against math professor C.W. Dukes, government professor Travis Spears, and numerous student competitors in ensembles, wigs and high heels. Durham's talent was to lip sync a song by then popular vocalist Vicki Carr, while Gerstenberger, in combat boots, performed a spectacular dance routine. "We put on an act," said Gerstenberger. Durham, now assistant superintendent of schools in Van Vleck, Texas, said, "I weighed 150 pounds and Gerstenberger weighed 280. I thought I did pretty well until I saw the runner-up. I had to come back the next year and do my talent again and crown the next year's winner." Durham completed his graduate studies at Sam Houston State University and joined the English Department in 1969. Durham said, "Looking back I really enjoyed my years at SPC. The students were mostly young-sters from rural West Texas and they were a pleasure to teach."

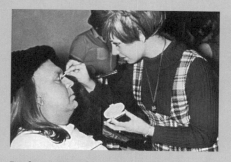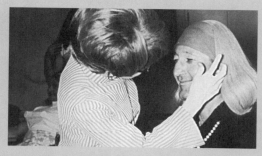

In the spring of 1970, the Kadettes Club sponsored the first "Mr. Caprock" contest. Four faculty members, Earl "Gertrude" Gerstenberger, C.W. "Cutie" Dukes, Travis "Goldie" Spears, and David "Bulletta" Durham, and several students donned high heels, wigs and formal attire for the pageant. Durham, then an English professor and later an assistant superintendent of schools in Van Vleck, Texas, was crowned "Mr. Caprock." Gerstenberger was selected runner-up.

with us about being "aware" of the ramifications of rooming together. "Although we were setting a precedent, we didn't really think of it in that light back then. I came to SPC to be a student, not a black student."[5]

Jackson graduated from SPC in 1971 and completed his degree at Texas Tech University in 1973.[6] Jackson was active in numerous organizations across the campus, including The Flaming Spurs, a student spirit organization, the Young Democrats, and student government. Panhandle, Texas, native Parker McCollough moved into Stroud Hall with Jackson in the spring semester of 1970. McCollough attended SPC on a track scholarship for Coach Clint Ramsey. According to McCollough, "rooming together may have been a novelty (to some), but it wasn't to me. Fred became a great friend of mine, sang in my wedding and we continue to keep in contact. His home became my home and my home became his home."[7]

A decade later, Tahoka High School graduate Ira White left her mark on the SPC student body while involved in the Fine Arts Department. White was reared singing Negro spirituals, performed in several SPC theatrical productions and was a cast member in several of the college's musical troupes.

Similarly, three Levelland Hispanic students – Seimon Mendez, Geneva Dominguez Gomez and Irma Quezada Guerra – organized the Los Tejanos Club under the sponsorship of foreign language instructor Frank Gonzales. "In 1969, we went to Dean Tubb and he said he wholeheartedly supported our idea for the club," said Mendez. As the number of SPC Hispanic students increased, the Los Tejanos Club has grown into one of the most active student organizations on campus under the guidance of Irma Bollinger, assistant professor of foreign language. In the early days "we didn't have any financial support from the college so we held enchilada dinners, dances and car washes to raise money for the Los

---

[5] Jackson was named to the Dean's List four semesters and received numerous departmental awards. As the eldest of six children, Jackson said he "set the pace" for his siblings. Five of the six graduated from college.

[6] Jackson has worked with BASF Corporation in Houston since 1987.

[7] While at Texas Tech, Jackson and McCollough continued their friendship and rented a home together while completing their degrees. McCollough later graduated from Texas Tech Law School and served in the Texas Legislature from 1988 to 1993. McCollough served with Representative Jim Rudd on the House Appropriations Committee. During one session when attempts were made to cut community college funding, McCollough told Rudd, "SPC is my alma mater; let me take the heat," and thus, with Rudd as chairman of the committee, funding was not decreased for community colleges. McCollough, one of track coach Clint Ramsey's athletes, later became a Lone Star Conference and Southwest Conference football official.

Tejanos," said Bollinger who sponsored the organization from 1979 to 1990. Testing coordinator Gracie Quiñonez and counselor Elizabeth Hoey Barham have sponsored the organization since then. According to former Administrative Vice President Earl Gerstenberger, "We worked to keep communication open with all minority students on campus."

As the college's enrollment increased rapidly during the late 1960s, new instructors joined the faculty and sponsored on-campus social clubs. Like most of the social clubs, the Vochais, the black student club, and Los Tejanos sponsored dinners, dances and fund raising events for their members. A growing student population encouraged a variety of student activities.

Interestingly, the minority student organizations worked closely with the various religious groups during the academic year. According to Gerstenberger, "We had very few racial problems."

"What few problems we did have disappeared with joint committees that staged interracial activities," said Arlano Funderburk, director of the Baptist Student

A Family Affair

During the past four decades, several West Texas families have vied for top honors in enrolling the largest number of family members at SPC. The Roberto Quezada family of Levelland, the Fred Albus family of Pep, the Robert Bradford family of Levelland, the R.H. "Buck" Bryant family of Whitharral and Brownfield and the Henry Franklin family of Pep have sent succeeding generations to SPC's classrooms.

The Quezada family sent 14 students to enroll and has had numerous family members employed at the college. Likewise, the Bryants, an extended West Texas family, enrolled 18 students at SPC. Judy Bryant, chairperson of the Physical Education Department, has been a faculty member for three decades. Glenda Bryant is an assistant professor of English.

Six Bradfords attended SPC during the 1970s and 1980s. Deborah, Class of 1974, majored in accounting while the remaining five were engineering majors. Barbara graduated in 1978. Two years later, Kathryn completed her studies at SPC. A third engineering Bradford finished SPC in 1982, followed by twins, Ronald and Donald, Class of 1984.

Steve and Debbie (Hammerle) Maines met while at SPC in the early 1970s. Their daughters Melissa and Stephanie both attended SPC. Melissa was a member of the SPC Lady Texans basketball team in 1995. Lloyd Maines served on the SPC music faculty and daughter Natalie attended the college. The Maines family, like so many others from across the South Plains, continue to place their confidence in the SPC faculty and administration. Interestingly, second and third generations of former SPC students are enrolling at SPC as we enter our 40th year.

Union. A musical program, "The Soul of Christmas," in 1972 was a concerted effort at eliminating any tension that had developed.

A Christmas Tradition

Each yuletide, SPC's Office of Student Activities has sponsored the arrival of Santa Claus in the Student Union Building and the tree lighting on campus. In 1969, a Christmas tree made of Douglas fir branches brought in from Cloudcroft, N.M., was decorated to establish a yearly tradition on the college campus. In 1984, after the college's main entrance was redesigned, an eldarica pine tree donated by the James Lattimore family was planted. At each yuletide, the tree is decorated with more than 1,500 light bulbs. After the tree and campus buildings are illumi-

nated, the crowd welcomes Santa and Mrs. Claus in the Student Union Building.

Current Board of Regents Chairman Mike Box and fellow student John Hammerle, with the cooperation of Student Activities Director Tom Selman, placed the first Christmas lights on the outside of the SUB in 1968.[8] According to Box, "We bought every red light bulb we could find in Levelland and then went to the Lubbock TG&Y and bought them out. We came back, dangled over the edge of the roof and stretched out the lights to decorate the building."[9] Box and Hammerle decorated the building the

The annual Christmas tree lighting ceremony had its origins in December 1969 with the construction of this 20-foot tree constructed of Douglas fir branches from New Mexico. The 1970 *Caprock* reported that nearly 2,000 area residents attended the first tree lighting ceremonies on the SPC campus that Christmas.

[8]   Hammerle was an SPC track and field competitor from Garland, Texas.

[9]   Box, a 1968 Whiteface High School graduate, was active in Student Government while at SPC and joined the SPC Board of Regents in 1986. Since 1994, Box has served as chairman of the board.

next Christmas and in the following years decorations were installed by the Maintenance Department. Thus, a Christmas tradition of three decades began. Each Christmas season has begun with the lighting of the campus and the arrival of Santa Claus at SPC.

Spiritual and Academic Life

The original SPC Board of Regents, president and administrators believed an active religious presence on campus would strengthen student growth and citizenship. The Regents voted during their April 1958 meeting that "the authorized study of the BIBLE be taught in the college, whereupon the question being called," the Regents voted unanimously in the affirmative. Consequently, Bible courses appeared as part of the course offerings and during the early years of SPC's history, "Religious Emphasis Week" was held on campus.[10] The administration invited various ministers to present inspirational messages to the student body. Indeed, administrators invited Rabbi Joseph Levenson, from Oklahoma City, Okla., to join with the Protestant and Roman Catholic ministers to talk with students.[11]

In addition to the Regents' attempts at fostering a religious climate on campus, several faculty members began Bible study groups in their homes. Sycily Lattimore, an original evening school faculty member in the Business Department, and about 10 students met each Sunday morning for Bible study in the Lattimore home. Sycily and James Lattimore "developed a closeness with those students that we recall with great fondness."[12] In like manner, students such as Judy Hendrix Schlechten shared a friendship they maintain 40 years later. "We (the study group) discussed worldly and earth-shattering topics like predestination, and I thought it was so terrific and intellectual," recalled Schlechten.

---

[10] The first SPC yearbook, *Caprock '59,* listed three faculty members, Fred Brewton, Ward Gregg and Therman Healy as Bible instructors.

[11] Registrar and later Academic Vice President Nathan Tubb invited the Rabbi to stay at his home during the week of lectures. Tubb and the administration realized the unlikelihood that any Jewish students were then attending SPC, but Tubb believed students should be exposed to a variety of religious theologies.

[12] James Lattimore was held in a prisoner of war camp in Moulmein, Burma, for more than three years after being captured on the island of Java by the Imperial Japanese Army during WWII. Lattimore worked until war's end on the Siam-Burma Japanese railway. Lattimore's insightful look at life inspired many of the informal groups at the Sunday morning meetings.

Throughout the 1970s, a Woman of the Year Award was presented to an outstanding young lady selected by the faculty. The 1976 award winner was Mary Marina *(top photo)*. The college's second dean of women, Carole Long, presented the award while faculty member and long-time college supporter Sycily Lattimore is seated at left *(middle photo)*. Also pictured is former First Lady Nancy Reagan who was the guest speaker for the occasion and Mildred Baker, the college's First Lady.

SPC Woman of the Year

Joyce Stephens Carr, 1969

Ann Robertson, 1970

Kathy Decker Tilley, 1971

Ruth Anne Blankenship Bennett, 1972

Phyllis Blair Milton, 1973

Carleen Schlenker, 1974

DeAnn Bingham, 1975

Mary Marina, 1976

Kathy Roberts, 1977

Sandy Melcher Sanders, 1978

Natalie Berryhill, 1979

Nancy Herring, 1980

Annette Willingham, 1981

Debbie Atkinson, 1982

Penny Chaney, 1983

Kathy Roberts (Hutchinson) of Brownfield, Texas, was named Woman of the Year in 1977 by a committee of faculty women. She worked in the SPC Career Center program, the College Relations Office, taught in Levelland public schools and became assistant principal at Levelland High School in 1998.

As the buildings on campus increased to accommodate the new students and academic programs, across the street from the college two religious organizations sought to fill the students' spiritual needs. Both organizations, the Baptist Student Union and the Church of Christ Bible Chair, worked closely with the college administrators. The Church of Christ Bible Chair was established by the Austin Street Church of Christ shortly after the college was founded and almost immediately the Los Creados Club, a Church of Christ organization, was established on campus. Later, additional Bible Chair support came from the Cactus Drive Church of Christ when it expanded in 1963. Initially, members of the Austin Street church attempted to purchase land from the Post-Montgomery Estate. Although the estate had sold land to the college only months earlier, sale of the Bible Chair site could not be finalized.[13] In October 1963, the Austin Street Church bought land north of the college from Willis Breshears for the Bible Chair's location.[14] From the first SPC semester, the Los Creados Club and other student religious groups flourished.

In the spring of 1995, the Bible Chair building became the site of the Wesley Foundation when the Northwest Texas Conference of the United Methodist Church purchased the building from Austin Street Church of Christ. Nevertheless, from the college's first semester, religious student organizations on campus were sponsored by faculty members. Two English professors, Frances Watkins and Inez Grant, were prominent in sponsoring religious organizations. Watkins provided guidance for the Catholic students in the Newman Club while Inez Grant, later named a Piper Professor, sponsored the Baptist Student Union. In addition, Therman Healy sponsored the Church of Christ student club, and the Methodist Club was sponsored by speech instructor Lilbern Kendrick.

Later in 1966, the Baptist Student Union was completed with donations from area Baptist churches and a generous gift from Mrs. T. A. Hamill. Youth directors of the First Baptist Church served as directors of the BSU during the first three years until a full-time director, Palmer McCown, was hired in 1969. In 1972,

---

[13] In November 1959, the Austin Street congregation decided to "attempt to secure an option on one acre of property owned by the (Post-Montgomery) Double-U Company." Five months later the "Board of Post-Montgomery decided not to sell the property in which the church was interested."

[14] During the first two years of the college's operation, Therman Healy served as Bible instructor. He was followed in 1960 by Bill Robinson who remained the Bible Chair director until 1970.

A Letter to The Churches of Christ

Dear Brethren:

In 1955, there were only two million students in college; by 1960, it is anticipated that over four million students will be enrolled in institutions of higher learning. By 1970, the enrollment is expected to soar to a peak of twelve million. Surveys among the Churches of Christ seem to indicate that only one out of ten members of the Church attends a Christian college.

As a result of this expected enrollment, colleges have had tremendous expansion projects and will continue to enlarge their facilities. Colleges have been established to meet the demand. The most recent college founded to help take care of this tidal wave of students is the South Plains Junior College located in Levelland, Texas.

A few months ago the possibilities of establishing a Chair of Religion were discussed by the elders and deacons of the Austin Street Church of Christ, Board of Regents of South Plains College, and Dr. Thomas Spencer, president of the institution. All were in favor of the project, and the task of establishing a Chair of Religion was put in motion.

At the present time, the Bible Chair is under the direction of the elders of the Austin Street Church of Christ. A separate building for this work is not required since the students will not be living on the campus. The college will allow the instructors in religion to use its classroom facilities for instructional use. However, the Church must take care of all instructional costs.

This project affords a wonderful opportunity for the Church in this territory to do a magnificent work, and it will have far reaching effect and be of lasting benefit to the Church.

By offering religious education to interested students, a number of men and women will have the advantage of growing spiritually as well as academically. The result of this training gives the Church a continual output of ministers, teachers, Church leaders, strong Christian men and women. We, the elders, seek your moral support as we undertake to establish this Bible Chair at South Plains College, and invite you to enroll in a Bible course.

Sincerely yours,

Elders
Austin Street Church of Christ
Levelland, Texas

The elders of Levelland's Austin Street Church of Christ sought to firmly establish a religious frame of reference for SPC students. Therman Healy, minister at the Austin Street congregation, instructed four Bible courses at SPC. The Austin Street Church of Christ sought support for the Bible Chair from area congregations.

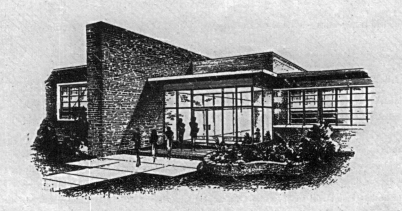

SOUTH PLAINS COLLEGE

RELIGIOUS EMPHASIS WEEK

Faith For Today

MARCH 27-28-29, 1961

The administration of South Plains College believed religion should be a part of the students' college experience. In March 1961, the first major Religious Emphasis Week was held on campus. Speakers from a variety of religious groups held lectures in the Auditorium and Library. The event concluded with a sunrise service in the quadrangle area and an assembly in the Auditorium. The program was an annual part of the student activities calendar until the early 1970s. *(Brochure courtesy Harley and Anne Bulls.)*

Arlano Funderburk became the full-time director.[15] For the past 20 years BSU members have traveled to Mexico for a mission trip and since 1972 students have participated in special retreat programs.

Indeed Levelland's churches contributed both monetarily and spiritually to the growth of students' lives. The Wesley Foundation's "Meal and Message" and the Baptist Student Union's weekly noon luncheons have provided a repast for college students.

The SPC Library

Dr. Spencer and the SPC presidents who followed his tenure have believed the cornerstones of higher education are a quality library and dedicated faculty members. Hence, Spencer quickly moved to establish a library of research, reference and contemporary books for SPC students, faculty and the community. Spencer's first request to the Board of Regents for $35,000 for the library received unanimous approval by the Board.

The South Plains College Librarians

Roger Mae Smith, 1958-1968

Joe Amis, 1968-1978

Jim Strickland, 1978-1989

Norman Spears, 1989-1998

Establishment of the SPC Library progressed slowly. Four years later, the college's 1962 Southern Association self-study listed 9,352 books in the SPC Library. This initial outlay became the nucleus of more than 72,837 volumes housed on two floors of the Library building. Currently, the college expends over $122,500 per year for books and periodicals.[16]

Dr. Spencer's librarian was Roger Mae Smith, a stern disciplinarian who until the arrival of her successor Joe Amis in 1968, demanded a library with an abundance of decorum and an absence of noise. According to long-time college business office employee Shirley Prothro, "Roger Mae told me I couldn't come to the library again wearing slacks. She possessed a sergeant's-like attitude, was very

---

[15] For the past 28 years, the South Plains Association and some Caprock Plains area Baptist churches have assumed the financial responsibility for the BSU. Levelland's First Baptist Church purchased the site for the BSU for $6,000 upon which was built a $44,000 student center in 1966.

[16] About 2,200 new volumes are added to the SPC Library's holdings each year.

strict and had her own dress code for students in the Library." Veteran chemistry instructor Jim Leggitt recalled "Ms. Smith didn't allow any foolishness and ran a tight ship."[17]

After the largest bond issue in county history received voter approval, the administration moved the SPC Library holdings in 1968 from the original location into the first two floors of its new location. The SPC Library, the only three story building on campus, contains 47,000 square feet and cost $551,495. The relocation occurred during the academic year. The Agricultural Club and Rodeo Club, then sponsored by Earl Gerstenberger, moved the 15,000 plus volumes into the new location. The club members loaded the books into pickup trucks and placed the books in proper call number order on the shelves in the new library.

---

[17] Roger Mae Smith ran "her" library similar to her previous life experience. She came to SPC after a career as a Navy officer. A former Science Department faculty member recalled that Miss Smith would not allow him to check out a book during the summer for use in a graduate class.

When Marvin Baker, Ph.D., assumed the presidency of South Plains College, the student enrollment was just over 500 students with classes held in the five campus buildings. As students and classes increased, Baker found himself working closely with architect Lavern Kirby to plan additions to the campus. In this mid 1960s photograph, President Baker examined blueprints for the new college library.

An Architectural Challenge

Transforming a flat sorghum field on the wind-blown Texas Plains into a college campus was no small order. Dr. Spencer consulted with Haynes and Kirby Architects and decided to arrange the five college buildings in a large diamond with a quadrangle area in the middle which could be used for social gatherings.[18] President Baker continued the relationship with Haynes and Kirby throughout his tenure at the college. All students' classes were within a short walk across the quadrangle. The architectural firm of Haynes and Kirby designed all the SPC buildings with the exception of the Baker Center. Laverne H. Kirby, who began his career in Lubbock in the early 1940s, drew plans for the college's structures. The well-known South Plains architect retired in 1972. According to Frank Wilson, an architect with the firm for many years, the most difficult project was the 1982 connection of the Student Union Building with the Women's Gymnasium. The construction involved the interconnection of seven previous college construction projects.

Bond Campaigns

After the original bond election to build the college, Hockley County voters approved three additional bond issues to expand SPC. First, voters approved a $690,000 bond issue in 1963 dedicated to expanding the Gymnasium, Student Union Building, Library and for construction of an Agriculture Building and a Physical Science Building. Two years later, Hockley County voters accomplished what many Hockley County political pundits said was impossible when they approved the first county-wide bond issue in excess of a million dollars. In fact, the largest building project since the college's inception was a result of the $1,750,000 bonds voted in 1965. The Board of Regents entered into a massive building program that charted SPC's course for the foreseeable future. The Technical Arts Center, Texan Dome, a new three-

South Plains College Bond Issues

1958	$ 900,000
1963	$ 690,000
1965	$1,750,000
1981	$5,500,000

---

[18] During the early years, SPC students used the quadrangle area for their campaign speeches while seeking student government offices.

99

floor Library, Biological Science Building, and further additions to the SUB and Fine Arts Building resulted from the bond issue.

In May 1981, the college's Board of Regents and the administration embarked on the most ambitious bond issue and building program since the college's inception. A $5,500,000 bond issue proposal was successfully presented to the college district's voters in a campaign that resulted in major renovations to nearly all of the Levelland Campus' buildings and facilities. President Baker and his administrative team spoke to every civic club and citizens group in the district, touting the benefits of supporting the proposed bond issue. Voters responded across the district with a 510 to 259 vote in support of the proposal. SPC Business Manager John Dickson wisely placed the bond proceeds in an investment program which yielded additional funds to renovate other facilities. Unlike the college's 1957 bond issue of $900,000 which took 20 years to retire, this tax obligation was retired in five years.

On July 4, 1987, current and former members of the SPC Board of Regents gathered to burn the last of the college's 1957 tax bond issue and declare the college free of any tax-supported bonded indebtedness. Regents each had a hand in tossing retired bonds into the barrel at the annual Levelland performance of the college's country music road show. Pictured at the gathering are *(from left)* Mark Wyatt, Gary Stacy, John V. Morton, Johnnie Keen, C.E. Bradshaw, Dr. Marvin Baker, and Pat McCutchin.

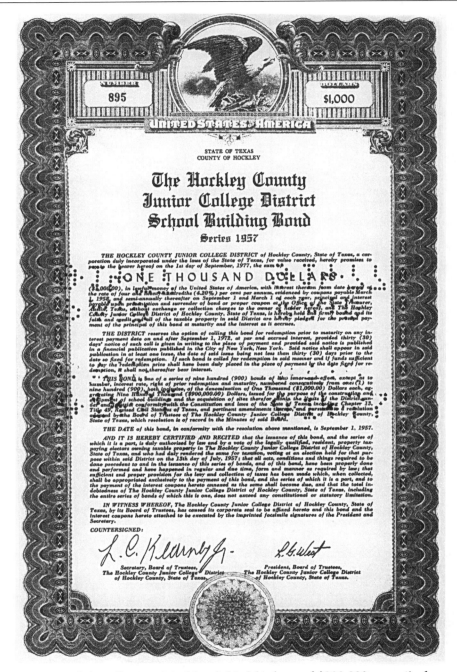

The last of the college's original bonded indebtedness of $900,000 was retired on Sept. 1, 1977, when bonds #895 through #900, bearing an interest rate of 4.20 percent, were paid.

The Distinguished Alumni Hall of Fame

In celebration of its 30th anniversary, South Plains College established the Distinguished Alumni Awards program to recognize and honor the noteworthy achievements of former students who have made significant contributions to their chosen professions. Since 1987, 20 former students have been accorded the honor and have been inducted into the Distinguished Alumni Hall of Fame.

1987 Recipients

*Dennis Deel, (1965-67), Manager, Analytical Mechanics Division, Martin-Marietta Corp., New Orleans.

*Leslie Lawrence, (1959-61), Professor of Art, Grossmont College, El Cajon, Calif., noted ceramic artist.

Thomas Spencer Jr., Ph.D., (1958-59), President of Garland County Community College, Hot Springs, Ark.

Terry Tubb, M.D., (1960-62), Plastic and Reconstructive Surgeon, Midland, Texas.

Kenneth Turner, Ph.D., (1965-67), Curator of No Man's Land Museum, Goodwell, Okla., noted forensic anthropologist.

1990 Recipients

Michael Balch, M.D. (1968-70), Doctor of Internal Medicine, private practice, Levelland, Texas.

*Don Boedeker, (1969-71), Quality Assurance Engineer, U.S. Navy Weapons Base, Ridgecrest, Calif.

*Larry McVay, (1958-67), Vice President and General Manager of Amoco Pipeline Co., Chicago, Ill.

David R. Stanley, (1958-60, deceased), former Professor of Government, South Plains College, Levelland, Texas.

*Royce W. Waltrip II, M.D., (1972-74), Research Psychiatrist, University of Maryland School of Medicine.

*William R. Wheeler, (1965-67), Engineering Consultant and Partner, Analysis and Design Applications, Co., Ltd., Bayshore, N.Y.

1995 Recipients

Bill M. Balch, M.D., (1973-75), Doctor of Internal Medicine, private practice, Levelland, Texas.

*Ruanna Myers Gossett, D.V.M., (1976-78), Post-doctoral Research Associate, College of Veterinary Medicine, Texas A&M University, Bryan-College Station, Texas.

S. Kent Harrison, Ph.D., (1975-77), Associate Professor of Agronomy, Ohio State University, Columbus, Ohio.

Sally Rowell Snow, B.S.N., R.N., (1969-71), Trauma Services Coordinator, Cook-Fort Worth Children's Medical Center, Fort Worth, Texas.

Thomas R. Watkins, D.D.S., (1972-73), Clinical Associate Professor, University of Texas Health Science Center School of Dentistry, San Antonio, Texas.

1998 Recipients

C. Donald Combs, Ph.D., (1970-71), Vice President for Planning and Program Development, Eastern Virginia Medical School, Norfolk, Va.

H. David Cook, M.D., (1967-69), Physician and Partner, Dallas Obstetric and Gynecologic Association, Dallas, Texas.

Gary Owen, P.E., (1974-76), Vice President of Engineering Services, Cliffs Drilling Co., Houston, Texas.

Robby Timberlake, R.Ph., (1966-68), Pharmacist and Partner, Baggett Pharmacy, Levelland, Texas.

* Professional career and corporate affiliations listed here are during the year of award and do not reflect changes which might have taken place.

CHAPTER 6

Expanding the College

Marvin Baker's administration of South Plains College can be described with one word, "growth." Enrollment figures indicate a steady increase in students from across West Texas and Eastern New Mexico. In the 1965 fall semester, 1,103 students enrolled in classes at SPC. Neighboring communities contacted President Baker during the mid-1960s expressing an interest in joining the college district. Citizens of Denver City, Plains and Muleshoe telephoned Baker with inquiries about possible expansion of the college district. Baker and his administration were interested in expansion, but they focused their attention on Yoakum and Gaines counties. Primarily, Baker had a keen eye on the potential tax revenues that would decrease the current district taxpayers' burden. In addition, an expanded district would solidify the college's ability to attract the area's high school graduates.

To this end, Baker spoke about annexation in March 1968 with various groups in the Muleshoe High School cafeteria. Following Baker's address, Muleshoe Chamber of Commerce President Robert Hooten asked the assembled group to consider circulating a petition to initiate the process.[1] Although the annexation of six additional counties into the college district did not occur, the college nevertheless extended its educational mission into more than a dozen surrounding communities.

---

[1] Baker asked that a majority of those in attendance endorse the annexation proposal and at the conclusion of the meeting more than 75 signatures were obtained.

With the expanding need for continuing education across the South Plains, Don Yarbrough became dean of continuing education in 1969 when the previous director, Charles Hays, accepted the position of dean of students at Midland College.[2] One year earlier, upon recommendation of Nathan Tubb, President Baker had hired Yarbrough to join the counseling staff. Yarbrough, having served as a Lamesa High School academic and vocational counselor, joined the Baker administration in guiding SPC into the next decade. Under Yarbrough's direction, the college's faculty began teaching across a nine-county area of West Texas. Both academic and technical instructors traveled as far north as Dimmitt and as far south as Seminole, Texas. Classes taught in Dimmitt were part of a unique educational program to meet the needs of migrant farm workers. The Panhandle Education Service Organization (PESO), with a grant from the United States Department of Labor, implemented a teacher aide education program with the courses taught by SPC faculty. Yarbrough realized the students' potential and encouraged the development of a program that would train not only teacher aides but also would establish the groundwork for higher education. Upon completing the SPC course of study, students could continue their education at a university to obtain teacher certification. The program was successful. It began in the fall semester of 1970 with fundamentals of math and concluded in the spring of 1976 with English composition. In the interim, more than 20 different courses were taught to complete the program.

The SPC Financial Aid Officers

Nathan Tubb, 1958-1963

Frank Hunt, 1963-1966

Charles Hays, 1966-1969

Mitchell Masters, 1969-1970

Paul Mackey, 1970-1972

Jerry Barton, 1972-1973

Glenn Pounds, 1973-1981

Bobby James, 1981-1982

Steve Beck, 1982-1987

Shirley Prothro, 1987-1990

Jim Ann Batenhorst, 1990-1998[3]

---

[2] Charles Hays, a Levelland native and a 1962 SPC graduate, was hired by Baker as the student financial aid officer and director of continuing education in 1966. He later served as president of Panola College, Howard College and New Mexico Junior College.

[3] During the early 1960s, student financial aid was limited. In the early 1970s, an expansion of Federal and State grants, in addition to the local scholarships and work study programs, increased monetary awards to college students. Federal guidelines stipulate that all student grants and loans are disbursed from one administrative office.

SPC and Reese Air Force Base

Probably the most productive continuing education effort engineered by Yarbrough was SPC's presence at Reese Air Force Base (RAFB). During the mid to late 1960s, an increasing number of United States Air Force airmen traveled the 25 miles to the SPC campus. Numerous Air Force personnel clad in green fatigues attended classes on the Levelland campus. It followed that additional students could be enrolled and taught on the base by the college's instructors. To that end, the college initiated Reese classes to meet the needs of the base's enlisted personnel. The program provided Reese's military and their spouses with priority registration times at each semester's registration. As a result, word of SPC's instruction on the base spread quickly and within a semester, students from the Lubbock area filled the Reese AFB classrooms. This established an educational relationship between Reese AFB and SPC that endured for 27 years.

In the spring of 1970, Yarbrough offered four college courses: English, history, government and speech. Initially, Yarbrough set up the Reese classes, but because of the rapid growth, additional personnel were added to direct the instruction. Bobby James served as director of career advancement at Reese AFB in 1973 and later became assistant to the dean of continuing education in 1976. During those years, both Yarbrough and James coordinated the Reese instructional program until the arrival of Jim Featherston. Featherston, former Seminole, Texas, high school principal, joined the college's administration in 1981 as director of special services. He served in that capacity until 1985 when he was named director of Reese programs. Featherston supervised the largest expansion of the Reese educational mission since its inception.[4] A former Marine Corps marksman, he understood the military way of life and worked closely with the Reese AFB commanders and base education officers. Featherston modified the SPC Reese schedule originally developed by Dean Yarbrough from a 16-week semester format to a quarterly, 11-week schedule in order to meet the USAF's educational and scheduling requirements.[5] The condensed schedule allowed the

[4] Featherston, a Snyder, Texas, native, attended SPC on a golf scholarship. He graduated from Texas Tech University and was a member of the Marine Corps rifle demonstration team prior to his career as an educator in Levelland and Seminole.

[5] Prior to Featherston's departure, the Base Realignment and Closure Commission deemed the flight training mission of Reese AFB unnecessary and the base closed Oct. 1, 1997. In typical organized "Featherstonian" fashion, the SPC facilities were moved from the closed Reese facilities to Reese Elementary School operated by the Frenship Independent School District.

college to offer a greater variety of college courses in the late afternoon and evening. The new schedule met with student approval as South Plains College Reese Center enrollment swelled to more than 900 students.

After Jim Featherston's 1998 departure, Judy Stocks became the Reese Center director. Stocks, who was coordinator of the Lubbock Campus Student Assistance Center from 1982 to 1985, rejoined the college after eight years as director of the Texas Tech University Learning Center and five years as assistant principal at Bayless Elementary School in Lubbock.

The Vice Presidents for Academic Affairs

Nathan Tubb, 1981

Luther Bud Joyner, Ed.D., 1982-1985

Robert "Bob" Cloud, Ph.D., 1986-1988

Orlo Sundre, Ph.D., 1988-1992

Gary McDaniel, Ph.D., 1992-1994

James Taylor, Ph.D., 1994-1998

Throughout the 27 years of SPC's presence on the base, the college's instructors used RAFB classrooms at the conclusion of each day's pilots' classes.[6] Faculty entering RAFB were required to show a gate pass and on occasion were subjected to searches.[7] With the closure of RAFB in October 1997, the college, while negotiating a continued presence on the former base with the Lubbock Reese Redevelopment Authority, quickly renovated and moved into the Reese Elementary school.[8] The area's students continue to enroll in a wide variety of classes at the newly named Reese Center.[9]

During the late 1960s, a number of factors caused a swelling SPC enrollment. Lyndon Johnson's Great Society programs expanded student grant and loan programs. In addition, the United States military presence in Southeast Asia brought numerous young men to the college campus. Student deferments encouraged young men to seek the classroom rather than military service. South

---

[6] Inclement weather, which cancelled pilot training in the T-37 and T-38 aircraft, "bumped" numerous SPC instructors from their classrooms. Former history instructor and Behavioral Sciences Department chairman Gary Wynn said ,"I taught my classes in the hallway many times."

[7] During international crises, such as the Iranian Hostage Crisis and Desert Storm, RAFB Air Police closely examined all vehicles entering the base.

[8] Computer instruction, first under instructor Darrell Grimes and then Roland Moreira, has become a cornerstone of the Reese Center programs. Fifty-one computers are networked in the instructional computer lab, open lab and adjacent offices. Moreira teaches Microcomputer Applications and all advanced-level computer science courses.

[9] The Reese Educational Center has 16 classrooms in addition to a resource center.

Plains College's student enrollment increased to 1,441 in 1967 and the expanding student population led to the largest new group of college faculty, 24, since the college's inception.

As South Plains College expanded during these years, Levelland and Hockley County enjoyed significant growth. Businesses along College Avenue flourished. As student enrollment increased, campus buildings, programs and activities were expanded and in turn attracted more students to the campus. The enrollment growth of the 1960s took SPC into another educational realm: technical, vocational and occupational education.

When Dr. Marvin Baker became SPC president in 1961, he began a long-standing tradition by hosting a faculty hamburger supper at the conclusion of each spring semester. Baker originally hosted the event in his backyard, but as the faculty and attendance grew, the cookout was moved to Texan Hall. In this 1971 photograph, Social Science Department member Bill Billingsley and Fine Arts Department Chairman Harley Bulls enjoyed the cookout. Several SPC faculty members can lay claim to the title of hamburger eating champion. Undoubtedly, math instructor Robert Pearce, automotive instructors Wayne Young and Mike Caroland, and athletic director Bill Powell were considered to be top competitors at each year's outing.

The First Faculty Forum

The first Faculty Forum was organized in 1971 by 45 faculty members who wanted to "strengthen communication between faculty, students and administrators." Travis Spears was elected president, C.W. Dukes, vice president, and Paula Bell, secretary. The Forum's 1971 meetings encouraged students to participate with faculty members in discussing common concerns. Student Senate President John Hammerle encouraged faculty members to spend more time in the Student Union Building associating with students. Spears met with the Administrative Council, and members invited the Faculty Forum to place a member on the council. After the first meeting, Spears said, "Every one of the members in the forum have a positive attitude which helps the organization that much more in achieving their proposed goals." Faculty members instituted a second Faculty Forum in 1976. Marketing instructor Buddy Moore served as president; Dianne Bridges, business administration instructor, was named secretary-treasurer; and Jeanelle Spears of the Physical Education Department served as vice president. Interest in the early Faculty Forum organization waned and it ceased to exist.

In 1997, faculty collegiality prompted renewed interest in a faculty organization, the SPC Faculty Senate. Business instructor and CIS Department Chairman Darrell Grimes was named president; Leann Ellis, Communication Department chairperson, was selected vice president. The Senate, meeting monthly, is composed of one elected faculty member from each department on campus.

The 5000th Graduate

At the May 13, 1983, commencement, Jana Bilberry was recognized as the 5000th graduate of South Plains College. When the Elida, N.M., accounting major walked the stage during the college's 25th graduation ceremony, she joined 583 other graduates completing their SPC education. Now, Jana Bilberry Terry, the mother of twins, resides in Portales, N.M., and works as an accountant.

Board of Regents Chairman L.C. Kearney Jr. congratulates Jana Bilberry as the 5000th graduate and presents her diploma at the 1983 Commencement Exercises.

CHAPTER 7

The Growth of Technical, Vocational and Occupational Education

T he 1960s transformed community college education from an academically oriented college climate to a broad-based education which stressed both the academic and the technical. SPC implemented federal and state programs designed to train a highly technical workforce for the nation.

South Plains College's first steps in technical education sought to alleviate a nursing shortage that existed across West Texas. The vocational nursing program began when the college opened it doors in 1958 and has experienced continued success the past four decades. Shirley Kennedy Cathey, then just completing her training at the University of Houston, joined the SPC faculty and established the program.[1] From its inception, "We had everything we needed – equipment, the president's backing and willing students," said Cathey. The program was a success from the start; her entire first class passed the State Licensed Vocational Nursing Exam. The growth of the Lubbock medical community created a demand that ensured the continued expansion of the program.

With the construction of the Technical Arts Center in the late 1960s, the nursing program began an expansion which continued into the college's 40th year. Nevelle Danner joined the nursing program faculty in 1964 and was joined by Helen Brown in 1971. Brown would direct the program until her retirement

---

[1] Shirley Kennedy Cathey directed the vocational nursing program for six years.

in 1983 and would begin the initial studies for implementation of a registered nurses program. During the early 1970s, SPC nursing students trained at St. Mary of the Plains Hospital in Lubbock, Texas, after their initial six months of classroom instruction. Nursing students completed rotations in psychiatric nursing at the Lubbock State School.

In 1984, South Plains College instituted the associate degree nursing (ADN) program under the direction of Marla Cottenoir. The two-year course of study initially enrolled 24 students. Fourteen years later the enrollment had expanded to 91 students in the ADN program. Students complete their studies during two years of course work and upon passing the state exam become registered nurses. During the instructional period, students work closely with St. Mary of the Plains Hospital. In 1998, Cottenoir served as president of the Texas Organization for Associate Degree Nursing and its representative for the 50 ADN programs in the state to the Texas Higher Education Coordinating Board on health care issues.[2] Cottenoir was named dean of the technical division in the spring of 1998.

With construction of the new Technical Arts Center, SPC entered a new era in education. In fact, SPC was on the cutting edge of technical, vocational and occu-

---

[2] Cottenoir has been in nursing education since 1974 and received her education at the University of Wyoming.

In the mid-1960s, South Plains College expanded its mission into technical, vocational and occupational education. Voters in the college district endorsed a $1,750,000 bond issue that, coupled with a federal grant, was used to construct the Technical Arts Center. The building, with 55,064 square feet, has housed almost every TVO program during its 30-year history.

pational education within Texas, a position achieved under the leadership of President Marvin L. Baker.

In the early 1970s, technical and vocational education expanded to meet the requirements of business and industry. Consequently numerous on-campus programs were researched, developed and implemented by the college administration. The Industrial Technology Department was originally created under James Carroll, agriculture technology instructor, who served as first chairman of the department. Darrel Raines became chairman at Carroll's retirement. Raines, drafting instructor since 1969, directs the eight different courses of study within the department.[3] Raines and fellow drafting instructor Bob Wilson teach about 70 students per year in the drafting program.

Although refrigeration and air conditioning technology had been an evening school course offering from the college's inception, with the 1970s a full-time program was instituted under the direction of Russell McDonald. He served as the instructor until 1976 when Wayne Young became the coordinator of the program. In 1978, Bill Gregg assumed control of the refrigeration program, working

---

[3] The drafting technology and commercial art programs enroll about 100 students per year in 19 separate courses. Students choosing the academic tracks of the various programs receive an associate in applied science degree after graduation.

Drafting instructor Darrel Raines received the Excellence in Teaching Award in 1976 from First National Bank President Bill Barnett. Raines joined the faculty in 1969 and was named chairman of the Industrial Technology Department in 1981. Raines taught seven years in the Borger public school system before coming to SPC.

with numerous part-time and evening school instructors. In 1990, the refrigeration program moved into facilities on the south end of the campus. More than 20 full-time students and 15 half-time students attend each semester in eight separate refrigeration, heating and air conditioning technology classes.

SPC's Occupational Training Programs

In 1969, the Baker administration initiated an expansion in technical education that would encompass the southern end of the college campus. Preliminary studies indicated a need for graduates trained in automotive repair. At the time South Plains College introduced the automotive program, only San Antonio College exceeded South Plains College in the field of automotive repair education. Initially, the dean of the TVO Division, Frank Hunt, learned from fellow faculty member and math instructor Kieth Mixon of the talents of Claude Kirkpatrick of Aztec, N.M. In January 1969, Kirkpatrick joined the faculty and welcomed 19 students into the new automotive mechanics program. "I had 10 work tables and two quarter-inch drill motors. That was the extent of the equipment I had to start the classes. More equipment arrived and in a few days most all of it was in," said Kirkpatrick. That first year, "out of the 19 students, we graduated 12."

The program began to grow as Kirkpatrick actively recruited students from the area's high schools. In the fall of 1969, the auto-diesel program enrolled 32 students and additional instructors were added to the program. By 1975, 95 students were enrolled under the guidance of seven instructors. With the increase in

Claude Kirkpatrick joined the Technical, Vocational and Occupational Division faculty in 1969. "Mr. Kirk," as he became known, served as coordinator and instructor of the automotive and diesel mechanics program for 16 years. In addition to his teaching duties, he directed transportation for the college's traveling country music road show for eight seasons. He served as a spokesman for the TVO programs in the high schools of West Texas and Eastern New Mexico and helped raise scholarship funds for the programs. Kirkpatrick *(at left)* receives a scholarship donation from long-time Levelland businessman Billy Williams of High Plains Transmissions. Kirkpatrick retired from the college in 1984.

diesel powered vehicles across America, a new diesel curriculum was also created. After investigating the job market, students who initially entered the automotive repair course of study would complete the auto program and continue their studies in the diesel program.

Kirkpatrick, Hollis Shewmake, Jesse Hittson and numerous part-time instructors conducted a two-shift educational track for students. The first shift began at seven o'clock in the morning with classroom instruction. A second shift arrived at one o'clock in the afternoon with groups alternating classroom and workshop study. This use of the 60 by 100-foot Auto-Diesel Mechanics Building continued during the 1980s and into the 1990s when enrollment declined.

Today, the automotive-diesel program averages about 60 students each semester. SPC auto-diesel graduates completing the program are awarded an associate degree or certificate of proficiency and are highly sought within the industry.

Since the inception of the automotive mechanics program in 1969, countless innovations have occurred in the automobile industry. "Back then electronics made up a 20th of the curriculum; now it is more than 60 percent of the course," said former TVO Dean Frank Hunt. Additionally, a special program was instituted

Gone Hunting

A special camaraderie characterized the early faculty and administration of South Plains College. Nathan Tubb, Frank Hunt, Earl Gerstenberger, Charles Hays, Don Yarbrough and occasionally other members of the faculty not only worked together, but they relaxed together. Accounts of hunting and fishing trips, surely embellished, enlivened the Monday morning coffee table discussions. SPC's history would not be complete without recounting the most incredible. Amazingly, on a quail hunting excursion near Post, Texas, TVO Division Dean Frank Hunt brought back a hunting vest full of trophies. As Hunt displayed the birds to his administrative colleagues, one magically flew up and landed 150 yards away. Hunt and Nathan Tubb went to get the bird; both shot, the bird went down, and an argument ensued on who should get the trophy. Hunt's reasoning for claiming the prize: "I shot him twice." Thus Frank Hunt's nickname, "The Hunter."[4]

[4] Accounts of Frank Hunt's abilities with shotgun, most certainly exaggerated, abound. He is rumored to have "peppered" several administrators and faculty with birdshot while hunting dove and quail.

for handicapped students. During the 1980s, women entered the auto-diesel program, a career field previously thought to be reserved for men. Said Hunt, "I asked one young lady why she was in the program. She was under the car and working and said, 'I can do the job and I can make a whole lot more money working on a motor than I can typing on a typewriter.' The curriculum changed as the role of the mechanic changed," added Hunt. Current program coordinator Eddie Cox and instructors Rob Blair, Tony Ortiz and Whitney Owens work closely with General Motors, Ford and Chrysler representatives in providing detailed state-of-the-art education of automotive and diesel mechanics.

In 1981, South Plains College initiated the automotive collision repair technology program with Joe Beesinger as the coordinator and Jerrell Claborn as instructor. The two-year educational program was housed in a 13,941 square-foot facility on the south end of the college campus. The building, originally called the Metals Technology Building, was expanded to 17,240 square feet in 1990 to accommodate a new automotive painting system. Although other programs are contained in the building, it continues to be called the Metals Technology Building because the machinist trades program directed by Bill Richards was originally housed in the building. In 1988, the machinist trades program was relocated to the Lubbock Campus. The current automotive collision repair program coordinator Rodney Hudson joined the program in 1986 as assistant instructor to Joe Beesinger. Hudson became program coordinator when Beesinger retired in 1991. As the program continued to expand, James Puente and Will Dodd joined the program's instructional staff.

Corporate Instructional Donations

South Plains College's automotive technology program has been the beneficiary of numerous donations from corporate sponsors. General Motors Corporation and Alderson Cadillac, Lubbock, have donated several new vehicles. Most recently, General Motors donated a 1998 Z-91 Chevrolet truck, the first to emerge from a new assembly line. These vehicles, with slight body-paint blemishes, are excellent training tools for the SPC students. Detroit Diesel Corporation, Caprock-Vermeer and Deutz Corporation have made valuable educational donations to the college. In addition, Bruckner Truck Sales and Tiner Machine Company have maintained an instructional presence at SPC by their generous support of the program. Once donated equipment arrives, the automotive-diesel instructors modify the equipment to create problems in the "training module." Students face "real-life" diagnostic and shop repair situations.

Each year, the 25 students enrolled in the program repair as many as 100 cars. "We train students to repair everything from minor scratches to major frame and body damage," said Hudson. The veteran instructor added, "The biggest leaps in technology in our program have been the Black Hawk frame repair rack and the Blowtherm downdraft spray paint booth. Both have increased accuracy, safety and efficiency in our instructional program. We have been on the technological cutting edge with our equipment, and I expect the new sonar repair systems will be on the horizon to further improve our program."

In 1991, the Auto-Diesel Mechanics Building was extended and connected to the Welding Technology Building to house new labs and classrooms for the electronics service technology program. The program has, during the past four decades, changed from the age of vacuum tubes to transistors and integrated circuits. More than 35 students are involved in the two-year, hands-on training of electronics repair. Louis Hernandez initially directed the program until instructor Odus Hawkins accepted the position. Hawkins developed the program and brought it into the age of computer circuitry. When he retired in 1995, J.D. Harrell, an SPC graduate in 1976, assumed direction of the program. In addition to classroom study, students are trained to repair electronic equipment. Fellow instructor Raymund Elizondo graduated from the SPC electronics program in 1974.

The Technical, Vocational and Occupational Division instructors work closely with advisory committees composed of area individuals working in their respective industry. Committee members serve a two-year term. In this 1983 photograph, welding instructor Pete Stracener, far right, meets with welding technology advisory committee members *(from left)* Jet Thomman, Tony Hord, Russ Jones, Ron West and H.D. Gregory. Since the college's founding four decades ago, welding and metal fabrication have been part of the technical curriculum. Stracener has been a member of the faculty since 1981.

SPC's electronic servicing technology program maintained a working relationship with Texas Instruments Corporation. More than 280 former SPC electronics graduates from programs on the Levelland and Lubbock Campuses have worked at the Texas Instruments plant in Lubbock.

The Law Enforcement Program

During the late 1960s, increased law enforcement personnel certification requirements prompted the college to implement the law enforcement program. The college's first instructors were associated with the criminal justice section of the South Plains Association of Governments . In the fall of 1972, James Harner served as the first full-time coordinator of the program that enrolled about 25 students in Levelland and 18 students at Reese AFB and a similar number in Brownfield. In 1973, George Lawless became program coordinator, and later in 1975, the college hired Larry Nichols to oversee the Reese AFB portion of the program. Enrollment grew rapidly with more than 350 law enforcement majors in 1985.

The tremendous increase in law enforcement students in 1982 prompted construction of the Law Enforcement Building with an indoor pistol range, com-

In 1982, law enforcement instructors George Lawless *(left)* and Larry Nichols *(right)*, began teaching defensive driving courses with the National Safety Council curriculum. As student enrollment in the law enforcement program increased, three additional instructors, Randy Fesperman, James Richey and Joe Wise, joined the faculty. The program offers an associate degree curriculum, basic firearm safety courses and inservice short courses for professional peace officers. Law enforcement classes are held in the Law Enforcement and Petroleum Technology Building on the south end of the SPC campus. As originally constructed in 1982, the building was equipped with five pistol firing lanes. In 1992, five additional lanes were added to the firing range to meet expanded peace officer training courses and public interest in handgun proficiency and safety.

pletely automated shooting booths and classrooms. Renovations in 1992 doubled the size of the shooting range and completed a facility that would be the envy of many law enforcement academies and educational programs across the nation.

In 1986, the State of Texas certified the SPC law enforcement program to offer credit short courses through the Texas Commission on Law Enforcement Standards and Education. In 1995, the law enforcement program received an exemplary rating from the Texas Higher Education Coordinating Board. Two Southern Association site visit accreditation teams have given the program exemplary reviews as well. SPC law enforcement graduates hold positions with law enforcement agencies across North America. Three graduates have joined the United States Federal Bureau of Investigation, while numerous SPC graduates are members of the Texas Department of Public Safety and the Bureau of Immigration and Naturalization. All told, more than 500 persons have graduated from the SPC program.[5] Since 1994, Lawless has chaired the Professional Services and Energy Department.

---

[5] Currently, Lawless is joined by fellow instructors Larry Nichols, Randy Fesperman, Jimmy Richey and Joe Wise. The latter two are SPC graduates.

The American Petroleum Institute (API) has generously supported South Plains College with student scholarships. Since 1982, the API has contributed $238,500 to the SPC Foundation. Dr. Marvin Baker *(center)* accepts a scholarship donation from Hank Low of Brownfield. Pictured are *(from left)* Charles Miller of Levelland, Coleman Williams of Brownfield, Low, Baker, Paul Musslewhite of Levelland, Jacque Hunter of Brownfield, and Frank Hunt, dean of the Technical, Vocational and Occupational Division.

When the college began in 1958, the oil industry in Hockley County was well established. College instructors taught "oil field instrumentation" to students that first year. As the progressive oil field industry modernized, it demanded trained welders, computer technicians and metal fabricators during the oil boom of the 1970s. SPC instituted the petroleum technology program in the fall of 1981. SPC officials expected about 20 students to enroll in the new technical program and were "overwhelmed" when the enrollment figures for the program turned out to be five times the original estimate. Kim Williamson was hired to launch the new two-year associate degree program. One year later, the new Petroleum Technology Building, a 14,000 square-foot facility which was shared with the law enforcement program, was dedicated as Hockley County celebrated the production of the billionth barrel of oil. The 1982 celebration included a oil field equipment show on campus that involved more than 50 local and area companies. Williamson left the college in 1993 and Terry Brown was hired to direct the petroleum technology program. Brown worked to adjust the program's curriculum as the petroleum industry adjusted to the global marketplace. Paul Harbin succeeded Brown as program coordinator in 1997.

Welding technology, like most technical, vocational and occupational fields, joined the computer revolution. Complicated programmable welding equipment was added to the program when it was moved into the current Welding Technology Building in 1983. Pete Stracener instructs about 20 students each semester in computer-operated metal fabrication, gas tungsten arc welding and other welding systems. About 20 additional students are enrolled each semester in continuing education classes offered one night a week in the Welding Technology Building.

After Hockley County voters approved a $5.5 million bond issue in May 1981, the administration transformed part of the original college band hall into facilities for a new cosmetology program.[6] Linda Coats became the first instructor, enrolling 25 students in the first class September 1984. The program grew steadily with more than 200 graduates completing the program. Carolyn Newkirk became the full-time instructor in 1987. The 12-month program requires students to complete 1,500 clock hours of instruction in nine major fields of study in preparation to take the Texas Cosmetology Operator Licensing Exam. In January 1997, a manicurist program was implemented to complement the program.

---

[6] The old Band Hall had previously been used for country and bluegrass music instruction.

CHAPTER 8

The SPC Lubbock
and Plainview Campuses

S outh Plains College's educational presence in Lubbock became a reality in the summer of 1973 when South Plains College opened an extension center. B.P. Robinson was named director of the center. Classroom facilities were leased at the various high schools and at Reese Air Force Base for allied health and short course instruction. The small Lubbock facility was headquartered at 2402 Ave. Q.

Frank Hunt, dean of the Technical, Vocational and Occupational Division on the Levelland Campus, established the initial framework for vocational training in Lubbock during the early 1970s. Hunt and SPC electronics instructor Louis Hernandez worked with Litton Industries to initiate a start-up training program for 400 electronics workers. The 40-hour training course developed by the college met Litton's Lubbock staffing needs for a Polaris missile guidance system government contract. The success of the program pointed to the importance of a technical-vocational school in Lubbock, and Hunt continued to work with Litton and Texas Instruments on other projects to provide a skilled Lubbock workforce.

A South Plains College campus in Lubbock moved closer to reality in 1977 when American Medical International (AMI), the corporation that owned West Texas Hospital, donated the hospital building to South Plains College for use as a vocational branch campus. AMI had just completed the construction of a new West Texas Hospital building one block northwest of its 1302 Main Street location. By then, Lubbock business and industrial leaders and the Chamber of Commerce recognized the need for a vocational education training center. John Logan,

119

Lubbock chamber president and a close business colleague of Dr. Marvin Baker, was a driving force in the campaign to establish the SPC branch. Working with Mark Soderquist, who served as chairman of the Lubbock Campus Advisory Board, he orchestrated the chamber's drive to raise $142,000 in contributions and pledges from local businesses to retire the existing mortgage on the building. Logan, according to former Lubbock Campus Provost Ronnie Glasscock, was a quiet "mover and shaker" who preferred to stay in the background while promoting Lubbock, the chamber and education.

SPC Lubbock Administration

B.P. "Robbie" Robinson, 1973-1978

Luther Bud Joyner, 1978-1981[1]

Ronnie Glasscock, Ed.D., 1981-1992[2]

Dick Walsh, Ed.D., 1993-1998

Logan's tireless efforts served to revitalize the downtown area which had been ravaged by the 1970 Lubbock tornado.

With the help of Congressman George Mahon, a $2 million federal grant through the Economic Development Administration was obtained to refurbish the building. Congressman Mahon and his newly elected successor Kent Hance cut the dedicating ribbon Nov. 12, 1978. Lubbock pioneer broadcaster R.B. "Mac" McAlister was honored for his contributions in obtaining the facility. The Lubbock civic leader's portrait has been prominently displayed in the building.[3]

The branch campus opened in the fall of 1978, enrolling 550 students in the 16 associate degree and certificate programs that were offered at the Main Street location. Luther Bud Joyner was selected to serve as dean of the new SPC Lubbock Campus. Robinson, who had worked to gain local support for the new campus, continued to work with Joyner to help get the new campus started.

"We opened (for classes) two weeks late with six full-time employees, eight new calculators and some old typewriters that fall semester in 1978," said Margaret Ingraham, one of the original SPC Lubbock faculty members. Ingraham had joined the Business Department faculty on the Levelland Campus in 1972 and

---

[1] Joyner loved the interaction with students in the classroom and taught English during his tenure with SPC. Since 1992, Joyner has been president of Amarillo College.

[2] In 1988, Ronnie Glasscock, dean of the Lubbock Campus, assumed the title of provost.

[3] McAlister, first as owner of KSEL radio and later KAMC-TV, Channel 28, had been a tireless supporter of SPC's educational mission. His presence in the Texas Legislature provided a constant voice for SPC and the community colleges of the state.

welcomed the challenge to join Robinson and Joyner at the new SPC Lubbock location. South Plains College bought "furniture and work tables from Texas Tech University after they were declared surplus by the university," said Ingraham.

According to Ingraham, the six faculty members began preparations for the fall semester in August, but remodeling of the facility delayed the semester's start. "We had one telephone per floor and a mimeograph machine to duplicate our tests." The business vocations teacher was joined in the Business Department by Kathlene Hall, dietetic instructor Ann Thompson, mid-management instructor Glenn Roach, respiratory therapy instructor Gordon Wanamaker and automotive repair instructor Bob Melvin. Larry Rice served as counselor and Mary Rooker coordinated the continuing education program.

Finally, the move into the former hospital building and the coordination of the classes "could not have been done without Bud Joyner," said Ingraham. Joyner had the "charisma and drive to get things done." Ingraham retired from South Plains College in 1988.

One instructional program destined for the Lubbock Campus temporarily remained on the Levelland Campus. Veteran SPC instructor Frances Bly helped

Prior to his retirement from the United States Congress, George Mahon encouraged the establishment of the speakers series at South Plains College. The aptly named Mahon Lecture Series speakers included Texas Governors Bill Clements, Mark White and Lt. Governor Bill Hobby. Mahon loved the interaction with students and welcomed their questions about government. The Congressman was instrumental in securing a $2 million economic development grant for the college which was used to transform the vacant West Texas Hospital into the SPC Lubbock Campus in 1978.

move the radiologic technology program from the Levelland Campus to the new downtown Lubbock facility in February 1979. "We loaded our rad-tech equipment from the college Administration Building into Doyle Davis' station wagon and in my car and moved to the new building during a weekend. We continued our classroom work on Monday morning because the eight students in the (radiologic technology) program were excited about moving into the building," said Bly. "We started with that first Lubbock class of eight students, and the program has grown to 30 students a year now," added Bly. Prior to the program's relocation to the Lubbock Campus, Bly taught an 8:00 a.m. class in Levelland, supervised students in a Lubbock clinical setting at 10:00 a.m. and then returned to Levelland to teach a 3:00 p.m. class before concluding her instructional day.

"When I began working in 1974 with Doyle Davis at the Levelland Campus, we had the typical high school graduate entering the radiologic technology program, learning on newly installed equipment. We now have older career-change individuals who are going back to school," said Bly. New computerization technology looms on the horizon for the SPC Lubbock rad-tech program.

Denny Barnes joined the program in 1981 and was named program coordinator in 1990 when Bly left SPC to

Lubbock Campus Excellence in Teaching Awards Recipients

In 1982, the Lubbock Campus instituted the Excellence in Teaching Award to honor an outstanding SPC Lubbock instructor. The honorarium was first sponsored by a number of local businesses and later by First National Bank in Lubbock. It is now sponsored by Norwest Bank Texas, Lubbock. A similar award, sponsored by Southwestern Bell, is presented annually to a part-time instructor on the campus.

Frances Bly, Radiologic Technology, 1982

Ann Thompson, Food Industry Management, 1983

Margaret Ingraham, Office Occupations, 1984

Barbara Jones, Vocational Nursing, 1985

Jamie Biggers, Accounting, 1986

Nancy Benz, Child Development, 1987

Richard Walker, Respiratory Care, 1988

Glenda Pedigo, Surgical Technology, 1989

Pat Dennis, Office Occupations, 1990

Donna Womble, Vocational Nursing, 1991

Ken Tunstall, Mathematics, 1992

Al Sechrist, Real Estate, 1993

Mollie McCook, Human Services, 1994

Jill Mertes, Mathematics, 1995

Denny Barnes, Radiologic Technology, 1996

Jimidene Murphey, Office Technology, 1997

Dick Shannon, Electronics Technology, 1998

attend radiation therapy school at Baylor Medical Center in Dallas. Bly returned to SPC in January 1994. More than 250 students have graduated from the rad-tech program since it began on the Levelland Campus in 1974.

When Bly and her dozen colleagues from the Levelland Campus moved to the Lubbock Campus, they established a new educational avenue for Lubbock's college students. Bly said, "Although I missed the camaraderie of being in Levelland with faculty members I had befriended, we (the Lubbock Campus faculty) made the adjustment and formed our new faculty friendships."

By 1980, enrollment at the Lubbock Campus had jumped to 750 students enrolled in the allied health and technical arts programs. By 1982, four additional degree and certificate programs had been added to the curriculum. The allied health programs included child development, human services associate, nursing home administration, radiologic technology, respiratory therapy, surgical technology, vocational nursing and nurse aide/orderly. The 12 technical arts programs included automotive apprenticeship, dietetic manager, dietetic technician, mid-management, real estate, supermarket management, electronics technology, fire technology, accounting associate, medical secretary, legal secretary and secretarial science.

As the new programs were implemented, full-time faculty were hired to coordinate the development of the curricula. The child development program was

 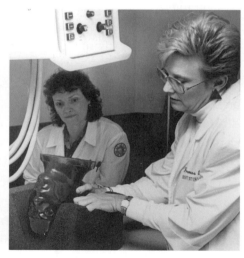

Dick Shannon *(left)* joined the Lubbock Campus faculty in 1982 as instructor in electronics technology. Frances Bly *(right)* began her teaching career in 1974 on the Levelland Campus and helped move the radiologic technology program to the Lubbock Campus in 1979.

developed by instructors Anne Deardorf and Nancy Benz. The human services associate program was implemented by Mollie McCook. The program was later changed to human services and rehabilitation science. The surgical technology program was moved from Methodist Hospital to the new campus building, and Glenda Pedigo served as director of the program. The vocational nursing program, previously offered by the Lubbock Independent School District, was relocated to the SPC campus and Barbara Jones and Mary Ruth Forman served as nursing instructors. A medical records technology program was implemented in the fall of 1981, and Ann Maddox, R.R.A., was hired to direct and teach the program. Dick Shannon joined the campus in 1982 to develop the electronics technology program.

In June 1981, South Plains College announced the hiring of Ronnie L. Glasscock, Ed.D., as the new dean of the Lubbock Campus, replacing Joyner who was named dean of arts and sciences on the Levelland Campus. Glasscock previously served as associate director of student financial aid at Texas Tech University and had been an administrator at Vernon Regional Junior College.

"Our most successful programs were our allied health programs," said Dr. Glasscock, who served as dean of the campus and later provost for 11 years. During this period of development, the allied health programs went through individual accreditation processes as well as maintaining standards for the Southern Association of Colleges and Schools.

Two Lubbock health care leaders, George Brewer, president of Methodist Hospital, and Charles Trimble, then president of Lubbock General Hospital, "were very supportive of our educational mission," added Dr. Glasscock. "The Lubbock Campus faculty originally wrote the associate degree nursing program proposal and defended it at Austin before the Texas Higher Education Coordinating Board. Although it was approved for implementation on the Levelland Campus, we felt a sense of accomplishment at leading the way in expanding nurse education for the college. Brewer really pushed hard for that program," said Dr. Glasscock.

During the initial years of Glasscock's tenure at the Lubbock Campus, "we were filled to capacity with students each semester." By the fall of 1984, enrollment had grown to a record 1,173 students at the campus, and new programs had been implemented.

In addition to the highly successful allied health programs of radiologic technology, surgical technology, vocational nursing and respiratory therapy, the business education curriculum also attracted large numbers of college students to

124

the Lubbock Campus. "Our biggest challenge was always scheduling and classroom space for students," Dr. Glasscock said.

Under Dr. Glasscock's leadership, the Lubbock Campus curriculum was organized into three instructional departments: Allied Health, Business Administration and Industrial Technology. A fourth department was created in 1989, the General Studies Department, when South Plains College incorporated a general education core of academic courses into its associate of applied science degree program. Previously, specialized general education courses had been developed for each technical program on the Lubbock Campus.

Prior to 1986, Dr. Glasscock had served as chief academic officer of the Lubbock Campus. As the campus grew in enrollment, administrative demands led to the hiring of Sam Hill as associate dean of instruction in 1986. Hill oversaw the development of new programs and curricula options which expanded the Lubbock Campus offerings from 26 to 36 associate degree and certificate programs. Hill left SPC in December, 1990, to take the position of vice president for instruction at Kankakee (Ill.) Community College. Herlinda Coronado was promoted to dean of instruction the following January. Coronado had joined the SPC Lubbock Campus in 1986 as a learning specialist to direct its student assistance center. Under Coronado's supervision, the Lubbock Campus programs underwent exten-

The SPC Lubbock Campus was originally the old West Texas Hospital.

sive review and revision in the early 1990s. Additionally, she worked with faculty to establish program articulation agreements with area schools in support of new statewide Tech Prep initiatives. Coronado left SPC in 1996 to become academic vice president at the Community College of Denver in Colorado. Jamie Biggers, who joined the Lubbock Campus faculty in 1980 to teach business courses and became chair of the Business Administration Department in 1985, was named to succeed Coronado.

Throughout the 1980s, the Lubbock Campus programs adapted to the changing workforce training demands of Lubbock business and industry. Advisory committees of local business and industry representatives guided the curriculum revisions. Nursing home administration and nurse aide/orderly programs were converted into continuing education programs as licensing requirements changed. The campus dispensed with its food industry management program, dietetic management programs and postal service administration in 1993 when workforce demand dropped. Similarly, the electronics program, under the close guidance of Dick Shannon, added an electronics manufacturing technology program when Texas Instruments expanded its production of semiconductor electronics at its Lubbock plant. The program was phased out a few years later when the TI Lubbock plant downsized.

The need for additional classroom space in order to expand existing programs prompted college officials in 1988 to attempt to gain voter approval to establish a branch maintenance tax to support the Lubbock Campus. College officials had hoped to take advantage of a newly passed piece of legislation allowing for the establishment of a maintenance tax for community colleges. From its opening in 1978, the Lubbock Campus operations had been funded by state appropriations based on contact hour formulas, student tuition and fees and its auxiliary enterprises. Campus faculty, administrators and local supporters worked to obtain more than 6,000 names on petitions to call the election. The petitions proposed a one and one-half cent tax on every $100 property valuation. The tax would have generated an additional $630,000 annually to support the establishment of a regional industrial training center and maintenance of the Main Street physical plant. The vote was held May 6, 1989, and the measure failed by a two-to-one margin, 2,769 to 6,219. While the proposal had garnered the support of every major public entity in Lubbock, including the *Lubbock Avalanche-Journal*, several factors contributed to its failure. Lubbock voters three weeks earlier had rejected a $58 million bond proposal for the Lubbock Independent School District. The legislation required Lubbock voters to approve a ballot which established a five-cent tax rate even though Lubbock County Commissioners had passed a resolution to limit the levy to one and a half cents. Additionally, opponents to the measure had placed a full-page ad in the *Avalanche-Journal* the day before, falsely claiming that the maintenance tax would be "totally controlled" by the SPC Board of Regents in neighboring Hockley County. In actuality, the law required the tax to be collected, budgeted and disbursed by the Lubbock County Commissioners Court. Light voter turnout, only eight percent of the county's registered voters, also contributed to the defeat. If anything, the campaign heightened awareness of the need for vocational training in the Lubbock area and the impact such training would have on future economic development.

In the fall of 1988, the campus leased the vacant E.K. Hufstedler Trucking Company facility located at 1941 Texas Ave. to house its industrial technology programs. The campus' automotive apprenticeship technology program, directed by instructor Neal Barnes, was immediately moved to the facility. The program had been housed previously in an old service station garage located one block east on Avenue J. SPC officials also relocated the machinist trades and automotive machinist trades programs from the Levelland Campus to the new Lubbock location in hopes of revitalizing the programs. The South Plains College Industrial Training Center opened to much fanfare in December 1988.

The campus obtained additional facilities in the spring of 1992 when the college received a donation of property from the estate of Ernestine Payne Welborn. The facility, located at 2415 6th St. in Lubbock, had served as a clinic for Lubbock surgeon Dr. Clifford E. Payne Sr. Payne had practiced in the Lubbock community for 24 years, 12 of which he spent at the 6th Street location. The 3,500 square-foot facility was renovated into classroom and lab space for the Lubbock Campus' continuing education program in nurse aide training and other allied health technician programs.

In the fall of 1992, SPC also leased additional classroom and office space in the 1200 block of Main Street, one block east of its seven-floor building. The facility, owned by the Lubbock Masonic Lodge, was opened as the Center for Cooperative Learning. The campus library, microcomputer classrooms and continuing education offices were moved to the location to ease some of the crowding on the Lubbock Campus and to allow computer information systems instructors Carol Peterson and Bob Haynes to address computer education and training in a new way. Peterson was hired in 1983 to teach office technology and data processing. Haynes, who had worked in the administrative computer center on the Levelland Campus since 1979, joined the Lubbock Campus faculty in 1984.

Continuing education programs have always played an important role in the Lubbock Campus curriculum. When the SPC Lubbock program began in 1973 with director B.P. Robinson, the college's offerings centered around continuing education short courses. When the Lubbock Campus opened in 1978, Mary Rooker was hired as director of special services to manage the college's continuing education programs. In her 11 years as director, Rooker developed many short-term training programs to address local workforce needs. When she retired in 1989 as dean of continuing education, the Lubbock Campus served more than 600 students annually through continuing education short courses.

SPC Lubbock Instructional Department Chairpersons

Allied Health Department
Peggy Wheeler, Director, 1982-1984
Ray Young, Director 1984-1985
Richard Walker, Director, 1990-1996
Deborah Wiggins, Ph.D., Director, 1996-1998

Business Administration Department
Jamie Biggers, Chairperson, 1985-1996
Jimidene Murphey, Chair, 1997-1998

General Studies Department
Ken Tunstall, Chairperson, 1989-1992
Jill Moore, Chairperson, 1992-1998

Industrial Technology Department
Dick Shannon, Chairperson, 1989-1998

Gary Schwantz was hired to replace Rooker. Under his direction, South Plains College played a leadership role in the development of the Center for Innovation which opened in early 1991 in the vacant Time DC building just off Southwest Loop 289. The center was a cooperative effort of the SPC Lubbock Campus, the continuing education program and Small Business Development Center at Texas Tech University and the Lubbock Board of City Development to create an educational training center in support of small business. The venture was short-lived, however, when the City of Lubbock decided to reorganize its economic development efforts and offices. Even so, Schwantz worked to expand the campus' continuing education efforts. New allied health training programs in phlebotomy, EKG interpretation, dental assisting and physical therapy aide were established. The number of continuing education courses offered quadrupled from 26 to 104, and enrollment nearly tripled from 603 to 1,562.

Schwantz left SPC in 1993 to enter private business, and Jim Walker was hired as director of continuing education. That same fall, the Workforce and Economic Competitiveness Act became law, restructuring and expanding Texas' workforce training system and the delivery of short-term technical training. The legislation shaped a new direction for SPC's continuing education efforts and allowed the college to expand its efforts in the area of contract training. Walker was named associate dean of technical and continuing education for the Levelland Campus in May, 1995. Roxanne Gross joined SPC that summer as director of continuing education and workforce development. The continuing education program has been focused on maintaining a skilled workforce for the South Plains region and annually serves more than 3,400 students through its program of short courses and contract training programs.

While Dean Glasscock managed student services on the Lubbock Campus, he hired Claudine Oliver in 1981 to run the campus bookstore and library. A year later, Oliver was promoted to assistant to the dean and was asked to supervise all student services for the campus. Larry Rice served as a vocational counselor on the Lubbock Campus until he was appointed to direct the campus' evening college program. Leesa Taylor and Rick Hudson were hired in 1980 to serve as vocational and career guidance counselors. Hudson left the college in 1983, and Weston "Bo" Kennedy was hired as vocational and placement counselor in 1984. Enrollment growth in the mid-1980s prompted the formal organization of a student services unit at the Lubbock Campus in 1986. Oliver was named director of student services.

The challenge of the 1980s, said Oliver, was providing student services not only for day students, but for evening students, as well. "More than half of our enrollment were adult evening students," said Oliver. "We worked to accommodate their special needs. Nearly all of them were working adults who wanted to go to college one night a week, so our emphasis was on scheduling student services to fit their needs. What made our efforts successful was how closely instructors and staff worked together. With everyone located in a single building, communication was easier." From the early 1980s until his retirement in 1994, Dr. Ron Reed worked part-time with Dr. Glasscock and Oliver by serving as evening administrator. Dr. Reed was an English professor at Lubbock Christian University.

One of the most innovative student services programs developed by the student services area was the First Step Program which was initiated in 1986. Rooker wrote the original grant proposal to fund the program which provided career counseling, short-term training and support services for displaced homemakers who wanted to enter the workforce with a marketable skill. The program was piloted on the Lubbock Campus and achieved great success. The service was expanded to the Levelland Campus the following year.

Taylor left the counseling program in 1988, and Stacy Elliott was hired as a vocational counselor. After serving nearly 28 years in public education and counseling hundreds of SPC Lubbock students, Bo Kennedy retired from SPC in December 1991. He had developed the campus' placement services for graduates. "I worked with students who are now attorneys, counselors and teachers," Kennedy said at his retirement. "Many of the students I helped find a job come back to see me, and they're smiling. That's worth it."

Oliver was named director of guidance and counseling on the Levelland Campus in 1990, and Susan Symons was hired as director of student support services in Lubbock. Both Oliver and Symons would direct the college's counseling efforts to expand services to meet the needs of special populations. The Carl Perkins Vocational and Applied Technology Act of 1991 directed federal dollars from developing high technology infrastructure to ensuring technical education was accessible to special populations of students. The Carl Perkins Act funded Tech Prep initiatives and special services programs for displaced homemakers, single parents, and economically disadvantaged technical students. The new programs allowed the counseling and guidance programs on both campuses to address student needs in new ways. Symons left SPC in 1994, and Linda Gober was named associate dean of student services.

In 1983, Beth Glass, although native to Levelland and a student at SPC from 1965-67, was unaware of the existence of SPC in Lubbock until her sister-in-law read her a two-line advertisement in the *Lubbock Avalanche-Journal* for a librarian for the Lubbock Campus. Living in Mansfield, Texas, at the time, she applied for the position and was hired as the campus' first professional librarian.[4]

When Glass arrived at the college in August 1983, the library was housed in the same area with the college bookstore. Prior to that fall semester, one clerk

---

[4] Beth Glass is from a family of Hockley County pioneers. Her mother and father, Mary Jane and Preston Marcom, were public school teachers. Her uncle, O.W. Marcom, one of the founders of SPC, was superintendent of Levelland schools for many years. Her maternal grandfather, David Elbert Magee, moved with his family to Levelland in 1925 to become county judge. Magee Hall, a men's dormitory on the Levelland Campus, is named in honor of Judge Magee. He was always interested in learning and took a speed-reading course at the college at age 82, the year before he died. Active until the end, Judge Magee did legal work on the day of his death in the West Texas Hospital. The hospital ironically is the same building which was remodeled to become the South Plains College Lubbock Campus where Glass has worked for more than 15 years.

had been responsible for the library and bookstore together. The lack of space had created problems for both the bookstore and library operations. Library books were stacked on the floor with cards intended for the card catalog tucked inside the books. At that time, the library subscribed to 50 magazines which were placed on a periodicals shelf. The library claimed one shelf in a small back room to hold back issue periodicals. Even with a bookstore manager and librarian in two new and separate positions, confusion existed for a time because books were both sold and circulated over the same counter. The situation was eased about 18 months later when the bookstore was housed in a different location.

"The area for the library was still extremely small," said Glass. "One student came in, walked to the door of the small storage room and poked her head in. When asked if she needed help, the student replied, 'No, I am just looking for the rest of the library.'" In the beginning, Glass ran the library by herself. This was a challenge with a population on the Lubbock campus of more than 1,200 stu-

Food industry management instructor Ann Thompson *(center)* and SPC Lubbock Campus Dean Dr. Ronnie Glasscock *(right)* receive a scholarship donation from Bruce Tilley, president of the Lubbock Restaurant Association. Thompson joined the college in 1971 as a part-time instructor in nutrition. Later in 1979 she joined the Lubbock faculty to direct the restaurant management program. Dr. Glasscock became dean of the Lubbock Campus in 1981.

dents. A part-time library aide was hired to keep the library open in the evening and eventually this position was replaced with a full-time library secretary.

In 1988, the secretary position was staffed with a full-time library technical assistant, Tracey Pineda. Two years later, Pineda was promoted to librarian when she completed her master of library science degree. More space became available when the library was moved in 1992 into the Center for Cooperative Learning, one block east of South Plains College on Main Street. The college leased this space for five years. In 1997, because the Co-op would close when its other occupants moved to the new Advanced Technology Center, the library was moved a second time, back into the Main Street campus building. A space usage committee on the Lubbock Campus had examined the total building and recommended that the third floor be remodeled to accommodate the library.

The library has expanded in 15 years in the number and types of services offered. Collections have grown beyond paper journals, books, and multimedia to include electronic databases and the many forms of electronic equipment needed in the transfer of information. Journal subscriptions which numbered 50 in 1983 exceeded 1,800 in 1998, including those available in full-text or full-image electronic format. Even in the midst of the wonders of the electronic age, the technology of the book has not been lost. The most frequently circulated books on the Lubbock Campus are from the collection of children's literature. These ever-popular books have been carefully selected (many donated by students in the child development program) to support literacy and the love of learning in children.

When Dr. Glasscock left the Lubbock Campus in October 1992 to accept the presidency of Cooke County College in Gainesville, Texas, the campus had grown to 1,311 students enrolled in 36 different associate degree and certificate programs. Richard Walsh, Ed.D., was hired in January 1993 to serve as the campus' new provost. He had previously served 25 years at Eastern New Mexico University in a variety of administrative positions and two years as executive director of a non-profit mental health agency. Dr. Walsh and the administrative staff and faculty would take the Lubbock Campus to a new prominence in the Lubbock community by working closely with business and industry to position the college as the primary source of technical training on the South Plains.

The efforts to collaborate with other community entities achieved success in August 1997 when South Plains College, the Lubbock Independent School District, Market Lubbock, Inc., and nine other community partners announced the opening of the Byron Martin Advanced Technology Center (ATC). The center, a

$5.5 million training facility, featured state-of-the-art computer and instructional equipment. The Lubbock Campus relocated its business administration and industrial technology program to the 84,000 square-foot facility which was remodeled from a long-vacant K-Mart retail store. The new facility provided the much-needed space for the campus to grow. The allied health programs, which have been the cornerstones of the Lubbock educational programs, remained at the 1302 Main St. location. In addition, general education classes and developmental programs in math, English and reading are taught at the downtown campus. With the opening of the ATC, the Lubbock Campus enrollment has grown to more than 1,400 students.

A newly coordinated emergency medical service program is on the forefront of SPC instruction. In April 1998, the Texas Higher Education Coordinating Board approved a joint emergency medical services training program between South Plains College and the Texas Tech University Health Sciences Center. In 1997, the Texas Legislature mandated an extensive training system for emergency medical technicians. New state licensing will take effect in 1999. The new EMS course of study initially will use Texas Tech University's equipment and program faculty and SPC will award semester-hour credit applicable toward the associate in applied science degree. The director will conduct the classroom portion of the two-year program at the Texas Tech University Health Sciences Center with the liberal arts curriculum taught on the SPC campus. Additional instructors for the program will be members of the SPC faculty. A similar degree program at Temple College in cooperation with Scott and White Hospital was approved by the Coordinating Board at the same time SPC's proposal was adopted. SPC administrators believe similar programs will be developed statewide in the near future.

Ann Maddox, R.R.A., joined SPC in 1981 to develop the medical records technology program on the Lubbock Campus. She retired in 1988.

The growth of the college's Lubbock Campus has been a story that is marked by unique challenges and great accomplishments. The campus has grown from the original six full-time faculty and a handful of staff members in 1978 to 94 full-time employees and 62 part-time faculty in 1998. In their desire to serve students, Lubbock Campus faculty and staff have been innovative in their approach to providing technical education and workforce development programs which are meaningful and which address community needs. SPC's presence in Lubbock has opened doors for educational partnerships which will take the college into the 21st century.

The Plainview Extension Program

One year after South Plains College opened its educational program in Lubbock, the college entered into a unique technical, vocational and occupational training consortium with Wayland Baptist College and the city of Plainview, Texas. The SPC-Wayland-Plainview agreement was instituted March 5, 1973, when the Central Plains Higher Educational Authority was created by an ordinance of the Plainview City Council. The authority contracted with South Plains College to provide post-secondary technical training, while facilities would be furnished by Wayland Baptist College. Originally, the consortium's campus facility was called

An Administrative Mystery

With the SPC-Wayland Baptist College consortium and the Plainview Regional Occupational Center well established, Leon Harris became the Plainview Campus administrator in 1974. Mysteriously, five years later, Harris disappeared, never to be seen or heard from again. Harris' automobile with keys in the ignition was found at the Lubbock International Airport. He had telephoned an SPC administrator with news that he intended to evaluate some technical-vocational programs in the Dallas metroplex. An SPC administrative audit team painstakingly examined the college's financial records and found nothing missing except the administrator. Said one SPC administrator, "We balanced the books to within a nickel." Harris' whereabouts continue to befuddle both faculty and administrators. Rumors of his amnesia, his residence in California and alleged return to Plainview and mysterious reappearances continue. Some measure of suspicion circled about the mystery, but the college's internal audit and the State Auditor's Office scrutiny revealed complete financial accountability. Apparently Harris' final fiduciary act in Plainview was a bank deposit that balanced the books. Nevertheless, the mystery remained.

the Regional Occupational Center and was located at 708 Yonkers on the Wayland Baptist College campus. The facility included an administration building, a classroom building and two shop buildings.

At the time of the dedication, the consortium was the only agreement in the United States between a comprehensive community college, a municipality and a church-related college. The consortium's goal was to provide vocational and technical education programs, adult and continuing education course offerings and specialized training programs in cooperation with business and industry in the Plainview area. South Plains College was to develop one-year and two-year curricula, while Wayland was to develop parallel programs which would result in a bachelor of science degree in occupational education.

Leon Harris was appointed to direct the Plainview program. He had joined the college in 1971 to teach mid-management on the Levelland Campus. The extension program opened in the fall of 1974 and enrolled 95 students. SPC officials had worked with local advisory committees to develop eight TVO programs. They included mid-management, office occupations, radio and television servicing, child development, human services, automotive mechanics, vocational nursing and welding. The following fall, enrollment jumped to 414 students at the

Donna Womble, R.N., has seen 17 classes of vocational nurses graduate from SPC's Plainview extension program. Womble joined the Plainview program in 1980, one year after SPC took over the vocational nursing program taught by the Plainview Independent School District. Kathleen Turner, who had taught in the Plainview ISD nursing program for many years, directed the program for one year prior to Womble's arrival. Faye Dickens taught with Womble for five years and retired in 1986.

center, and by the fall of 1977, 525 students were enrolled in college-credit courses in Plainview. As the program grew, Dan Shockey was hired in 1977 to assist Harris in administering the program.

Harris left the college in 1979, and Shockey was selected to direct the Plainview program. Bill Pohl, who had served as guidance counselor on the Levelland campus and at the Plainview Center, was charged with directing a program of adult continuing education courses there in a wide variety of interest areas.

By 1977, the center employed 10 faculty members in the eight program areas. Among the most popular programs at the Plainview center were the secretarial sciences and vocational nursing. By 1981, plans were being made to offer cosmetology, auto body repair, teacher aid training, sales training and a general business program.

Shockey left the college in the fall of 1981, and Dr. Vance Clapp was appointed to serve as acting dean of the Plainview center. Dr. Clapp was a member of Wayland Baptist College's staff. Declining enrollments at the center, a change in the workforce training needs in the Plainview area, difficulties associated with administering the program from SPC's main campus in Levelland and the desire of Wayland officials to expand their own technical and vocational offerings, prompted the partners in the consortium to agree to transfer the center's programs to Wayland Baptist University. In June of 1983, Wayland assumed direction of the educational programs at the Regional Occupational Center.[5]

South Plains College retained one program at the Plainview Regional Occupational Center, its vocational nursing program, because state law does not allow the funding of vocational programs at private colleges and a need existed in the Plainview community for vocational nurse training. Donna Womble, R.N. and a graduate of Iowa Lutheran Hospital School of Nursing, began her teaching career at SPC-Plainview in 1981 as vocational nursing instructor. Her program enrolls about 36 nursing students each year at the Plainview center. Suzanne Griffin, R.N., joined the nursing faculty at Plainview in 1986. Womble and Griffin have helped maintain SPC's program in the Plainview area. Additionally, since the inception of SPC's presence in Plainview in 1974, Amelia Cline has been associated with the college in secretarial support.

---

[5] In 1981, Wayland Baptist College was renamed Wayland Baptist University. The Regional Occupational Center was renamed the Lifelong Learning Center in 1983.

CHAPTER 9

Guidance, Counseling and Other Student Services

From the time Dr. Thomas Spencer wrote the first college catalog and Nathan Tubb envisioned the various educational departments, the counseling of students received a positive emphasis at SPC. Initially, "the guidance program of South Plains College involves the administration, the entire faculty and the student body. It aims at the maximum development of the student." An orientation course was established to "assist the student to make adequate personal and social adjustments to college life."[1]

SPC administrators quickly realized that counseling and guidance, if done properly, should be the domain of trained professionals complementing the academic and technical, vocational and occupational programs on campus.[2] In early 1963, John Yates, former counselor at Port Arthur High School, was hired to oversee the program. He was followed by academic counselor Don Melton and vocational counselor Don Yarbrough in 1967. Melton and Yarbrough expanded the orientation program and began working closely with the many small schools in West Texas and Eastern New Mexico. The two men traveled across the area talking with students, presenting South Plains College to the public school coun-

---

[1] The first college catalog stressed that all faculty were to take part in "becoming the student's guidance counselor."

[2] During Registrar Nathan Tubb's direction of faculty counseling and guidance, his student secretary was Claudine Campbell. Campbell, a freshman from Anton, worked for Tubb in assigning students to their respective advisors. She later would become director of guidance and counseling at SPC.

selors and encouraging young people and their parents to visit SPC. Melton and Yarbrough realized that if the high school graduates' families toured the SPC campus, enrollment soon followed.

With new community colleges like Western Texas College in Snyder and Midland College attracting students, SPC counselors began serving in the dual role of counselor and recruiter. Sherley Foster, a counselor from Petersburg High School, was hired as academic counselor in 1970.[3] Foster's knowledge of West Texas and her friendship with counselors across the area helped reinforce SPC's service to many college students for several decades.[4]

In an attempt to gauge students' opinions on social and moral issues, Yates circulated a campuswide questionnaire in February 1967. Of special interest to

The Morals Committee

In 1967, amid the turbulent unrest and social disarray found on many college campuses, SPC administrators established a special committee to study, assess and foster "good morals" of the SPC student body. Apparently, after speakers at a Southern Association of Colleges and Schools meeting addressed the "moral decay" on campuses, a cross section of SPC administrators, faculty and Levelland religious leaders met during the academic year and discussed fostering good "morals" on campus. "South Plains College is already to a great degree presenting a wholesome, moral and religious atmosphere due to the fine faculty and administration presently employed," the minutes of the January 1967 meeting of the Morals Committee reported. Apparently the college's professorial ranks were to inculcate a proper moral code. "An instructor's 'personal orientation' could be presented in the classroom at will. It was pointed out that this could be a slight problem at times in a small college situation. Everyone agreed that one of the most important things that instructors could do to present a wholesome atmosphere was to 'live' a proper example in front of students at all times."[5]

---

[3] Foster was named "Outstanding Counselor in 1984" by the West Texas Association of Counseling and Development. Foster, the first All-State basketball player from Abernathy, began her teaching career as assistant girls basketball coach at Abernathy High School in 1958. During her tenure, the Abernathy girls won two state championships. Foster completed her bachelor of education degree at Abilene Christian College and her master's degree at North Texas State University.

[4] Foster and her colleagues developed a photographic slide presentation that explained SPC to high school students and counselors. Foster explained, "We took that slide show thousands of miles to tell the SPC story."

[5] Minutes of the Morals Committee meeting.

From South Plains College's initial 1958 entry into education, guidance and counseling of students have been pre-eminent. Originally, Registrar Nathan Tubb directed all faculty to counsel the college's students. However, as the college grew, a director of counseling position was created in 1963 when John Yates, who also served as SPC baseball coach, arrived at the college. Later in 1967, Don Melton *(above left)* **became director of counseling. Melton was later joined by Don Yarbrough who served as the college's first vocational counselor, and by Abernathy, Texas, native Sherley Foster** *(above right)* **who served as the academic counselor. Foster, believing a "step on the right foot" was the best beginning of any college education, instituted the freshman orientation program.**

the committee was the students' requested list of prospective speakers on campus. In May, the tabulated results revealed SPC students were primarily interested in the Vietnam War, college life and careers. The committee proposed a Lyceum Speakers series with committee members gathering lists of prospective lecture guests. Further discussion about college funding for career education within each academic department was suggested.

The college's counseling staff, Melton, Foster and newly hired Bill Pohl, expanded their efforts into career education, the administration of the College Level Examination Program (CLEP) and embarked on a new method of freshman orientation.[6] When Melton left the college in 1976, Sherley Foster was named direc-

---

[6] Yarbrough, having been hired as vocational counselor, became the dean of continuing education in 1969. In 1994, he was named dean of technical and continuing education. He retired in 1998.

tor of guidance and counseling. Foster and her staff greeted more than 500 students enrolled in orientation each fall semester. A pre-enrollment orientation seminar was instituted during mid-August prior to the beginning of classes. Students participated in on-campus activities prior to their first day of college classes.

SPC's enrollment growth on the Levelland Campus paralleled the educational expansion taking place at SPC Lubbock and the college's extension program on the campus of Wayland Baptist College in Plainview, Texas. SPC counselors Larry Rice of Lubbock and Vernon Smothers of Plainview joined the college counseling program. The off-campus growth required an expansion of services and centralization of counseling, guidance and testing on-campus that led to the opening of the third floor of the SPC Library. The unfinished 6,000 square-foot room, constructed in 1967 to accommodate future growth, was completed and became the center of all SPC student services. Renamed the Student Assistance Center in 1980, the third floor of the Library logged more than 7,000 student visits the first semester. Additionally, the Learning Center was also moved into the area.

During the late 1970s, the SPC counseling department participated in the Comprehensive Employment and Training Association (CETA) program. Addi-

The SPC counseling staff, with offices on the third floor of the Library, assists students in career guidance, orientation and degree planning. In 1979, the staff included *(from left)* Cydney Farrar, career project guidance associate; Kathy Huthinson, career project; Aileen Lindley, secretary to the counseling staff; Keith Bratton, guidance associate and counselor; Sherley Foster, director of guidance and counseling; Janet Griffith, coordinator of the career project; Mike Mullen, vocational counselor; and Karen Mitchell, career project secretary.

tionally, the Career Center expanded to assist students with career decisions. After President Ronald Reagan was inaugurated in 1981, the CETA program appropriations were diminished and the program ended. The Learning Center staff grew to fill the career education void caused by the CETA grant cancellation.

Orientation and assessment of the SPC students' academic abilities became the focus of the guidance and counseling and Learning Center staff in the early 1980s. Upon entering orientation, freshmen students took reading tests and were required to provide a writing sample. Counselors and Learning Center staff then assessed the students' abilities and provided advisement to the students.

In 1983, Janice Joyner became the director of guidance and counseling as assessment, testing and pre-registration activities increased the work load of the counseling staff. The college's student population increased each year, creating the need for an expanded counseling area. Counselors at the SPC Lubbock Campus continued to coordinate their duties with the director of guidance and counseling on the home campus.

With Joyner's departure in 1985, Gayla Truelock-Williams directed the counseling department. The state-mandated Texas Academic Skills Program (TASP) was phased into the educational program for new college students in 1989. The counseling department took the leadership role in implementing the TASP concept of assessing a student's reading, writing and math skills. Testing an incoming freshman's basic skills was not unfamiliar to the SPC counseling staff. Academic testing had been a part of new student orientation at SPC for many years.

In 1991, a full-time special services coordinator was added to the counseling staff to meet the needs of disabled students. First, DeZane Errico, then Zoe Bradley and Tamara Golden coordinated assistance for SPC's special needs students. In addition, the First Step Program, having been successfully piloted and implemented at the Lubbock Campus, was added to the counseling department's program. The program provides special support services for single parents and displaced homemakers who want to return to college for career training. Elizabeth Hoey Barham coordinates the program.

The Career Center, equipped with seven computers, is constantly updated with career education information. Job placement services are also centered in the counseling department. Gracie Quiñonez has served as testing coordinator while Lorea Belle has worked primarily as the Reese Center counselor. Truelock-Williams, Lynn Whitfield, Christi Anderson, and Counseling Center Director Claudine Oliver assist students in their educational decisions.

The Learning Center

South Plains College instituted a new concept in student services in the fall of 1980 when the Department of Learning Resources and the Learning Lab opened on the third floor of the Library, along with the Counseling and Guidance Office and the Office of Financial Aid. Gail Platt, hired in August 1979, had come to the college to coordinate Project BEFORE (Bilingual Education for Occupational Research and Education), a federally funded program that resulted from a Texas Education Agency proposal written by Sam Parker, an employee of the SPC Plainview Campus. Long-time college faculty member Bill Powell served as the program director.

The administration distributed Platt's duties among the three SPC campuses. She worked two days a week in Levelland, two days a week in Lubbock and one day a week in Plainview. Initially, her primary responsibilities involved implementing the program objectives (requiring that program applicants be tested for literacy skills and be provided with English-language instruction) and writing progress reports for the project.

Although the program was housed in an interior office in the Administration Building, a classroom in the northwest corner of the Administration Building was available in the afternoons for the classes and tutoring sessions. Sociology

In 1993, South Plains College's directors of guidance and counseling gathered to celebrate their friendship and the retirement of long-time counselor Sherley Foster. Pictured from left are Claudine Oliver who became director of guidance and counseling in 1990, Sherley Foster, Gayla Truelock-Williams and Janice Joyner.

professor Gary Wynn, whose office was directly across the hall, suggested to Platt that "It would be a good thing to test students' reading skills to find out if they can read these textbooks we require. Could you test all the students?" Platt said, "Sure. I don't see why not, if the faculty want me to." That was the originating idea of an entity, first called the Department of Learning Resources and the Learning Lab, and later renamed the Learning Center.

In the spring of 1980, Powell resigned from the college and recommended that Platt direct the program. President Baker approved the change and assigned Platt to the Levelland Campus with consulting responsibilities for the Lubbock and Plainview campuses.

Working with Sherley Foster, director of guidance and counseling, Platt visited with Baker and the departmental chairs to promote the idea of a Student

An Older and Wiser SPC Graduate

"My classes helped me rediscover the beauty of West Texas," said Marcellette O'Callaghan, the oldest SPC graduate. O'Callaghan walked the SPC stage May 10, 1985, just 13 days before her 80th birthday. She holds the distinction of being SPC's oldest graduate and she epitomized a cornerstone of SPC's philosophy of life-long learning. On her way toward graduation, O'Callaghan was twice named to the Dean's List. She eloquently penned her thoughts to Sherley Foster, then director of guidance and counseling, when she wrote,

"SPC has given me a new outlook upon life. I will be a happier person, much more tolerant and understanding than I would have had I not had the opportunity to learn of subjects I had merely heard of. The years I have spent at SPC have been the happiest years of my life. I have proved to me I can function and enjoy life as any normal person should. I owe much to the people who have had a hand in helping me learn to live life unafraid of life."

The Texas House of Representatives passed a resolution commending O'Callaghan on her remarkable achievement and pioneer spirit. O'Callaghan commuted 30 miles each day from her home in Brownfield, Texas.

Assistance Center to be housed on the (then vacant) third floor of the Library building. During the summer of 1980, the college remodeled the third floor and the Learning Center began operation. The new facilities included two offices and three temporary classrooms on the top floor of the Library building. Cherilyn Perryman, wife of the newly-hired SPC men's basketball coach, who had experience tutoring and teaching math, was hired as a lab instructor to work with Platt.

In August of 1980, Platt, Perryman and their secretary Beatrice Murillo assessed the reading skills of freshmen orientation students with the *Nelson-Denny Reading Test*. They evaluated more than 475 students that first year and conducted additional assessments of students who were recommended for testing by college faculty members. Platt and Perryman taught reading, math and study skills classes, in addition to tutoring students who came for assistance. By the end of the 1980-81 academic year, four student peer-tutors had been hired to supplement student learning.

The Department of Learning Resources and the Learning Lab assumed responsibility for basic skills assessment, instructional programs in basic skill areas such as reading and math, private instruction by a lab instructor and tutors, and an independent-study lab with audio-visual equipment and self-instructional programs.

In 1981, Platt authored the "Learning Resources and Learning Lab" manual that described procedures for the center's operation. Organizationally, Platt reported directly to President Baker. When Dean of Arts and Sciences Bud Joyner was later promoted to vice president for academic affairs, the Learning Center came under his direct authority. At that time, the program was renamed the Learning Center. Gail Platt, Ph.D., was named the director of the Learning Center in 1983.

The organizational structure of the Learning Center developed by Joyner continued throughout his tenure and that of his successor, Dr. Robert Cloud. Dr. Orlo Sundre, during his term as academic vice president, recommended that the director of the Learning Center report to the dean of student services. Although when this realignment was first proposed in the spring 1990 it met with critical resistance (outlined in the 1990 Annual Report), the Learning Center faculty and staff subsequently embraced the benefits associated with the change.

Finally, during the last decade, Platt has written annual reports detailing operations in the Learning Center. Most of these reports are available through the ERIC Clearinghouse for Community Colleges, University of California at Los

Angeles. The 1990-91 Annual Report revealed that the Learning Center served 2,403 students, approximately 47 percent of the entire student body on the Levelland Campus. In comparison, the most recent Annual Report (1996-97) indicated that 3,872 students were served with over 27,946 individual student contacts.

The most recent Annual Report explains the Learning Center's purpose: "The Learning Center is an academic support activity providing reading and learning strategies, development courses, collegiate instruction in reading and human development, peer-tutoring, computer-aided instruction, independent-study opportunities, workshops and seminars, and a variety of learning assessments for students and prospective students of South Plains College."

During the past decade, the Learning Center has adapted to a rapidly changing educational world. Professional staff members have been awarded faculty rank and tenure. Three assistant professors of reading, Glenda Shamburger, Anne Solomon and Marla Turrentine, joined the program. A lab instructor and the reassignment of English and math faculty from their respective departments provide a seamless curriculum for students. Moreover the implementation of the Texas Academic Skills Program, a statewide assessment, advisement, instructional and evaluation program, required additional Learning Center changes. Four developmental reading courses, a TASP reading lab, and two college-level reading courses plus a college-level human development course were implemented. Technologically, the college opened a 20-station networked computer lab with a full curriculum of basic skills instruction in 1988.

Finally, a nationally certified tutor training program, with CRLA certification, trains 20 tutors each year. More than 35 students are employed each semester. The Learning Center faculty and staff routinely make presentations at state and national conferences, serve in state and national leadership positions within their professional organizations, publish their writings and speak to various groups. These leadership roles have been supported and encouraged by the administration of South Plains College throughout the history of the Learning Center. In addition, Deanna Hines, secretary in the Learning Center, chronicles and maintains data concerning the services provided and the students served by the Learning Center.[7]

---

[7]   Gail Platt, Ph.D., documented and compiled the history of the Learning Center.

Student Health Services

South Plains College administrators instituted a student health care clinic in September 1986. The part-time clinic, located in the Student Activities Office of the Student Center, originally opened to meet student health needs each weekday at 11:00 a.m. Mary Jane Dishion, R.N., served as student health nurse and coordinated the Levelland medical doctors' daily visits with ailing students. Dr. Praeshart Punhong served as the primary care physician when the SPC clinic began operation.

In 1989, Irene Lamb, R.N., joined the college in the full-time position of coordinator of student health and wellness. In the early 1990s, five local physicians rotated duty in the college health care clinic. Dr. Bill Balch and Dr. Richard Aguas serve as the SPC primary care physicians.

South Plains College students who need medical attention contact the health clinic office each weekday morning to schedule a medical appointment. The student health services program has been effective for both students, faculty and staff. Lamb administers weekly allergy injections and more than 300 influenza vaccinations each fall. Lamb's duties involve coordinating health care for students at the SPC main campus in Levelland, the extension program at the Reese Center and the Lubbock Campus.

The College Relations Office

Maintaining close ties with the community and presenting a positive image of educational excellence have been at the forefront of the college's marketing and public relations efforts from the college's inception. That effort has developed into the present-day Office of College Relations which is responsible for public relations, communications, marketing and student recruitment. Dr. Thomas Spencer managed much of the college's public relations activities during his tenure as president.

The college's first effort to inaugurate a public relations office came in 1961 when Dr. Marvin L. Baker employed Maurine Elkins to staff a news office and write stories about the college. Elkins, a newspaperwoman who had previously worked 10 years as a reporter for the *Levelland Daily Sun News*, operated a one-person shop from 1961 to 1971. "The original concept was to get the good news out about the college in the form of news releases," recalled Earl Gerstenberger,

Two SPC Texans

Anton High School honor student, Claudine Campbell, enrolled at SPC in the fall of 1961 and fortunately, Claudine's salutatorian scholarship and her National Defense Science Foundation Loan covered most of her college expenses.[9] Campbell opted for a work-study job in Registrar Nathan Tubb's office. Tubb, the college's first "real counselor," assisted Campbell in arranging her first college class schedule. She continued her education at Texas Tech, and after her marriage to Smyer resident Wayne Oliver, received her bachelor's and master's degrees. Oliver rejoined the SPC educational family in 1981 and became the director of student services on the Lubbock Campus in 1986. In 1990, Oliver became the director of guidance and counseling on the Levelland Campus overseeing 12 staff members. She and her husband have two sons, Warren Todd Oliver with United Cotton Company in Lamesa and Jeffrey Wayne Oliver, M.D., at Texas Tech University Medical Center in Lubbock.

Levelland resident Thomas Jerry Barton entered SPC in the fall of 1959. After his SPC graduation, Jerry completed his degree work at West Texas State University and Texas Tech University in business administration. Barton joined the SPC faculty in 1970 teaching mid-management courses. He later became financial aid officer in 1972, SPC registrar in 1974 and succeeded Earl Gerstenberger as dean of students in 1982. Barton and wife Mary Beth (Wofford) have two children, a son, Dr. Scott Barton, and a daughter, Robin, both of San Antonio, Texas. As dean of students, Barton supervised the deans of men and women, the residence halls, the Counseling Center and the Learning Center. In addition, Barton coordinated the University Interscholastic League events held each spring on the college's campus. Seventeen academic events, the one-act play, and the Region I-A track and field, golf and tennis meets continue to be coordinated through Barton's

office. More than 80 public schools participate in regional competitions held at SPC each year. Winners have been certified by Barton, as overall meet director, for subsequent state contests. Barton began his association with the Kiwanis Club when he joined the SPC Circle K Club in 1959. Barton retired from SPC in 1998.

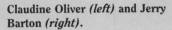

Claudine Oliver *(left)* **and Jerry Barton** *(right)*.

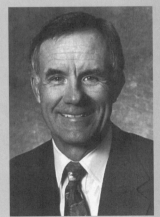

---

[8] Claudine Campbell, with yearbook experience, was editor of *The Caprock* and assisted with drama department presentations.

who supervised the Office of College Relations as vice president for administrative affairs before he retired in 1994. "Mrs. Elkins was a one-person office with some student help. She did all the writing and had the materials published all on her own." Now 90 and married to J.R. Arnold, she lives in Temple, Texas.

When Elkins left SPC, Thomas Selman, who served two years as director of student activities, was appointed to take over the preparation of news releases and public relations work in addition to his other duties.

In the summer of 1973, the college began a concerted effort to expand its public relations activities with the establishment of a bona fide Public Relations Office. Jack Brown was employed as director of public relations, and Dianne Whisenand Lawson was employed in September 1973 as his assistant. For the first time in the college's history, the office expanded its news coverage to include the college's athletic events and special features about students, faculty and events. Brown and Lawson also worked to develop recruitment literature and program brochures as the college developed its marketing and student recruitment efforts. Both employees handled photography duties as well, giving the college's communications and news program a new dimension of reporting.

Brown continued as director of public relations until the office was reorganized in early 1977. In the fall of 1976, college administrators began to evaluate

During the past four decades, South Plains College's facilities have been the central meeting place for many Hockley County study clubs. Maurine Elkins *(left)*, Irene Ellis and Sycily Lattimore, members of the Levelland Woman's Club, meet in a college lecture room. Elkins was the college's first public relations officer.

the organization of student recruitment, public relations and marketing activities at the college. With the establishment of educational extension centers at Reese Air Force Base (1970), Lubbock (1973) and Plainview (1974), new demands were being placed on these functions, and there was a growing desire to manage enrollments at the off-campus locations.

In January 1977, the Office of College Relations was created and Eddie Trice, who had been dean of men, was named dean of college relations. Creation of the new office centered responsibility for student recruitment and public relations in one office. SPC pioneered the idea of an administrative unit charged with student marketing, public relations and communications. The college was probably 10 years ahead of many other educational institutions in Texas. Within the community college movement, similar offices began to become widely organized in the mid to late 1980s. Much of the student recruitment groundwork had been laid by SPC counselors and administrators who had worked closely with area high schools in prior years.

While Trice served in an administrative capacity and helped with recruitment, the staff expanded to include a full-time sports writer and photographer. Steve Lindell was hired for that job in the summer of 1977. Lawson continued to fulfill her duties in handling general news and media relations for the college.

In the summer of 1977, the Office of College Relations moved from two small offices in the east wing of the Administration Building to a central office at the main entrance to the Administration Building. The office was given responsibility for the college telephone switchboard and employed a number of students to operate the system. "The office matured and went from the original concept of simply getting out good news in the form of news releases to the consolidation of several facets of college communications," said Gerstenberger.

The Office of College Relation's first major project centered around planning and coordinating the 20th anniversary celebration which was conducted during the 1977-78 school year. It was during a planning committee meeting that the college's present motto "Dreams Precede Realities" was proposed and adopted as the anniversary theme. J.G. Stacy is credited with brainstorming the motto years earlier and sharing it with Dr. Baker. The central focus of the celebration was a Campus Open House and Parents Day, the first large-scale special event to be organized by the Office of College Relations. That event was held during the anniversary year and defined for the office the future role it would play in organizing and coordinating major special events for the college.

One highly successful aspect of the office's marketing effort was promotion of the college's unique program in country and bluegrass music. Under Trice's direction, the story of the unusual program was picked up by the Public Broadcasting System, *Texas Monthly*, United Press International, *Bluegrass Unlimited*, and other major publications. Trice engineered the presentation of an honorary degree in bluegrass music to the legendary Bill Monroe which took place on a PBS television special hosted by country music artist Tom T. Hall. The publicity event began Hall's 20-year association with the college's program.

When the Lubbock Campus opened in 1978, expanding SPC into a multi-campus system, the Office of College Relations extended its role to include public relations efforts for the college's newest addition. As the college grew, so did personnel in the office. Terry Isaacs was hired in July 1980 to coordinate student recruitment and assist with sports writing and promotions. Trice continued to serve as dean of college relations until November 1980 and was succeeded by Isaacs who served as interim director until he accepted a position as a history instructor in May 1981.

As South Plains College experienced its greatest growth in the 1980s, the Office of College Relations mirrored that growth and entered a third stage in its development. Stephen John was employed as director of college relations in August 1981, coming to SPC from Sul Ross State University where he had served as assistant director of news and information. Prior to his arrival that summer, Kathy Hutchinson, an SPC graduate who had worked the previous year with a federally-funded career counseling program for high school students, was appointed as the college's first full-time student recruiter. The office quickly intensified its student recruitment efforts in area high schools and began a systematic program for developing a full complement of recruitment materials and program brochures. Efforts were also initiated to develop a system for responding to the information needs of prospective students who inquired about the college and its educational programs.

Under John's direction, the Office of College Relations focused on the college's institutional image as it was portrayed in its publications, recruitment efforts, special events and publicity activities. During a 10-year period, the office continued to refine its role and scope in promoting the college. In addition, newswriting activities were formally organized into a news service and the office launched a campus photography service. Recruitment activities were guided by a unified marketing plan which was developed by the office staff and endorsed by the Recruitment Committee in 1986.

To facilitate its growing role in serving the college community as an "in-house public relations and advertising agency," the Office of College Relations physically moved in 1984 into the newly-remodeled Visitors Center, previously the president's home at the main entrance to the campus. This new location gave the office greater public visibility in greeting visitors and prospective students to the campus.

The size of the college relations staff remained stable until the summer of 1987 when state budget cuts forced the college to downsize its workforce for the first time in the college's history. The Office of College Relations lost one staff position as a result of those cuts and operated understaffed for 24 months before receiving approval to fill a new position of communications assistant. Fully staffed, the office continued to expand its external and internal communications activities, launching for the first time a multi-page employee newsletter in September, 1990. *Format* debuted as an effort to foster a sense of unity and family among a faculty and staff which was growing in numbers and diversity. It has continued in publication and was redesigned and renamed *NTouch* in September 1997.

In 1991, another staff position was approved, and Charles Ehrenfeld was hired to coordinate sports publicity and assist with internal communications projects. He fully developed the office's sports marketing and promotions efforts and expanded the office's news and promotions services to the Lubbock Campus.

The advent of electronic desktop publishing, which the Office of College Relations embraced in 1987, allowed the office to produce first-class publications and other printed materials to promote SPC. The new technology enabled the office to build a unified institutional image which spanned all external publications. In 1990, the office took responsibility for publishing all course schedules and the production of the college's general catalog which was computerized using electronic publishing hardware and software. Continued application of computer technology in design and production has allowed the Office of College Relations to develop the capability of designing all publications in-house and has led to the development of new publications and communications pieces which have been added to the college's promotions efforts.[9]

---

[9] *Dreams Precede Realities* was designed, typeset and completed entirely within the College Relations Office.

The Office of College Relations took a leadership role in the development of the college's official logos. The logos were developed by three visual communications specialists who worked at SPC. The position of visual communications specialist, originally created in 1982 with the employment of Steve King, provided graphic design support for presentation projects directed by the Office of the President and other administrative offices at the college. The position reported first to the college president and later to the vice president for administrative affairs. In August 1994, it was incorporated into the Office of College Relations.

The five individuals who have held that position since its creation have worked with the Office of College Relations to shape the visual image of the college in many ways. The "intertwined SPC" logo was developed by Steve King and was adopted and incorporated into general use in 1983. King, a New Mexico native hired in 1982, was the college's first visual communications specialist. The "windmill logo" was developed by Angie Abernathy in 1988 when the decision was made to redesign the college's letterhead stationery and bring a more contemporary image to college communications. The logo, used widely in college publications,

College recruiting brochures in the mid to late 1970s featured variations of the two logos on the left. The top incorporated the three-column edifice which Dr. Marvin Baker used on occasion to illustrate the comprehensive community college concept. The same symbol appears on the college's flag. The intertwined SPC *(bottom left)* was used from about 1978 -1982 before it was replaced by a more contemporary SPC logo *(top right)*. The windmill logo *(bottom right)* was designed in 1988. The two logos on the right have been used consistently in college publications for the past 15 years.

advertising and other promotional materials, has become the recognizable symbol of the college.

The college's official seal was redesigned by Annie Austin in 1992 at the request of John. The original college seal prominently featured an architectural rendering of the front entrance to the original Administration Building constructed in 1958. The Administration Building entrance was completely remodeled and changed in 1983 as a result of an extensive campus renovation project. That change, coupled with the desire to create a more collegiate symbol for the college, led to the design proposal which was approved by Dr. Marvin Baker.

The new seal's heraldry featured the three-column edifice which appears on the college flag and which represents the basic components of a comprehensive community college. The edifice rests on an open book, symbolizing knowledge and the college's open admissions policy. A single star, representing the state of Texas, rises above the edifice which is framed on the left by an olive branch, representing honor and valor, and on the right by an oak branch, representing strength and longevity. The college's motto, "Dreams Precede Realities," appears on the

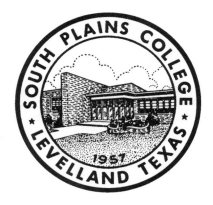

The college's original official seal was designed by college architect Lavern Kirby in 1958. The seal featured the architect's rendering of the front entrance to the Administration Building. By 1983, the building's entrance had changed dramatically due to campus renovations and the picture on the seal was no longer recognizable. A new official seal was designed in 1992, incorporating symbols which reflect the college's comprehensive community college philosophy.

lower edge of the circular seal. The new seal's first official use was on the diplomas for the Class of 1993.

In the past 17 years, the Office of College Relations has played a major role in shaping the college's public image through a multitude of public relations activities. The staff has assisted in coordinating three anniversary celebrations, including the college's 25th, 30th and 40th anniversaries, in addition to hundreds of other special events and programs which have become a tradition at the college. It has brought a level of excellence to the college's publications which has resulted in numerous regional and national awards for publication design, special events planning and news and feature writing from the National Council for Marketing and Public Relations, the National Junior College Athletic Association and the Texas Association of Continuing Education. It has developed thematic advertising and promotional campaigns based on data and input from student focus groups and members of the college community. In 1995, the College Relations Office incorporated new technology in telling the college story, including the production of a public affairs program, "The College Connection," which aired on Levelland's local cable system, and now the Internet and World Wide Web with the development of the college's web site.[10]

Over the years, the volume of work produced by the staff has grown in proportion to the growth of the college. In 1997 alone, the Office of College Relations researched, wrote and distributed 1,554 media releases through its news bureau. It was called upon to coordinate the promotion of 105 special events and projects. Through its photography services, it completed 336 photo assignments and work orders which resulted in 217 scheduled photo shoots, 336 rolls of film and 2,816 photo prints. It directed the production of 303 publications and graphics projects and coordinated 167 advertising projects. Additionally, the office coordinated and participated in 253 student recruitment events, processed 9,058 inquiries about the college from prospective students, hosted and/or toured 1,881 visitors to campus, and distributed 19,405 pieces of literature about the college and its programs.

---

[10] The college's network administrator, Tim Winders, joined the college staff in 1995 and has engineered SPC into the computer age. Fourteen SPC academic and administrative buildings are interconnected with the latest fiber optics technology. In addition, the Reese Center, the Lubbock Campus and the Byron Martin Advanced Technology Center are also interconnected to the main campus.

The office has matured in its role and scope and become an integral part of college operations. "Through its public relations efforts, the Office of College Relations has told a very positive story about South Plains College and kept a positive image before the public," said Earl Gerstenberger.

A Stolen Victory Bell and Toga Parties

During the past 40 years, SPC's deans of men have maintained order and discipline on campus. Their recollections of students' antics could fill volumes. Long-time SPC employee and 16-year veteran of the Dean of Men's Office, Darrell Grimes, held the primary disciplinary position longer than any other person in the college's history. His recall of the stolen SPC victory bell during the mid 1980s is but one example of problems the dean faced.

The Deans of Men

Earl Gerstenberger, 1966-1973
Mike Jones, 1974-1976
Eddie Trice, 1976-1977
Buddy Moore, 1977-1978
Darrell Grimes, 1978-1993
Ron Mayberry, 1993-1995
George Cormack, 1995-1996
David Jones, 1996-1998

After the construction of Texan Dome, the SPC victory bell was placed on a pedestal in front of the Dome. Charley Sanders, a member of the Board of Regents and close personal friend of President Baker, had given the bell to the college. After 20 years of prominent display, the bell mysteriously disappeared after a Texan basketball game. Dean Grimes and the college administration unsuccessfully scoured the campus and surrounding area for the bell. Weeks later an area farmer found the bell in his field and returned it to the college. The bell was secured to its mounting, and no one was punished for the crime. Only years later did news of the culprits surface. Ironically, several law enforcement students were guilty of the bell caper.[11]

---

[11] The alleged victory bell culprits are current employees of the Flower Mound, Texas, Police Department. One, as the chief investigator for the department, denied any knowledge of the bell caper, but did name a colleague, a sergeant with the department, as having some knowledge of the event. The sergeant, in turn, denied any knowledge and named the investigator as the person with information of the event. Both denied any involvement but did confirm the possibility that the bell was heisted after a basketball game into the back of a pickup. The bell is large and would have required the strength of several men to remove it from its pedestal.

Likewise, several unknown students stole the ornament from atop the live Christmas tree and damaged the top of the tree. Although Grimes attempted to locate the culprit, Vice President Gerstenberger, known for his devotion to the college's landscape, took the event "personal" and, according to Grimes, "wanted blood on that event." Luckily the students were never caught and Gerstenberger, a former dean of men, did not vent his wrath.[12]

On occasion, SPC students became creative entrepreneurs in their social conduct. Forrest Hall and the entire SPC track team staged a toga party at the Levelland National Guard Armory in 1984. Needing music for the event, the SPC cheerleaders volunteered their sound system speakers for the gathering. After the highly successful event, ("We made enough money to feed pizza to the entire dorm," said organizer Alex Torrez) the speakers were being returned to the Women's Gym when the campus police brought an end to the party. Again, the dean of men responded appropriately and the offending students answered for their actions.[13]

Finally, Grimes recalled his tenure as dean of men with a rather unique outlook. "It was like being sheriff and a plumber; nobody wanted to do the job because it can be unpleasant. You have to be slow to anger because tomorrow you'll feel differently about what happened." Grimes' attitudes toward discipline and his manner of dealing with students proved successful. His teaching and administrative career have spanned 23 years at SPC.

---

[12] The men's dorms were frequently the site of mischievous events. Probably the most embarrassing was Frazier Hall's construction of a snowman. After a winter storm, the dorm's young men prominently displayed their sculpture in front of the dorm. The snowman, a bit risque, drew the ire of the dean of men. Indeed, his round-the-clock duties required his residence on campus. Dean Grimes recalled, with a chuckle, the famous water fight between the athletes of Frazier Hall and the cowboys of Magee Hall. The event began with innocent water balloons but culminated with the creative genius of the Magee Hall cowboys. It seems they began mixing their water in buckets with material obtained from the agriculture farm. The dean of men, unscathed, put an end to the entire event.

[13] In 1981 - 82 a four-officer, full-time Campus Police Department was created to provide security at South Plains College. Randy Neill was selected as the first chief of SPC police.

In 1967, Texan Dome was constructed on the South Plains College campus. In addition to the home of the SPC Texans and Lady Texans, the Dome has been the site of indoor tennis, boxing and symphonic concerts. The Texan victory bell was placed on its pedestal after Charley Sanders, an original member of the Board of Regents from Pettit, Texas, found the bell near San Angelo, Texas. Sanders, whose hobby was collecting bells, paid for the bell and donated it to the college. Two years after the bell was placed at the Dome, a "mystery ringer" would toll the bell each evening. When the campus police officer checked the area, no one could be found ringing the bell. The police officer, inquisitive as to how the bell was being tolled, stationed himself inside the Dome and waited for the bell's sound. After the bell began ringing, the officer discovered two students had tied a long twine cord onto the bell and were located on the west side of the Dome.

Levelland Campus Recipients
of the Excellence in Teaching Award

In 1965 the Excellence in Teaching Award was created to honor an SPC teacher for outstanding classroom instruction as a "master teacher." Faculty members are nominated by their peers and the recipient is selected in a campuswide vote. The award and honorarium were originally provided by First National Bank in Levelland. It is now provided by South Plains Bank in Levelland.

Earl Gerstenberger, Agriculture, 1965
Don Appling, History, 1966
Don Stroud, Art, 1967
Wilburn Wheeler, Mathematics, 1968
R.E. "Bob" Beck, Chemistry, 1969
J.B. Balch, Science, 1970
David R. Stanley, Government, 1971
Robert Pearce, Mathematics, 1972
Polly Parmer, Science 1973
Paula Bell, Business 1974
Richard James, Mathematics, 1975
Darrel Raines, Drafting, 1976
Helen Roberts, Speech and Drama, 1977
Clint Ramsey, Physical Education, 1978
Jim Blassingame, Science, 1980
Kieth Mixon, Mathematics, 1981
Travis Spears, Government, 1982
Lee Weldon Stephenson, English, 1983
Jim Leggitt, Science, 1984
Glenna Cooper, Science, 1985
George Lawless, Law Enforcement 1986
Scott Couch, Science, 1987
Larry Nichols, Law Enforcement, 1988
Jeanelle Permenter, Physical Education, 1989
Irma Bollinger, Foreign Language, 1990
Jim Young, Science, 1991
Marla Cottenoir, Registered Nursing, 1992
Larry Roberts, Physical Education, 1993
Bill Billingsley, History, 1994
Judy Bryant, Physical Education, 1995
Bob Wilson, Drafting, 1996
Scott Yarbrough, English, 1997
(Tie) Darrell Grimes, Computer Information Systems, 1998
(Tie) John Hartin, Creative Arts, 1998

CHAPTER 10

A Musical Tradition

From the college's opening semester, music has been a part of the South Plains College educational program. In fact, during the past four decades, choral, band and country music have prominently placed the college in the national media and in local communities across the Southwest.

In addition to Texan Band Director Wilburn Wheeler, Dr. Spencer persuaded Anne Bulls to teach voice and choral music.[1] Soon thereafter, Harley Bulls joined the faculty teaching students in the fledgling music program. The Bulls, along with speech instructors, staged numerous musical productions such as *Carnival, Flower Drum Song* and *Oliver* in the SPC Auditorium. During Spencer's tenure, Harley and Anne Bulls held preparatory music classes in the afternoon for the area's pre-college students for "$1.00 per lesson to students wanting piano or voice lessons. We built our classes by working the registration table and encouraging youngsters to sign up for the chorus."

As the music program grew, Larry Don Wiley was hired to teach piano and formed the Baker's Dozen, a choral group of 13 students who performed across

---

[1] Spencer hired Doreen Grimes as the first piano instructor at the college. Although Grimes initially agreed to join the faculty, family illness required her to decline Spencer's offer to lead the Music Department. She informed Spencer of her decision during the first registration and he asked Anne Bulls, who had taught at Southwest Texas State College in San Marcos the previous year, to join the faculty. Bulls, with 18-month-old twins, reluctantly agreed and began an SPC teaching career that ended with her retirement in 1984.

President Spencer selected Levelland native Wilburn R. Wheeler to direct the SPC band. Wheeler, in addition to his band directing duties, also taught mathematics. Wheeler, a musical taskmaster, served as Texan band director until the arrival of Jack Nowlin in 1968. In this 1961 photograph, saxophone player Doug Macon *(left)* listens intently to Wheeler's directions. *(Photo courtesy of Harley and Anne Bulls)*

The 1959 South Plains College Band was directed by mathematics instructor Wilburn Wheeler. Members of the band were Bob Bowers, Leon Tatham, Louise Vaughn, Victor Ward, Tommy Martin, Eddie Hale, Robert Vialle, Ronald Rhodes, Brenda Cooper, Davie Mitchell, Lyndon Smith, Sandra O'Conner, Thomas Taylor, Carlene Glover, Duane Duncan and Jerry Myatt. *(Photo courtesy of Harley and Anne Bulls)*

the South Plains.[2] Prior to the mid-1970s, the choral and classical music programs grew by leaps and bounds. The Fort Worth Symphony Orchestra performed in Texan Dome March 17, 1974. A grant from the Texas Commission on the Arts and Humanities funded the symphonic program.

The Texan stage band and jazz band came under the tutelage of bandmaster Wilburn Wheeler. Wheeler traveled across the South Plains encouraging outstanding musicians to visit SPC. Wheeler believed if students toured the music facilities, they would have a favorable impression of the college and would enroll in the Fine Arts Department. Wheeler's health prompted his reassignment to the Math Department on a full-time basis in 1968. Jack Nowlin joined the Fine Arts Department as the band director. His 10-year association with SPC resulted in an expanded concert program. Nowlin was joined by noted musician Bill Snodgrass in the early 1970s to develop the jazz band program. Interestingly, Nowlin managed the SPC Bookstore during the morning hours and directed the SPC bands and taught private lessons during the afternoons. Nowlin's bands and those of his successors enlivened the Texan Dome crowd at each Texan basketball game.

Fine Arts Department Chairpersons

Harley Bulls, 1968-1980

Don Stroud, 1980-1988

Jon Johnson, 1988-1998

Creative Arts Department Chairperson

John Hartin, 1986-1998

In the early 1980s, Mark Rogers, concert band director, Dan Hanson, keyboard instructor, and Jan Jessup, choral director, joined in the music program. In 1984, Bruce Keeling, D.M.A., assumed direction of the SPC jazz band, and in 1990, percussion specialist Al Gardner became director of the SPC pep band.[3] Lynda Reid, a woodwinds instructor, joined the music faculty in 1986 to direct the SPC symphonic band. Reid, with the assistance of Keeling, has conducted a junior high school band camp each summer. More than 150 students from across the South Plains and Eastern New Mexico attend the week-long camp in mid-

---

[2] Many believed the Baker's Dozen was named by the college's second president, Dr. Marvin Baker. Instead, Wiley found a group of musically talented college students and tagged them with the name.

[3] The SPC pep band performs at Texan basketball games throughout the season.

June. Traditionally, the jazz and symphonic bands make their spring concert tour of area high schools each year.

Members of the SPC bands traditionally have been selected for competitive scholarships by the music faculty. Program scholarships, awarded for participation in a particular choral or music group, and endowed scholarships, such as the Wilburn Wheeler Music Scholarship, are awarded through the SPC Foundation. The symphonic band, under the direction of Reid, includes more than 50 students each semester, while the jazz band and pep band are comprised of 25 performers. Piano instruction, a tradition at SPC, is under the tutelage of Sally Barfield and Wilma Turner. Noted vocalist Ruby Moultrie and Fine Arts Department Chairman Jon Johnson instruct voice students. Numerous ensembles in both vocal and instrumental music are active in the Fine Arts Building. During the past decade, nine SPC band students have won national auditions and have been named to the All-American Community College Jazz Band. In 1989-90, Mike Morrison, a baritone saxophone player from Levelland, transferred to the University of Texas at Arlington and joined the jazz combo and jazz band. Morrison's combo received a "Downbeat" Award for the best college jazz group in America.

Trombone Tradition

SPC's band directors have a tradition of being trombone players. The first band director, Wilburn Wheeler, played the trombone and wielded the director's baton. His successor, Jack Nowlin, who now plays the bass trombone, served as director of the SPC bands for 10 years. Dr. Bruce Keeling can frequently be seen on the stage with his slide trombone in hand at the Lubbock Symphony, at church musical performances, and at musical events throughout the year. Nowlin, now retired in Slaton, performs with several musical groups and occasionally teaches music.

The Fine Arts Department awards more than $30,000 in scholarships to music, art and theater students each year. More than 350 students enroll each semester in the department.

No discussion of the SPC music directors would be complete without mentioning the SPC assistant band director, Scott Couch. Although Couch taught his full class load of biology students in the Science Department for 26 years, he could be seen throughout the week in the band hall assisting the brass students.

Couch finished his bachelor's degree in music education and served as Levelland High School's band director for three years. He returned to the University of Central Arkansas for his advanced degree and began teaching science. Al-

One of SPC's original faculty members, Anne Bulls, joined the faculty as the first week of classes began. The music teacher hired by President Spencer declined employment and Mrs. Bulls agreed to teach the already registered students. Two of Bulls' first students in 1958 were Kay Marlar and John Andrae. *(Photo courtesy of Harley and Anne Bulls)*

In the spring of 1959, Harley Bulls became the SPC choral director. President Spencer frequently called upon Bulls to display the choral talents of the SPC students. Bulls retired as Chairman of the Fine Arts Department in 1980. The spring 1959 choir was composed of *(front row from left)* director Harley Bulls, Barbara Butler, Kay Marlar, Anita Burnett, Betty Terrell, Donna Burnett, Sibyl Goode and Bob Ewing; *(back row from left)* Jerry Tyler, Betty Turney, Mary Beth Sims, Jan Dowlin, Reba Gayle Willis, Wanda Balch and W.B. Snodgrass. *(Photo courtesy of Harley and Anne Bulls)*

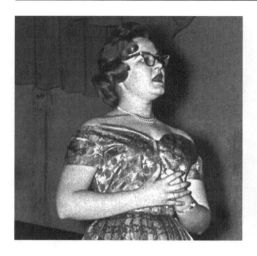

Frequent recitals were given by the college's music students under the direction of Harley and Anne Bulls. Carolyn Thompson (Reno) performed her recital on the SPC Auditorium stage during the spring semester of 1962. After teaching in public schools, Thompson completed her master's degree at Texas Woman's University in Denton, Texas, and returned to SPC in 1981 as a librarian. She coordinates student use of audio-visual and computer equipment in the SPC Library.

In the spring semester of 1962, Larry Don Wiley of Levelland and Linda Cotten of Whiteface were named Mr. and Miss Music at SPC. Wiley later joined the SPC faculty and is currently professor of music at the University of Texas-Arlington.

The 1965 Texettes choral group sang for numerous civic groups and clubs in the area. The sextette was composed of *(from left)* Sheri Faulkner of Levelland, Sandra Dalton of Levelland, Barbara Baldwin of Levelland, Elaine Stokes of Sundown, Janice May of Whiteface, and Marcheta Ownby of Levelland. Harley Bulls directed the musical group. In the spring of 1965, the Texettes performed at the Junior College Convention in Dallas, Texas, with Mike Martin, a music student from Pecos, Texas, *(not pictured)* performing the guitar accompaniment for the group. *(Photo courtesy of Harley and Anne Bulls)*

though he was an outstanding science teacher and was accorded the Excellence in Teaching Award in 1987, Couch's love of music and the high brass instruments could not be denied. His ability on the trumpet and coronet was impressive. Couch served as the assistant band director to Wilburn Wheeler and Jack Nowlin from 1967 until 1978. During his quarter century as a member of the Science Department and in the years since his 1993 retirement, Couch performed with the SPC bands.

The music instructors of the past four decades, like Wheeler and Nowlin, have found within the Fine Arts Department a most enjoyable teaching experience. The "students were interested; the friendships we made in the community and the camaraderie with fellow faculty members made my years at SPC the most pleasant of my career," said Nowlin.

The South Plains College Texettes presented numerous Christmas musical programs at the college for civic clubs and for the surrounding communities. Members of the group included *(seated)* Vivian McDaniel of Morton, *(standing from left)* Diann Conway of Levelland, Cindy Dykes of White Deer, Lynda Packard of Springlake, Phyllis Gibbs of Brownfield, and Gail Evans of Whiteface. Harley Bulls, chairman of the SPC Fine Arts Department, was the group's director. *(Photo courtesy of Harley and Anne Bulls)*

The South Plains College Texan Band has traveled across the South Plains performing for music enthusiasts. Each year the music program conducts a performance tour of West Texas public schools. The Fine Arts Department sponsors jazz, symphonic and concert band programs.

In the spring of 1968, the SPC Faculty Men's Quartet was composed of *(from left)* Bob Beck, chemistry professor; Henry Adair, psychology-sociology professor; Harley Bulls, music professor; and Charles Sylvester, college registrar. *(Photo courtesy of Harley and Anne Bulls)*

A Country and Bluegrass Phenomenon

As the music world changed in the 1970s, so did the college's fine arts curriculum. Academic Dean Nathan Tubb had previously initiated short courses in guitar, which to the administration's amazement, received an astounding reception among musicians and lovers of country music.

Eventually, students from around the world would come to the SPC campus and the country and bluegrass music program. Tubb hired professional guitarist John Hartin, who joined the SPC faculty in 1975, and originated the first country and bluegrass music education program in the United States. Hartin, having already established a guitar instruction program at Wayne State University in Wayne, Neb., met his first class of eight country music students in the fall of 1975. "Toby Hise, a U.S. Army veteran from Haskell, Mary Beth Ashburn from Meadow, and Debbie Wells from Morton were among the first students to enroll," said Hartin. "The number of students in the program increased rapidly, and two years later we hired steel guitarist Tim McCasland and fiddle instructor Ed Marsh in 1978."[4]

McCasland first arrived at the campus in 1976 as a student in the new country music program. "We only had one country band and just the beginnings of a bluegrass band. I became a part-time teacher in the spring of 1977 and joined the faculty full-time in 1978. John (Hartin) had so many students, they needed another teacher," said McCasland.[5] "I had learned to play the Dobro, and one of my first students was Beverly Byers from Lubbock. One of my best students was Tab Scott, a kid from Kentucky who was a gifted player. I gave him an assignment to play a 'lick' in 5/4 time, a Dave Brubeck song, and he couldn't handle it. It was a time signature he'd never really heard before and it was at the edge of his envelope. He broke his Dobro against the wall in the old Women's Gymnasium where we held class," said McCasland. "It was a visceral reaction to playing the guitar."[6]

Finally, McCasland, gazing back at the past two decades said, "Teaching and learning the guitar require the same skills and level of commitment that they did when I began work here. Although the students have much more technical feed-

---

[4] Hartin, talking with noted Lubbock musician Lloyd Maines, learned of a talented guitarist in Lubbock, Tim McCasland, who was attending Texas Tech University.

[5] McCasland had taught private guitar lessons for seven years prior to his association with SPC.

[6] Of the shattered Dobro event, McCasland said, "I know what a guy looks like when he goes postal." Occasionally, the student still corresponds with his former teacher.

back to help them to master the instrument, teaching guitar hasn't changed much. I still try to challenge and test them to learn the instrument."

Nevertheless, the country music program became a popular musical attraction for South Plains residents.[7] Thus was born a 20-year musical experience that traveled from coast to coast and vaulted SPC onto the television screens of American households. South Plains College's innovative country and bluegrass music program pioneered the teaching of a unique musical curriculum.

"The Land and a Man"

What began as a tribute to wild west show legend Dick Dudley, *The Land and a Man,* developed into a traveling country music road show in 1976. Speech and drama instructor Helen Roberts had wanted for several years to produce a musical program that replicated the wild west show.[8] After more than 75 interviews and a year of researching the topic, Roberts elicited the help of numerous SPC instructors to produce the show. The original musical opened at the SPC Track to celebrate the nation's bicentennial in the summer of 1976.[9]

The success of *The Land and a Man* prompted college officials, while making theme changes, to duplicate the college's successful production. President Marvin Baker envisioned a tribute to the country music legends of Texas. Thus was born *Texas: Cradle of Giants* with its 40-page script that traced the history of country music in Texas from the early 1900s to the modern day. A two-hour program of song and dance was performed on a self-contained stage, the SPC showmobile. The success of the 1977 musical production prompted a second season of *Texas: Cradle of Giants* the following summer.

Firmly established as an outstanding entertainment program across the South Plains and West Texas, the traveling country music show would for the next 17

---

[7] Lynn Daniel, bass instructor, and then Randy Ellis, sound technology instructor, joined the program to complete the original SPC country and bluegrass music faculty.

[8] Roberts, Joe R. Baulch, Jim Jenkins, Jack Nowlin and Dr. Baker formed the original "committee of five" that began plans for *The Land and a Man.*

[9] Instructors from almost every department on campus assisted in the production at the SPC Track. Art instructors Don Stroud and Burl Cole built and painted the sets, agriculture instructor Jim Jenkins provided the horses and tack, and history instructor Bill Billingsley assisted Roberts with the script. The musical was set to run July 2, 3, and 4; however, inclement weather forced postponement of the first night's performance. Overflow crowds prompted Roberts to hold over the program for a final performance on July 5, 1976.

In 1977 and 1978, the college's traveling musical road show, *Texas: Cradle of Giants,* featured the music of the nation's country music stars who were natives to the Lone Star State. Later the road show was renamed *The Golden Years of Country Music,* then *Raisin' a Ruckus,* and through much of the 1980s and 1990s, *Country Caravan.*

The Golden Years of Country Music traveling road show entertained many West Texans during the spring and summer of 1979. Cast members included *(top row from left)* Freida Berry, Randy Ellis, *(middle row from left)* Rocky Reynolds, Scott Yarbrough, Jerry Lawson, Tim McCasland, *(bottom row from left)* T.J. Spears, Dan Hanson, Barry Canter, John Hartin and Leann Ellis.

years play an integral part of summer entertainment for more than 30 communities.[10] *Cradle* gave way to *The Golden Years of Country Music* followed by *Raisin' a Ruckus* and *Country Caravan* as each summer show played to tremendous crowds in Andrews, Floydada, Lamesa, Texas, and Fort Sumner, Artesia, Alamogordo and Lovington, N.M. Throngs of country music enthusiasts greeted the SPC traveling musical troupe. As was the tradition, the roadshow concluded its summer tour at the Amphitheater in Roswell, N.M., on July 3 and was welcomed home for the traditional Independence Day performance in Levelland at the SPC Track. Each year's show schedule forged lasting friendships among the cast members.

Ed Marsh, trained in classical violin, developed an interest in fiddle music in the mid-1970s while studying at Western Kentucky University. Marsh, through a series of coincidental acquaintances, learned that SPC had originated a country

---

[10] West Texas farmers, while busy irrigating their cotton crops, found time to gather at their community's courthouse square for the yearly road show performance. Each community centered their summer trade days, old settlers reunion, or Chamber of Commerce special event around the SPC roadshow performance.

In 1983, the country music road show adopted the name *Country Caravan*. By 1987, the show's cast had grown in size and professionalism. That season featured one of the largest casts for the summer show which included *(seated left to right)* Joe Carr, Paula Horton, Ed Marsh, Marcia Miller, Judy Wilson, Crystal Finley, *(middle row from left)* Jennifer McCasland, Tim McCasland, Steve Loveless, Eli Cardona, Jackie Howard, John Hartin, *(back row)* Mike Huffman, Ricky Turpin, Bruce Keeling, Shelby Hines, Scott Schmitz and Toby McWilliams.

and bluegrass music program and had advertised for a fiddle instructor. Marsh flew to Levelland, interviewed and "played *Orange Blossom Special, Arkansas Traveler, Faded Love* and a Handel or a Bach piece" for Academic Dean Nathan Tubb. "Nathan asked that I talk with Chairman Harley Bulls and he put on his stamp of approval and I got the job," said Marsh.

"The night I got into town, I checked into the Levelland Motel and heard banjo and fiddle music coming down the hall. I met two fellows who were enrolling in the program, Steve Joseph from Maryland and Joe Alger from Oregon, and we picked together that night. They asked if I was a student and I said, 'not exactly.' I still keep in contact with both those students. I was 25 years old beginning my career," said Marsh. The fiddle instructor completed his master's degree in music at Texas Tech University and has taught fiddle and music theory in a unique musical program.

When the semester began, Marsh said, "Mildred Baker introduced me to every faculty spouse and teacher at the back-to-school supper in August; she knew every one of them. I detected a real sense of what we do and who we are. Every time anyone gathered on the South Plains, John Hartin, Tim McCasland and I played music for them. We played at the chambers of

THE 1994 TOUR

Here's where Country Caravan will be playing this season.

April 24, 25	Ocala, Florida
May 16	Sundown, Texas
May 17	Smyer, Texas
May 20	Henrietta, Texas
May 21	Gainesville, Texas
May 22	The Colony, Texas
May 23	Athens, Texas
May 24	Seymour, Texas
May 27	Whiteface, Texas
May 28	Floydada, Texas
May 28	Crosbyton, Texas
May 30	Fredericksburg, Texas
May 31	Kerrville, Texas
June 1	Junction, Texas
June 3	Lubbock, Texas
June 4	Post, Texas
June 6	Slaton, Texas
June 7	Canyon, Texas
June 9	Tulia, Texas
June 10	Amarillo, Texas
June 11	Sweetwater, Texas
June 14	Denver City, Texas
June 17	Ropesville, Texas
June 18	Seagraves, Texas
June 21	Lamesa, Texas
June 23	Andrews, Texas
June 24	Seminole, Texas
June 25	Brownfield, Texas
June 28	Lovington, N.M.
June 30	Alamogordo, N.M.
July 1	Cloudcroft, N.M.
July 2	Artesia, N.M.
July 3	Roswell, N.M.
JULY 4	LEVELLAND, TEXAS

The 1994 *Country Caravan* schedule began with two shows in Ocala, Florida, and concluded July 4 at the SPC track. The 35 shows on the schedule attracted countless country music fans. Through its 18 seasons, it is estimated that more than 400,000 music fans saw the shows in hundreds of locations.

commerce, pie suppers and goat ropings. We were constantly looking for students and patrons for the college," said Marsh.

In 1986, the Creative Arts Department became a separate entity from the Fine Arts Department. In the mid-1980s "two world class musicians," Joe Carr and Alan Munde, joined the program.[11] They, along with Cary Banks, Steve Garner, Rusty Hudelson, Jay Lemon, Randy Ellis, Stuart Moody, John Reid, Jerry Stoddard and Steven Wohlrab, teach more than 500 students each semester in the commercial music, performing arts and sound technology programs.

In addition to music theory, band, piano, orchestra and jazz, the college's musical tradition expanded into the sound technology program in the fall semester of 1980. The original Agriculture Building was renovated to become the recording studio. Ellis, an SPC graduate who trained at Belmont College in Nashville, Tenn., joined the faculty. In 1982, the college named the studio in honor of SPC benefactor and country music star Waylon Jennings.

Country music star Tom T. Hall, performing at the South Plains Fair in Lubbock, noticed the SPC country music program's performance and talked with Ed Marsh and Tim McCasland. Hall's interest in the innovative music program flourished. Later, Hall hosted and produced a Public Broadcasting System special, *Bluegrass Spectacular,* and he wanted to honor Bill Monroe, the legendary father of bluegrass music. South Plains College conferred an honorary associate degree on the country music legend. The PBS program, through numerous encore telecasts, brought increased national exposure to the SPC country and bluegrass music program.

To fully blend the world of music and video in the various music programs, the performing arts technology program was added to the Creative Arts Department in 1987-88. Pat McCutchin served as the first faculty member of the program which teaches video technology, lighting and staging associated with musical productions.[12] The performing arts technology program is a two-year course of study culminating in an associate of applied science degree. One hundred-twenty students are enrolled in the program's courses with 40 students majoring in the

---

[11] Professors Carr and Munde are the authors of *Prairie Nights to Neon Lights: The Story of Country Music in West Texas.* Carr and Munde interviewed 100 musicians from West Texas and documented the growth of country music on the plains of Texas. The 230-page book contains 50 photographs of West Texas music pioneers.

[12] McCutchin served on the SPC Board of Regents from 1980 to 1985. McCutchin graduated from the University of Texas in 1963 and has been associated with the college since 1978.

field. Instruction centers around the lighting, staging and production of musical and theatrical events in the Tom T. Hall Production Studio. The facility is a 3,600-square-foot recording studio constructed in 1986, capable of seating 400, and dedicated by Tom T. Hall. The inaugural event received national publicity on March 26, 1987, when what was promoted as the World's Largest Bluegrass Band picked out *Foggy Mountain Breakdown* in the new studio. Hall continued his support of the college's unique music program with scholarships. "We named the concert hall and recording studio in his honor," said Ellis. The studio is equipped with digital video cameras and nonlinear editing equipment capable of recording entertainment performances of all the creative and fine arts programs. Moreover, numerous fashion shows, political receptions and television shows are staged in the hall. Later, an additional production studio was named to honor country music songwriter Redd Stewart. The composer of the *Tennessee Waltz*, Stewart frequently visited the SPC Creative Arts Department.

In April 1998, the Lubbock Arts Council honored Creative Arts Department Chairman John Hartin for his work in promoting music and entertainment in West Texas. The organization placed a commemorative plaque honoring Hartin's musical career and "the development of the Creative Arts Department at South Plains College" at the Buddy Holly Terrace at 7th Street and Avenue Q.

Helen Roberts taught speech and drama at SPC for 26 years. In 1975, Roberts researched, wrote and directed an original musical, a dramatization of the life of Dick Dudley. In 1978, Roberts joined English professor Inez Grant as one of two SPC instructors accorded Piper Professor honors by the Minnie Stevens Piper Foundation. Roberts scripted and staged eight seasons of SPC's country music summer shows. In 1983, she collaborated with John Hartin to write another original musical, *O.I.L.*, commemorating the production of the billionth barrel of oil in Hockley County. Before she retired in 1994, she wrote a third musical, *Black Rose*, the story of a young slave girl during the Civil War which featured Tahoka student Ira White in the lead role. During her tenure at SPC, she directed many memorable musicals and theatrical productions which featured college and local talent.

On March 26, 1987, 187 bluegrass enthusiasts joined country music star Tom T. Hall in forming what was promoted as "The World's Largest Bluegrass Band." SPC dedicated a new state-of-the-art audio and video recording studio in Hall's honor during the festivities. Ten years earlier, Hall had given SPC's country and bluegrass music program national exposure on a PBS special "Bluegrass Spectacular."

Country music outlaw Waylon Jennings, whose son Buddy attended SPC, held a benefit concert for the college May 6, 1982, at the Lubbock Municipal Auditorium. President Marvin Baker presents Jennings a token of appreciation after the show.

Redd Stewart *(right)*, country music song-writer best known for composing *The Tennessee Waltz*, has been a benefactor of South Plains College. Stewart produced one of his last recording albums at South Plains College. Playing with Stewart are John Hartin and Ed Marsh.

The Creative Arts Series

South Plains College initiated a unique lecture and performance symposium in 1982 with the Creative Arts Series. "It was an event with a lot of people; I only put the structure to some brainstorming," said former Arts and Sciences Dean Bud Joyner.[13] Noted lecturers and performers made their presentations in the Theatre for the Performing Arts to interested students and community members who enrolled in the humanities class. Speech and drama professor Helen Roberts coordinated the series for five years. The successful program included such notables as actors Charlton Heston and Buddy Ebsen, Astronaut Pete Conrad, and Captain Gerald Coffee, a U.S. Navy pilot held captive in North Vietnam.[14]

1982-83 Events
Buddy Ebsen
An Evening with *O.I.L.*
Clarence Kincaid
The Music of Christmas
G. Gordon Liddy
Robert Blalack
Spring Band Concert
Hickman, Berline, and Crary

1983-84 Events
Dr. Daniel Keyes
Mike Cross
Tony Randall
Dr. William Westney
The Amazing Kreskin
Preservation Hall Jazz Band
Chris Carlson
SPC Choir

1984-85 Events
Actor Charlton Heston
North Texas State One O'clock Band
Violinist Eugene Fodor

Dr. Layne Longfellow
The National Shakespeare Company
The Alvin Ailey Dancers

1985-86 Events
The Shroud of Turin, by George Bortin
Riders in the Sky
Actor Steve Landesberg
Actor G. W. Bailey
Actor William Windom
Texas Boys Choir

1986-1987 Events
Musician Larry Don Wiley
U.S. Captain Gerald Coffee
The Flying Karamazov Brothers
Actress Louise Fletcher
The Glenn Miller Orchestra
Astronaut Pete Conrad
Actor Scott Keeley
The Famous People's Players
Artist Terry Morrow
The South Plains College Jazz Band

---

[13] Joyner began his tenure at SPC in 1978 after a seven-year stint at Vernon Regional Junior College. At Vernon "we had a series like the Creative Arts Series, but it was not as structured or as frequent as that presented by Helen Roberts at SPC," said Joyner.

[14] Professor of English Lee Weldon Stephenson substituted for an absent creative arts series speaker. Stephenson spoke on the foundations of the Western World.

The Marjorie Merriweather Post Collection

In 1965, Marjorie Merriweather Post, in the spirit of her father C.W. Post, provided "on loan" 13 paintings to the SPC Fine Arts Department. Mrs. Post frequently toured the area and visited the college. The art donation occurred after Mrs. Post's discussion of fine art on the South Plains with SPC President Marvin Baker. Several weeks later Mrs. Post called to inform Baker that a shipment would be arriving from the Smithsonian and her private collection. By 1973, Mrs. Post donated nine of the paintings to the college art department with the remaining four being donated to the Smithsonian Institution. Most of the artwork had been obtained by the late C.W. Post in 1915 when he purchased the Blakeslee Collection in New York. The college, established on land from the C.W. Post estate, displays the paintings in a climate-controlled area in the gallery of the Fine Arts Building and in the foyer of the SPC Library.

The paintings received as gifts from Mrs. Post included: *The Bacchanalian Feast*, obtained by Post in Italy; a rural scene by Dutch painter F. Van Paemel; *Napoleon's Retreat from Russia* by Joseph ven den Bussche, 1837 - 1908; *Sultan*

One of the early SPC faculty members left a visual legacy across the city and community. Don Stroud, professor of art and chairman of the Fine Arts Department, was presented the Excellence in Teaching Award in 1967. Stroud and fellow SPC art professor Burl Cole designed and constructed the mosaics that adorn the Hockley County Courthouse and Methodist Hospital-Levelland. Stroud's artistic talent decorated numerous SPC college yearbooks and catalogs. Dr. Marvin Baker looks on as Stroud is presented the award by Hobert Lewis of the First National Bank of Levelland.

HILLWOOD
4155 LINNEAN AVENUE
WASHINGTON, D. C. 20008

December 10, 1968

Dear Mr. Stroud,

Thank you very much for your letter of November 26 with the snapshots enclosed showing the paintings on display in your Fine Arts Building. I think they are most beautifully displayed and I am greatly pleased. They really look very handsome.

I am honored to know that you want to hang this plate regarding myself but I would prefer Marjorie Merriweather Post to Mrs. Merriweather Post, i.e.:

South Plains College is
deeply indebted
to
Marjorie Merriweather Post
for
her generosity
in giving and loaning
these works of art.

Regarding the history of the painting of Catherine the Great, I have checked with Mr. Ross, our curator here at HILLWOOD and enclose herewith a copy of a memo from Mr. Ross with particulars regarding this painting. This is all the information we have.

Again, my thanks for your thoughtfulness. All warm regards and every good wish.

Sincerely,

Marjorie Post

(Mrs. Merriweather Post)

Mr. Don Stroud
Art Department, South Plains College
Levelland, Texas   79336

In 1965, Marjorie Merriweather Post loaned four paintings and donated nine works of art to the South Plains College Fine Arts Department. In the ensuing years, four of the artistic works, including a Peter Paul Rubens portrait, were given by Mrs. Post to the Smithsonian Institute. Department Chairman Don Stroud frequently communicated with Mrs. Post's Palm Beach, Florida, and New York City offices. As heir to the Post cereal company fortune, Mrs. Post engaged in numerous philanthropic and educational endeavors. The land on which the college is built was obtained from the Post estate.

on Horseback by Charles Baskerville; and a portrait of the *Earl of Gower* by Sir Joshua Reynolds. In addition, Mrs. Post donated *Catherine the Great*, artist unknown; *Birds in Landscape* by Carl Lutz; *Caroline, Queen of George III* by Allan Ramsey; and a pastel by an unknown 18th century artist. The Ramsey portrait is actually a portrait of Charlotte of Mecklenburg-Strelitz, who married George III in 1761. The painter Ramsey, 1713-1784, painted several portraits of Charlotte, one of which hangs in the National Portrait Gallery in London.

Four other paintings were loaned by Mrs. Post for exhibit at South Plains College. They included *The Holy Family with St. Elizabeth* by Peter Paul Rubens; *Lady Esses as Juliet* by Sir Thomas Lawrence; *The Valley Farm* by John Constable; and *Outskirts of a World* by David Cox.

The *Earl of Gower* by Sir Joshua Reynolds is perhaps the most notable of the paintings and may be mislabeled. SPC art professor Don Stroud received several letters from noted English art critics in response to Stroud's inquiries. The subject of the portrait, the Earl of Gower, did sit to Sir Joshua Reynolds in the early 1760s; however, Professor Ellis Waterhouse at the Barber Institute, Birmingham University, after comparisons with other portraits, believed the portrait to be that of the second Lord Waldegrave who sat to Reynolds in 1760. Additionally, Kingsley Adams of London's National Portrait Gallery felt the *Earl of Gower* may have been a portrait of Waldegrave or Francis Seymour Conway, the Earl of Hertford from 1750 until 1793. Both critics based their opinions on the profile of the Earl of Gower and the fact that the Earl was not made Knights Garter until 1771 while the portrait was painted in 1760-1761, and paid for in 1764. The K.G. was prominent in the full-length portrait and according to Waterhouse, "It could have been put on later, but it doesn't look like it. The second Earl of Gower was made K.G. in 1771. This sitter isn't at all like him." Nevertheless, art devotees from around the United States tour the SPC Fine Arts Building and Library to view the Marjorie Merriweather Post Collection.

CHAPTER 11

English, Communications, Mathematics and Business

"If you love something, you want to share it"
Lee Weldon Stephenson

L ee Weldon Stephenson joined the English Department in the fall of 1969.[1] At that time, Inez Grant, Robert Slaughter, Betty Treadway, Frances Watkins, David Durham, Leona Dale, and Kathy Dominguez were grading freshman English themes. A short time later, Jim Cooper, Ph.D., joined the English faculty. Although SPC's student enrollment had grown during the 1970s, much of the growth occurred within other divisions of the college. It was not until January of 1983, when Leona Dale, Ph.D., retired that Patricia Cearley, Ed.D., was hired. In the following years, increased enrollment prompted the addition of other English faculty members.

Stephenson, during his almost three-decade tenure in the English Department, has taught English, philosophy, and sponsored the SPC *Caprock* yearbook as part of his academic duties. Stephenson taught English, first with Inez Grant as chairperson, then Robert Slaughter, Frances Watkins, and now Mike Felker, Ph.D. Stephenson, an eloquent master in the classroom, was named the recipient of the Excellence in Teaching Award in 1983. His thoughts about teaching English and philosophy during the past 30 years are a refined look at community

---

[1] During the early years, Deane Burks, Mary Nell Copeland, Inez Grant, Rosemary Kendrick and Hazel Sylvester taught English at the college.

college education. "When you love something, you want to share it," said Stephenson. And that he does. His explanations of words, thoughts and terms have motivated students during his tenure at SPC.

Always quick to recall an excellent student, Stephenson remembered his most memorable day with David Pharies, Class of 1971 and an outstanding student from Levelland High School. After explaining a philosophical concept, Stephenson noticed Pharies had turned pale and looked as if he might be ill. Pharies, after the class and still appearing pale and gaunt, returned to Stephenson's office. "I asked David what was wrong. He said, 'I've gone to school for 13 years and today I learned something for the first time.'" Pharies' quest for knowledge did not stop with his first SPC English class. He continued his education, received his Ph.D. from the University of Washington, and is a professor of English at the University of Florida in Gainesville.[2]

English Department Chairpersons

Inez Grant, 1958-1969
Robert Slaughter, 1969-1977
Frances Watkins, 1977-1979
Robert Slaughter, 1979-1991
Mike Felker, Ph.D., 1991-1998

Stephenson's comments reflect the attitudes of the English faculty. Although the ensuing four decades have brought retirements and a younger instructional

---

[2] Pharies has published numerous scholarly articles during his academic career.

Robert Slaughter joined the SPC English Department in 1969 as chairman and served in that capacity until 1977. As a Kellogg Fellow at Sam Houston State University, Slaughter met Dr. Marvin Baker when Baker was a guest speaker in the interdisciplinary post-master's program. They later had lunch at a well-known student hangout, Leslie's Chicken Shack. Dr. Baker and Tubb met with Slaughter at the Baker Hotel in Dallas for a formal interview and offered Slaughter his first SPC contract. In this photograph, Slaughter advises Letticia Quezada of Levelland, who graduated from SPC in 1981. She completed her B.A. degree at the University of Texas and is currently director of sales for Ramar Hispanic Media in Lubbock.

staff, they continue to stimulate students with a variety of teaching techniques. In 1998, English Department members included Chairman Mike Felker, Ph.D., Sandra Barnhill, Ph.D., Glenda Bryant, Patricia Cearley, Ed.D., Kay McClellan, Victoria McLure, Gary Poffenbarger, Sharon Race, Edward Sears, Robert Slaughter, Betty Stanley, Lee Weldon Stephenson, Teresa Trevathan and Scott Yarbrough.

The English instructors have addressed the technological age with the use of computer-assisted instruction. Four English classes are being offered on the Internet, one class is offered via interactive television, and 14 English sections are taught with computer technology. Still, Stephenson's adage, "If you love something, you want to share it," holds true. Members of the English Department believe in Stephenson's adage. Indeed, they do share their love for English literature with SPC students.

Developing the students' ability to communicate

In 1991, the college administration created the Communications Department due to continued enrollment increases. Chairperson Leann Ellis and eight faculty members teach in four program areas, with 29 courses in speech, forensics, journalism, telecommunications and foreign language. From the college's founding, foreign language

English Students' *Faux Pas*

All classroom instructors can relate dozens of humorous grammatical, spelling, and contextual mistakes created by their students. English instructors Lee Weldon Stephenson and Scott Yarbrough provided a list of their favorite malapropisms found in themes and essays. Herewith, several examples:

"To my dad, my uncle is just like a brother."

"Given a little more time, President Reagan will have unemployment, inflation and crime on the downrise."

"As you can see, I am no William Sheakspere."

"The judge handed down a sentence of guilty and was sentenced to jail."

"An outward going person would mostly wear clothes that show."

"He liked many of the things that people get out of college, like the neat people you get to meat."

And, "Friendship is not something that can happen in one eyesight."

Creative spelling and diction continue to amuse the English grammarian. It is of "up most importance," that we learn "techknowligy," as we go through our "teenagehood" years.

Correcting these mistakes requires an instructional vigilance for the slightest of grammatical errors. Naturally, the faculty promptly mark the errors. The English Department's budget for red grading pens was $162.48 in 1997.

181

courses have been offered to prospective students in the area. In 1958, Artie Fore-hand taught conversational Spanish. Later George Roberdeau and Jean Pierarts taught Spanish and French. Frank Gonzales, remembered for his brightly col-ored suits and love of the Spanish language and culture, joined the faculty in 1967. Currently, Spanish professor and past recipient of the Excellence in Teach-ing Award, Irma Bollinger, and colleague Jorge Zamora, teach more than 80 stu-dents in seven different course areas. Jorge Zamora, educated at the University of Mexico City, joined the faculty in 1997.[3]

In 1991, Bollinger instituted the South Plains Foreign Language Festival. Bollinger and Levelland High School foreign language instructor Sherri Barsch joined their talents and resources to initiate the festival. From the original four schools that attended the festival – Seminole, Seagraves, Denver City and Levelland – the festival has grown to more than 36 schools with more than 900 students in attendance. The festival is held each spring and stages competitions in nine dif-ferent areas of language expertise. The festival has resulted in the formation of the South Plains Foreign Language Collaborative, an organization of college and public school teachers. In 1998, 53 Spanish teachers and eight French teachers participated in the event. Public schools within a 100-mile radius of Levelland are invited to the event.

Although speech and drama were important facets of the SPC educational mission, forensics competition expanded in the early 1990s with numerous com-petitions in public speaking and oral interpretation events for the speech stu-dents. As members of the Texas Forensics Association, the SPC team competes in two tournaments each year. Additionally, the college speech program is a mem-ber of Phi Rho Pi, the junior college national forensics association. Each spring, the organization stages a regional qualifying forensics tournament and the sub-sequent national meet. The legacy of SPC's first speech instructor, a popular in-structor among students, Lilbern Kendrick, continues into the college's fourth decade with Ellis, Natalie Bryant, Janna Holt-Day and Julie Johnson. The speech instructors teach seven different courses within the department.[4]

---

[3] Zamora, after practicing law for 10 years, returned to Texas Tech University to obtain his master's in Spanish literature and linguistics.

[4] SPC's speech instructors train student judges for the wide variety of speech competitions held each year in University Interscholastic League and Texas Forensics Association competition.

Mathematics and Engineering

When Robert Pearce joined the Math Department in 1965, only three other faculty members taught college algebra and higher level mathematics courses. Math Chairman Wilburn Wheeler, Charles Sylvester and C.W. Dukes welcomed Pearce, a recent West Texas State College graduate. Pearce's career spans two widely divergent eras of math instruction. When Pearce joined the faculty, all the math classes were taught in the Science Building with instructors standing in front of a chalk board explaining equations and working problems.

Increased student enrollment contributed to the need for increased financial support of the Math Department during the 1970s. Four additional faculty members, Kieth Mixon, Gwyneth Wood, Glenn Pounds and Richard James, joined the math faculty to meet the increased instructional load. Thirty-three years later, with Pearce as the most senior tenured faculty member, the math and engineering instructors teach 32 different courses on the SPC campus and are experimenting with a new computer-structured software system.

In the past three decades, math instructors have taught in almost every building on campus. For a while they occupied the third floor of the Library and could

Mathematics instructor Charles Sylvester was one of the original faculty members. He, Wilburn Wheeler and C.W. Dukes "were the Math Department" until Robert Pearce, current chairperson, arrived in 1965. Sylvester later succeeded Nathan Tubb as the college's registrar.

Original faculty member Wilburn Wheeler taught mathematics as well as directed the SPC Texan Band. Wheeler served on the SPC faculty from 1958 until his retirement in 1974.

183

Mathematics and Engineering Department Chairmen

Charles Sylvester, 1958-1964
Wilburn Wheeler, 1964-1974
Robert Pearce, 1974-1998

Math Department professor Robert Pearce initiated a new technique for math instruction in 1974. Pearce, fellow instructors Richard James and Kieth Mixon began videotaping their lectures after President Marvin Baker obtained funding for the program. The video tapes were placed in the SPC Library and made available to students.

frequently be seen in any available classroom on campus. In 1992, the department moved into the new Math and Engineering Building located south of Texan Dome. What was planned as a building to serve the Math Department's needs for the foreseeable future has been filled to capacity in five years.[5]

Optimum instruction by the SPC math faculty has remained Pearce's goal since becoming chairman of the department in 1974. Although SPC has continually attracted a solid base of excellent math students, changing demographics, public school requirements and a diverse curriculum have altered the perceptions and opinions held by many math students who enroll at SPC. "We stress explaining the concept, then allowing the student work time in the classroom to learn the tasks," said Pearce.

South Plains College's Math Department pioneered the use of equipment to enhance instruction. In the spring semester of 1974, when instructional video technology was in its infancy, the Math Department developed a new mathematics teaching system. After viewing the video equipment obtained by the Athletic Department, Pearce talked with President Baker about funding to expand the use of in-

---

[5] One additional office was created by erecting a partition in a storage closet.

Mathematics professor Richard James, a graduate of Eastern New Mexico University in Portales, N.M., joined the SPC faculty in September 1968. In 1975, SPC faculty members selected him to receive the Excellence in Teaching Award.

structional video in the Math Department. Baker agreed; Pearce traveled to Purdue University to study their videotaping system, and a new mathematics teaching methodology began. After President Baker provided funding, Pearce taped trigonometry lectures and made them available to the students. The following year in a summer educational project, fellow math instructors Richard James and Kieth Mixon taped other math class lectures. As a result, the department placed the complete set of instructional tapes in the SPC Library and students could view the tapes to reinforce a math concept or review mathematical problems prior to an exam.

What began in 1974 as an idea for enhancing instruction resulted in more than 440 tapes supplementing classroom instruction.[6] According to Pearce, "We had little in the way of technology except for a stick of chalk those first years." As the years progressed, Pearce used all his persuasive skills with President Marvin Baker. "We both had math backgrounds (Baker had taught math at Southwest Texas Junior College), so I guess I could coax more resources out of him than some of the other chairmen." Moreover, students in 1995 used the first of three computer science laboratories within the Math Department. Technologically, the Math and Engineering Department currently has one of the finest learning environments in the entire Southwest. Students majoring in computer science have 52 computer workstations located within the Math Department's labs. Professor Charlotte Young, who joined the department in 1995 after teaching four

---

[6] The instructional tapes are available for student use on their home video cassette systems. Four VCR television systems are available for student use in the Math Department.

years in the Business Administration Department, uses a networked large-screen television as a teaching aid to instruct students in computer science.

A new instructional software program, written by instructor James Stephens, was piloted in the college algebra classes in the fall semester of 1998. The interactive system, touted as capable of increasing student success rates by 40 percent, utilizes computer instruction and video examples teamed with faculty explanation.

Forty years after Charles Sylvester walked into his first SPC classroom with slide rule in hand, the SPC Math and Engineering Department continues amid changing computer technologies to teach mathematics with a striking similarity. Veterans Pearce and James are joined by instructors Linda Campbell, Mark Damron, Jay Driver, Pat Foard, David Hobbs, Jo Beth Horney, Jim LaGrone, Don Lavigne, Alma Lopez, R.B. Pruitt, Sally Robinson, Caleb Rosson, Scott Shannon and Charlotte Young as they enter the classroom with graphing calculators and computers. No matter the equipment, an SPC math instructor stands at the front of each assembled class calculating, explaining and exhorting students to work harder. Four decades ago the SPC mathematics student had the same experience.[7]

---

[7] According to Pearce, one of the great joys of teaching occurs often in the Math Department. "One of our former students will call, write, or stop by and say thanks for that extra work we demanded."

In 1969, Tax Assessor-Collector John Dickson was awarded the Promotion of School Spirit Award. SPC math professor Glenn Pounds *(right)* presented the award to Dickson. Pounds served as SPC financial aids officer until 1983, when he returned to the Math Department to teach algebra and trigonometry. Pounds' wife, Shirley, worked as SPC reference librarian for 27 years. Dickson joined the SPC administrative team in 1962, became business manager in 1982 and retired in 1993. Lunette Dickson served as chairperson of the Business Administration Department for 18 years.

The Business Administration Department

"We began with the old manual rotary calculator that we called the coffee grinder. The old duplicating machines we used in the office procedures class included the fluid duplicator (purple masters, purple hands!), the stencil duplicator (black ink, black hands!), and the offset printer (black ink, black everything!). Now we have color printers and scanners," said Business Administration Department Chairperson Dianne Bridges. South Plains College's first business program consisted of six courses taught by Fred Stoughton, Michael Knowles and several part-time instructors from the community.[8] Initially in 1958, the business program included a broad variety of business courses that included typing, business machines and accounting. The department provided one and two-year commercial (secretarial) programs and a two-year transfer program that prepared students to complete a baccalaureate degree in business. For a while, SPC awarded the associate of business administration degree.

As technology changed in the early 1960s, the department added six electronic data processing courses and computer programming, which at that time could be a frightening concept to many college freshmen. In 1968, business classes, then taught across campus, were consolidated into the newly constructed Technical Arts Center. In the early 1970s, computer information systems technology expanded with COBOL, FORTRAN and assembly language programming classes. The college continually upgraded the computer system used in the Business Department. The first mainframe computer was an IBM 1620 added to the department in 1963. Currently, the Business Department offers 52 courses in three different program areas with nine separate curricula, while the newly created Computer Information Systems Department under Chairman Darrell Grimes offers 17 courses with two curricula options. More than 1,400 students are enrolled each semester in Business Department courses. Faculty member Paula Bell, who began her SPC teaching career in 1960, has continued her association with SPC. Although the veteran teacher retired in 1994, she enjoys the classroom environment and has taught computer classes part-time in the evening school each se-

---

[8] Local attorney E.W. (Bill) Boedeker, business law, and Sycily Lattimore, accounting, served as part-time instructors when the college opened. When additional classes were necessary, Lattimore taught American history for Social Science Chairman Don Appling and joined the Business Department faculty full-time in 1968. She retired in 1979.

mester. Bell, who received the Excellence in Teaching Award in 1974, said, "I've enjoyed teaching students during each of the four decades I've worked at SPC."

In 1997, the Computer Information Systems Department adopted a unique computer teaching system. ROBOTEL allows instructors in the program to take control of each computer screen electronically to demonstrate a specific computer task. Additionally, instructors may then display any student's screen to the entire class by using this Canadian-manufactured teaching system. The college installed a duplicate ROBOTEL system at the Reese Center computer lab in 1998. As a teaching tool, the "system is unequaled by any system on the market," said Grimes. The system was installed after college President Gary McDaniel, inquisitive about computer technology, enrolled in Grimes' computer course. The ROBOTEL system is the latest example of technological innovation within the CIS Department. Grimes and veteran instructors Karen Ramsey, Exa Kaye Ainsworth, Don Boyd, Deborah Lamprecht and Roland Moreira use the system to teach computer science students on the Levelland Campus and the Reese Center Campus.

As computer technology education made advances across the Business Department curriculum, faculty members continually updated their knowledge and skills through seminars at educational institutions across the Southwest. Although tremendous changes have occurred in the area of computer technology, an adaptive curriculum within the SPC Business Department has met the needs of an ever increasing student population.

In fact, the department with two instructors in 1958 has grown to more than 14 faculty members on the Levelland Campus and nine members on the Lubbock Campus, providing business education to SPC business students.

Students within the Business Department originally joined the college chapter of the Future Business Leaders of America. In 1960, the organization's name was changed to Phi Beta Lambda. In 1970, the campus club divided into the Office Education Association and the Mid-Management Club. Ann Gregory, associate professor of accounting, reinstated the Phi Beta Lambda chapter in 1988 with students participating on local, state and national levels.

The marketing and management program has included everything from traditional management courses to supermarket, service station and aviation management classes.[9] In 1970, student interest prompted creation of the fashion

---

[9] SPC administrators Jerry Barton, Darrell Grimes, Leon Harris and Buddy Moore began their careers as instructors within the mid-management program.

Phi Theta Kappa

In January 1960, South Plains College established the Kappa Mu chapter of Phi Theta Kappa, the honor society for junior college students. Initially, Rose Marie Pilcher and Deane Burks served as co-sponsors of the SPC chapter. Thomas Taylor was elected the first Kappa Mu president and Gary Grant was named vice president. During the past four decades, faculty members from various departments on campus have served as sponsors of the organization. An annual installation of new members has been held each spring since the first installation in April 1960. In 1961, six members – Barbara Golden, Shirley Hanley, Dean Marcy, Susan Roberson, Ann Tyer and Joe Wilson – attended the Phi Theta Kappa national convention in Sheridan, Wyo., with Inez Grant and Don Appling as sponsors. The following year, Registrar Nathan Tubb accompanied nine SPC Kappans to Biloxi, Miss., site of the national convention. In the ensuing years, SPC has continued to participate in the state and national conventions. In 1985, 17 members attended the national convention in St. Louis, Mo., with Kappa Mu selected to receive the organization's Milestone Award. This enabled two SPC Kappans, Mary Ann Sanchez and Bruce Turnipseed, to attend the Honors Institute in Mississippi. SPC's Phi Theta Kappa members have sponsored a variety of community service projects, fund raisers and student activities events during its history. The local chapter's membership is made up of the top academic and technical students on campus. As the chapter prepares to enter its fourth decade, English professor Gary Poffenbarger serves as the chapter sponsor.

When South Plain College opened its doors in 1958, Dr. Spencer believed a bus transportation system across the South Plains would encourage enrollment at the college. The college purchased several buses and hired students to drive them to the campus each day. Later to transport the SPC athletic teams, the college purchased eight-door extended pickups which seated 22. In this 1961 spring semester photograph, Registrar Nathan Tubb is pictured in the bus he drove to Biloxi, Miss., to the National Phi Theta Kappa Convention. According to Tubb, the air-conditioned bus afforded students a prime view of Bourbon Street as the students traveled through New Orleans, La., on the return trip to Levelland.

merchandising program. Originally, Carolyn Pults served as part-time instructor for the program, and as it expanded, Sharyn Godley offered six different course offerings in the fashion industry. In 1974, instructor and program coordinator Cindy Brown joined the faculty. Students are given "real world" experiences in off-campus study at the Dallas Apparel Market each fall semester. Brown and Kae Hineline of McLennan Community College jointly sponsor student tours to the New York City fashion market. The student-funded New York trip is conducted every other year. The fashion merchandising program presents a variety of fashion shows to interested clubs and organizations in the area.

Chairpersons of the Business Administration Department

Michael J. Knowles, 1960-1965

Richard Wood, 1965-1967

Paula Bell, 1967-1975

Lunette Dickson, 1976-1992

Dianne Bridges, 1993-1998, Chairperson of the Business Administration Department

Darrell Grimes, 1998, Chairperson of the Computer Information Systems Department

In 1990, the mid-management and fashion merchandising programs were revised to marketing and management and merchandising, respectively, to reflect current business trends and broaden the programs' scope. In 1998, an advanced marketing and management class was taught by Clyde Neff, who joined the faculty in 1987.

The secretarial courses have been a part of the curriculum since the college's founding. However, classes in typewriting and shorthand have given way to new computer technology. Under the leadership of Lunette Dickson, the longest-serving Business Department chairperson during the first 40 years of the college's history, the secretarial science program expanded to include classes for medical and legal secretaries. Bette Pitts was hired in 1977 to teach the legal secretary courses.[10] Later, Linda Hall, Ronnie Leiker and Susan Mills joined the faculty to instruct students in the latest computer applications within the office technology area.

---

[10] Accreditation criteria of the Commission on Colleges of the Southern Association of Colleges and Schools requires instructors of specialized courses to have at least three years' work experience in the field.

Lunette Dickson *(above left)* joined the South Plains College Business Department in 1969 and became departmental chair in 1976. During her tenure, the department experienced its greatest growth and expansion in programs, students and technology. Paula Bell *(far right)* began teaching data processing in 1960 when computers were the size of a typical classroom. She retired in 1994. Bell worked with Dickson to bring new technology to the computer information systems program.

The Old Punch Card Registration System

In the late 1960s, SPC's registration kept pace with the computer age with the new IBM 1620 computer punch card system. Each offered class and section would have pre-cut computer cards corresponding to the number of chairs in the assigned classroom. Cards were given to each enrolling student. When the cards were handed out the class was full. However, any student who pleaded with math instructor Robert Pearce could get him to cut another card to make room for "just one more." As a particular day's registration progressed, there clearly were more cards being cut than the available seating capacity in Gary Wynn's anthropology class. When Wynn asked the student where he got the card, the frightened student responded, "Mr. Pearce cut it for me." To which Mr. Wynn responded, "Have Mr. Pearce cut you a chair." Three decades later, allegations resurface at each registration that Chairman Pearce uses the computer terminal "override" in much the same manner as the punch card system of the late 1960s. On another occasion, English professor Lee Weldon Stephenson bemoaned the lack of general education in the United States with, "You can't even find anybody who'll teach Dostoyevski," to which history professor Bill Billingsley responded, "If he has a class card, I'll teach him."

The SPC Secretarial Staff

No college's history could be complete without including those individuals who provide the continuity and maintain the day-to-day operations of the college. SPC's secretarial staff has grown from two full-time employees, Jean Bowman, president's secretary, and Lena Parsons, registrar's secretary, to an impressive staff of veterans who are an integral part of the college's educational mission. In addition to the original two secretaries, two part-time staff members, a bookstore manager, three individuals in the tax office, a grounds keeper and three custodians composed the secretarial and classified personnel in 1958. Forty years later, the list of exemplary SPC classified and secretarial employees has grown to number 75 across three campus locations. Many staff members have served the college for more than two decades. Their contributions to the college's educational efforts can never be measured but should be recognized. Shirley Prothro began her SPC employment in 1966, Jeanette Grisby in 1976, Teresa Williams in 1978, and all continue their daily tasks at SPC. Jean Bowman, Jean Beck, Ruth Holland, June Gerstenberger and Billie Burtner all retired after decades of dedicated service to South Plains College. Their efforts, although many times not visible to the casual observer, have contributed to the success and reputation of South Plains College.

Long-time employee Billie Burtner worked as secretary to Nathan Tubb, Charles Sylvester, Jerry Barton, Don Stroud and Jon Johnson during her almost 20-year SPC career.

Secretaries to the President

Frieda Sonnenberg, 1958-1959

Jean Bowman, 1959-1968

Mary Robinson, 1969

Shirley Prothro, 1969-1970

Mary Robinson, 1970-1978

Barbara Gilley, 1978-1990

Brenda Dunlap, 1990-1995

René Heard, 1995-1998

CHAPTER 12

Maintaining the College Facilities

The SPC Maintenance and Grounds Department has grown to include 45 individuals who maintain the college's facilities. The department has been directed by five different individuals. The first superintendent of buildings and grounds was Orville Allison, followed by James Ferrell, Russell Townsend and L.C. O'Bannon. The most recent director of the physical plant is Joe Bollinger. All were familiar with the difficulties of maintaining the buildings.[1] Ferrell, as director of maintenance, also taught in the refrigeration and air conditioning technology program.

Originally, the Administration Building utilized a chilled water system to provide climate control. Few public buildings across the South Plains enjoyed the luxury of air conditioning during the late 1950s. As a result, the college's administration emphasized the new campus' air conditioned buildings to prospective students. The chilled water system worked well for the first decade, but as the chemical content of West Texas water worsened, the overhead pipes were constricted by sediment buildup. In addition, water leaks became commonplace in the buildings. The Gymnasium utilized space heaters suspended from the ceiling, but the faculty offices of coaches Bill Powell and Myrtle Lucke were not heated. "During several of the first winters, the commodes and pipes froze in the

---

[1] In 1998, the SPC Maintenance Department included one plumber, one painter, three carpenters, three heating, ventilation and air conditioning specialists, one electrician and more than 30 custodial personnel to maintain 38 buildings. The superintendent of buildings and grounds position was renamed director of the physical plant in 1993.

building," said Earl Gerstenberger. The original Library and Auditorium had refrigerated air and central heating. Later, chilled water systems were installed in other buildings, such as the Technical Arts Center constructed during the late 1960s.

Dale Stone became the first on-site manager for SAGA Food Service in Texan Hall. Greg Magill succeeded Stone as food service manager as the SPC student enrollment increased and additional demands were placed upon the food service. According to Earl Gerstenberger, then dean of men, "We almost had an uprising on our hands with student complaints. Dr. Baker, Nathan (Tubb), Hi (Walker) and I had a meeting with Magill concerning the food quality. Nathan had eaten a sandwich in the cafeteria a few days earlier and he, in typical Tubb fashion, said, 'Greg, your sandwiches just don't have any character.' Magill replied that he 'didn't know what gave a sandwich character.'"

Nevertheless, after Charles Ketcham replaced Magill as SAGA Food Service manager, students and faculty agreed that the food service improved. He was followed by Ed Smith, a native of the Northeastern United States. Smith experi-

The original Texan Hall lunch line, contrary to student opinion, catered to the tastes of students. Although complaining about the cafeteria food seems to be an obligatory freshman duty, numerous faculty members, who discern fine cuisine, are found daily in the dining hall. SAGA Food Services operated the dining hall until 1989 when the Marriott Corporation obtained the food service company. The 1960s lunch line was replaced with the food-court concept in the mid-1980s when Texan Hall was renovated.

enced difficulty with "chicken fried steaks" which he thought were a poultry dish and Reuben sandwiches which did not please the Texans' palates. Larry DeVoto then became food service manager and expanded the scope and service to the SPC students. DeVoto's wife was from Brazil and he took an interest in the foreign students attending SPC. DeVoto implemented the International Dinner in which foreign students prepared their favorite meals from their native countries. Generally, the International Dinner was a popular event on campus throughout the late 1960s and early 1970s when the foreign student population on many college campuses was significant.[2]

Later, Jim Wilkes, a Meadow, Texas, native, became cafeteria director from 1977-1986 when the SAGA Corporation was sold to the Marriott Corporation.[3] As the college food service industry became more competitive in the early 1980s, the college accepted bids to award the cafeteria contract. Both Professional Food

The College Food Service

Since the college's inception, a food service, first as a snack bar and a small lunch line in Texan Hall, has provided meals for SPC students. With the construction of the first dorms, a small kitchen was added adjacent to the SUB. Portable steam tables were rolled into the SUB, and the area became a cafeteria. Initially, Dorothy Christmas, wife of original faculty member and industrial arts instructor John Christmas, managed the SPC snack bar. Later, the addition of dormitories required the expansion of Texan Hall and construction of an enlarged kitchen. Basil Kolb served as food service manager until the college enlisted SAGA Food Corporation in the mid-1960s. SAGA, formed by three men in Hobart, N.Y., in 1948, approached college administrators about providing cafeteria services at SPC. With their experience at numerous institutions across America, college officials agreed to a contract with SAGA that began a three-decade relationship in cafeteria services.

Management and Aramark also submitted bids to win the SPC contract. Said Wilkes, "When they opened the bids Doc Baker just smiled. We got the contract,

---

[2] Minor problems beset the International Dinner each year. Most significantly, a bevy of students working in the SPC kitchen left the area in disarray. Moreover, on one occasion, two students from the Middle East engaged in a culinary argument that escalated into fisticuffs amid the pots and pans.

[3] Wilkes and wife Karen (Phillips) were long-time associates of SPC. Karen was a Texan Cheerleader from Sundown, Texas, in 1968 - 1969. Jim Wilkes, whose father was superintendent of schools at Meadow, Texas, for 28 years, tried out for the Texan basketball team under coach Dennis Patton.

South Plains College's first bookstore manager was Rachel Watson (right). She and Elouise Woodley (left) also ran the college snack bar. Although the snack bar has been moved and the Student Union Building renovated, the original snack bar griddle is still in operation in the current Student Center snack bar.

but Doc Baker was tough. You had to work double hard. Doc would tell you where he thought you could save money, but you always knew where you stood." After Wilkes' departure to Texas Lutheran College, Rene Silhan became the food service manager, and after a recent international merger, the SPC cafeteria management was contracted with Marriott-Sodexho, a French company.

The ritual of complaining about college dorm food exists worldwide, and SPC students have readily participated in the custom for four decades. As former students return to SPC and take the tray down the lunch line, it seems that their comments about the food are more positive. Numerous students, SPC faculty and staff can be seen in Texan Hall each day at lunch time. Throughout the year, numerous banquets, social events and luncheons are held at the college. Those events began 40 years ago with portable steam tables and a sandwich line.

The Most Expensive Book on Campus

Originally, the South Plains College Bookstore, as a part of the Student Union Building, occupied a small area adjacent to the snack bar. When the first bookstore manager, Rachel Watson, ordered the academic and technical faculty members' textbook selections, a chemistry book at $6.50 was the most expensive on campus in 1958.[4] Watson and those who succeeded her stocked the books during the summer months in anticipation of the student demand for the fall semester.

During the past four decades, the bookstore has expanded into merchandising textbooks, supplies, wearing apparel and a host of items to meet student needs. It has expanded to provide books and laboratory manuals needed by the SPC student population of more than 6,000 students.

Numerous managers employed by the college have operated the bookstore during SPC's history. Originally, Rachel (Watson) Nelson was assigned the duties of selling the textbooks, pens and some wearing apparel out of a storage room in the Administration Building. "I brought my coffee pot and made coffee for the faculty," said Nelson. Within a short time the SUB was completed and the SPC Bookstore was relocated. Nelson also managed the SPC snack bar in the SUB and after 10 years as bookstore manager, she became dorm matron at Stroud Hall and served in that capacity for another 10 years.

---

[4] The author tried unsuccessfully to locate the chemistry textbook used by Professor Henry Lucke that first year. A comparison of that text with the current volume would be astounding. A comparison of the price tags of the two books would prompt a similar response.

Bobbie Loving

For the past 33 years, Viver "Bobbie" Loving has graced the SPC kitchen. Her service skills have outlasted at least five different food service directors employed by the SAGA Corporation and Marriott Corporation. Remarked one faculty member, "Bobbie's gumbo is second to none." Bobbie has managed to work in a variety of circumstances. She was an employee in the 1960s when the kitchen was small and the work area confined. She has coped with the idiosyncrasies of corporate managers and student work-study employees. Moreover, she is an accomplished employee who reports to the SPC kitchen each day at 5:30 a.m. to prepare breakfast for the dorm students. Her efforts and contributions, although unnoticed in the day-to-day college operations, have been significant. Bobbie's presence in the cafeteria and her excellent skills have helped to brighten the SPC experience for the thousands she has served.

After Dr. Marvin Baker's arrival, Administrative Dean W.L. Walker coordinated textbook selection with the departmental chairpersons and ordered books from suppliers. The college deposited the bookstore's profits into the auxiliary fund which was used for student activities, services and dormitory refurbishment. Band instructor Jack Nowlin served as bookstore manager for 10 years. Jean Beck, who worked in the bookstore for 21 years, started as Nowlin's assistant and later assumed the role of manager.

After Beck's retirement in July 1996, South Plains College contracted with Texas Book Company, Greenville, Texas, to operate the bookstore. Texas Book is the largest wholesale textbook dealer in the Southwestern United States.

In May 1987, retired SPC government professor David R. Stanley established the David R. and Stephanie Stanley Scholars program. Stanley, a World War II veteran, graduated from SPC in 1960 and later Texas Tech prior to his 22-year teaching career at the college. Stanley was accorded the Excellence in Teaching Award in 1971 and retired in 1987. He was named a Distinguished Alumnus of the college in May, 1990. Fred Harris, director of development and secretary-treasurer of the South Plains College Foundation, assists Stanley and daughter, Stephanie, in the establishment of the scholarship program which benefits history and government majors. Harris directed the foundation for 12 years, helping raise the foundation corpus to nearly $2 million on deposit. Stephanie came to South Plains College in 1996 and served as president of the Student Government Association and Phi Theta Kappa and was a member of the Campus Ambassadors. She received the Presidential Student of the Year Award at the spring 1998 Student Awards Assembly.

CHAPTER 13

The South Plains College Foundation

I n June 1979, Board of Regents member Gary Stacy pressed for the establishment of a foundation to promote the growth and funding of South Plains College. Stacy, an SPC student during the first years of the college's existence, believed endowments would establish a solid underpinning of support. The first director of the SPC Foundation, B.P. Robinson, concluded the initial year with contributions of $28,000. Robinson remained director of the SPC Foundation for five years, during which time the foundation received more than $425,000 in contributions.

Fred Harris was hired in February 1984 as director of development. He had served previously as vice president for industrial relations at Burgess Industries in Dallas for 13 years. Harris served as director of development and treasurer of the SPC Foundation for 12 years, and it was during his tenure that the foundation became firmly established. By 1989, the foundation's endowed funds nudged the $1 million mark. Because of his background in corporate personnel services, Harris was also given the task of developing and directing the college's personnel services and employee benefits. He also worked to establish the student and alumni job placement office on the Levelland Campus. In an effort to establish an alumni association and maintain contact with former SPC students, Harris helped develop an alumni newsletter, first called *Texan Talk*. The publication later took on a magazine format and was renamed *Caprock* when the college discontinued publication of the college yearbook. Through the foundation, he established the Ventures, Investments, Innovations and Ideas Assesssment Center which provided objective evaluation and assistance regarding feasibility and marketing for

John L. *(right)* and Vergie Belle *(left)* Smallwood were active members of the Levelland community. Although the Smallwoods never had children of their own, they assisted many young people in beginning their college educations. The couple established the first significant scholarship program at the college in 1980.

small companies or individuals interested in producing new goods and services. Two years before his retirement in June 1996, Harris raised funds to establish several scholarship programs for non-traditional students, a group he felt had been somewhat neglected by donors. By 1996, the foundation's corpus amounted to $1,942,000 on deposit, 90 percent of which was endowed or restricted to specific uses. In the nearly 20 years of the foundation's existence, more than 8,000 scholarship awards have resulted from Stacy's vision.

To celebrate the college's 40th anniversary, the SPC Foundation launched the Founders Challenge Endowment Campaign in April 1998. With a goal of $3 million, the Founders Challenge has become the foundation's most ambitious fund-raising effort. The initial campaign was overwhelmingly received with generous donations from the area's citizens, faculty and corporate entities.

The Smallwoods and Other Scholarship Donors

In 1979, J.L. and Vergie Belle Smallwood established the Smallwood Scholars endowment. Their generous contributions have resulted in more than $1.2 million in scholarships to SPC honor students. The Smallwood endowment cre-

The heirs to the Mallet Ranch, Christine DeVitt *(seated)* and Helen DeVitt Jones generously supported the South Plains College agriculture program. Christine DeVitt, pictured holding a maize stalk from the Mallet Ranch in this late 1950s photograph *(inset)*, enjoyed West Texas agriculture. The DeVitt sisters donated numerous grain sorghum crops to fund construction of facilities at the college's agriculture farm and to provide numerous agriculture student scholarships. Both sisters were patronesses of the arts and also supported the college's art and music programs with scholarships. *(Inset photo courtesy of Nancy Carr)*

ated the most prestigious scholarship program on the SPC campus. The Smallwood legacy to education at South Plains College continues each year when more than 20 honor students from across the South Plains are designated a "Smallwood Scholar." As a tribute to the Smallwood generosity, the Smallwood Apartment Complex on the south end of the campus was dedicated in their honor.

Additionally, Christine DeVitt, Helen DeVitt Jones and the CH Foundation have been benefactors to the college's scholarship programs. The CH Foundation has provided donations to the art, music and agriculture programs of SPC with donations exceeding $250,000. Shortly after the college's establishment, Miss DeVitt, with a keen interest in South Plains agriculture, donated $10,000 to improve the SPC agricultural farm facilities. On numerous occasions, Miss DeVitt donated sorghum crops to finance the SPC Agricultural Department. In 1973, Christine DeVitt and Helen DeVitt Jones generously supported their favorite area of instruction, the Art Department. They donated funds to construct a "walk-in kiln" to be used in the department. The DeVitt sisters, heirs to the Mallet Ranch in southwest Hockley County, frequently visited South Plains College and expressed keen interest in art education.[1]

The Davidson Family Charitable Foundation has also generously supported numerous SPC departments. Steve Davidson and Susan Davidson McClenahan, formerly of Midland, Texas, have donated more than $100,000 to South Plains College through the Davidson Foundation. Their charitable support of SPC began in 1987.

A variety of generous benefactors have endowed scholarship programs at South Plains College through the SPC Foundation. Burnett Roberts and Sycily Lattimore, long-time Levelland civic leaders, have included SPC among their charitable donations. Roberts and Lattimore, although born in Alberta, Canada, made the Coble Switch area of the county their home in the early 1930s. As a farmer, Roberts established a life-long association with the Rotary Club and in 1985 celebrated a half-century of membership in Rotary International. He served as president of Levelland Rotary in 1958-59 and was instrumental in the Rotary Club's endorsement of SPC's founding. Sycily J. Roberts Lattimore, a Rotary Paul Harris Fellow

---

[1] The Mallet Ranch, established in 1895, is composed of about 55,000 acres of land with more than 1,000 producing oil wells. "The ranch still comprises one of the largest blocks of virgin high plains prairie still in existence," according to David R. Murrah, author of *Oil, Taxes, and Cats: The Saga of the DeVitt Family and the Mallet Ranch.*

The South Plains College Foundation and many students have been the beneficiaries of Mr. and Mrs. Z.O. Lincoln. The Lincoln scholarships, first established in 1981, were funded by the Lincoln family to promote South Plains College and education. As pioneers of the South Plains, Z.O. and Retha Lincoln exhibited a great love for the college, Hockley County and West Texas.

and a recipient of Rotary's Service Above Self Award, was named Levelland's Outstanding Senior Citizen in 1991. Mrs. Lattimore retired from the SPC faculty as associate professor of marketing and management in 1979. She chaired the advisory committee which helped establish the SPC Foundation.

Mrs. Z.O. Lincoln established the Lincoln Scholarships for deserving students in 1986 with a gift of $70,000. The program included seven scholars programs which honored her late husband, herself and each of her five daughters. She later established an additional scholars programs through the foundation which honored her brother, Jesse W. Wood. Mrs. Lincoln expressed her desire to fund scholarships for SPC students majoring in education, nursing, engineering, petroleum technology, theatre, agriculture, the sciences and history. She believed in South Plains College and its education of future teachers.

The Texan Cheerleaders were first organized in the fall of 1958, and five students were selected to build and promote school spirit. They included *(left to right)* Anita Burnett from Whitharral, Billie Robnett from Earth, Barbara Edwards from Levelland, W.B. Snodgrass from Whiteface and Linda Hill from Levelland.

204

Ol' Tex as he appeared on the cover of the 1969-70 basketball program.

CHAPTER 14

Texan Athletics

From a pickup game to national champions

Intercollegiate athletic competition held a prominent position among the SPC administration's initial goals. Presidents Spencer and Baker believed a strong athletic presence would increase the viability and visibility of the new college. Athletic rivalries among junior colleges in the area were intense and South Plains College's entry into juco sports would have a turbulent beginning. SPC's athletic teams met tough competition among the established West Texas and Eastern New Mexico colleges. Recruiting players for a new college would prove a formidable task for the new coaching staff.

Former University of Texas athlete Bill Powell came to Levelland from his graduate studies at Eastern New Mexico University in Portales, N.M.[1] Powell, a fiery person cut from the same authoritarian mold as Administrative Dean W.L. Walker, was a tall imposing basketball star at the University of Texas prior to his service in the United States Air Force. While directing all the SPC athletic programs, Powell coached basketball, track, golf and taught physical education.[2] His arrival in the summer of 1958 allowed him little time for recruiting a basketball team. Powell scoured the area's basketball pickup games for anyone with basket-

---

[1] Larry Roberts, former SPC golf and tennis coach, probably knew Powell better than anyone on campus. Roberts said, "Powell was a regimental type of person who strove for perfection. He was 100 percent SPC."

[2] Powell was son-in-law to University of Texas golf legend Harvey Penick.

ball ability. Fortunately, Powell saw a lanky Ropesville youngster, Don Crossland, shooting hoops with several Levelland teenagers. Powell asked Crossland to attend player tryouts when classes began, and Crossland made the first Texan squad.

The college's roundballers competed against the Texas Tech freshmen squad, Lubbock Christian College's team and the other junior college teams in West Texas and Eastern New Mexico.

The 1958 Texan Basketball Team Roster

Jesse Ballew, Levelland

Jackie Bass, Plains

Travis Bryant, Whitharral

Don Crossland, Ropesville

Weldon Curbo, Whiteface

Buddy Greener, Pep

Gary Grant, Ropesville

Tom McRae, Plains

Melvin Rowell, Optima, Okla.

Newlon Rowland, Plains

Johnny Valentine, Ropesville

Early competition in the Western Junior College Athletic Conference included such teams as Howard College, New Mexico Military Institute, Amarillo College, Lubbock Christian College and San Angelo Junior College. The conference was part of Region V of the National Junior College Athletic Association.[3] The Texan teams traveled in a "stretch limo truck" to the scattered locations.[4]

Powell and his first Texan team did not fare well in the Western Junior College Athletic Conference. When the season concluded, they had failed to break into the win column during the season. The first Texan squad lost games to Eastern New Mexico University, New Mexico Military Institute, Frank Phillips College and Howard College. Nevertheless, it was a beginning for the Texan basketball program. Powell's cagers improved on their record the second season and steadily developed into contenders in the WJCAC. Newlon Rowland, a former member of

---

[3] Texas, due to its size and the number of community colleges within the state, is divided into two competition zones for purposes of the National Junior College Basketball Championships held each March in Hutchinson, Kansas. Up until 1992, only one team from the two Texas regions could advance to the national basketball championships every other year. During the odd years a playoff was necessary to determine the single tournament entry from Texas.

[4] Initially, the Texans traveled to their conference games in a yellow school bus. Frequently, the winter trips to New Mexico Military Institute, Roswell, N.M., were hampered by the weather. During the first Texan season, Powell and his cagers were caught in a snowstorm between Roswell and Plains, Texas. One of his players from Plains, Tom McRae, drove the bus by his home and got blankets to make the remainder of the trip more comfortable.

that first team, recalled that the Texans won five games the second season under Coach Powell.[5] In 1964, only eight years after fielding players from a pickup game, Powell's Texans won the college's first conference basketball crown.

As the college's athletic programs grew, so did the coaching staff. In 1968, Dub Malaise, a flamboyant outside shooter and playmaker for the Texas Tech University Red Raiders, joined the Texan staff.[6] Malaise had coached the Red Raider

---

[5] Rowland lettered in basketball and baseball for the Texans. In addition, Rowland ran track the first two seasons. Because the college had not constructed a track, Rowland and his fellow tracksters competed at the Levelland High School track. He currently resides in Hart, Texas, and is Castro County Commissioner, Precinct 1.

[6] Malaise ended his four-year playing career at Texas Tech in 1966. Most notably, Malaise poured in 50 points, long before the three-point line, against the University of Texas in 1965. "We beat them in Austin, 112-80." According to Malaise, "My first year of coaching the Texans, we played in the old gym; then it was like we died and went to heaven when they built Texan Dome. It's probably still the premier junior college facility in the state."

The SPC Texans were coached by Athletic Director Bill Powell. At each Texan game, the Gymnasium was filled by faculty and students to cheer on the team. Powell recruited his first basketball team from among the student body. He placed a small article in the first edition of the school newspaper, *The Plainsman*, and invited any student to try out for the team. In 1974, SPC began a women's basketball team, the Texanettes, later renamed Lady Texans. Notice the crow's nest where several faculty members were perched to get a better view of the game. Industrial arts instructor John Christmas constructed the crow's nest as a summer project.

freshman squad the season prior to taking the SPC job. "I learned a lot more about the game of basketball by coaching it," said Malaise. In the late 1960s, competition became more intense in the Western Junior College Athletic Conference and across the state. According to Malaise, "Coaching in the junior college ranks was one of the toughest jobs. You were recruiting against the major universities, and you had to build a team with young players that might not have been ready for the college environment." Players were vigorously recruited by coaches from around the nation. The college's WJCAC competitors hit the recruiting trail each spring working to sign the most promising basketball players. Malaise signed Obezonia Garrett, a local standout from Levelland, Gene Perry of Haltom City,

The South Plains College Texans played their first 10 seasons in the original Texan Gymnasium located in the center of the campus. In 1968, with the construction of Texan Dome, the old gymnasium became known as the Women's Gym, and was primarily used for physical education classes. In this picture made by Photocraft Studios in Levelland, the Texans are probably hosting McMurry College's junior varsity. The photograph was taken in November 1967 at one of the final Texan games held in the old gym. When the Christmas semester break concluded, Coach Dub Malaise took his Texans into the Dome for their remaining season's contests. Texan standout Danny Sledge, 55, put in the shot as Obezonia "Little Boy" Garrett, 22, and Jim McCrory, 35, prepared to play defense. Garrett, from Levelland, lettered two years as a member of the Texan squad. A former Texas Tech Red Raider standout, Malaise coached the Texan squad from 1968 through 1970.

and Tim McClendon from Fort Worth, as the nucleus of his team.[7] Malaise's teams met stiff competition from keen rivalries with Howard College in Big Spring, Odessa College, and New Mexico Junior College in Hobbs. In 1968, Malaise's team finished the season with a 15-16 record. The next year his Texan squad went 21-12 and in his last year as Texan head coach, the SPC team finished the season with a 22-1 record. New Mexico Junior College became an increasingly difficult place for the Texans to play. SPC players would, after a rough night in Hobbs, report that when the scheduled official was late for the impending game, a rabid Hobbs basketball fan would be enlisted from the stands to put on a uniform and officiate the game. The Texans' assessment of NMJC officiating is no doubt exaggerated, but no one can deny that a game in NMJC's gymnasium almost always ended in a nail-biter.

After Malaise left the coaching ranks to enter private business, Coach D.E. (Buddy) Travis Jr. joined the SPC staff. After an 11-year stint at Howard College, Travis was well-versed in the intensity of West Texas competition. His previous connection with Howard College heightened the rivalry between the two schools. Travis, aided by assistant coach Dennis Patton, recruited George Pannell of Roanoke, Va., and Ron Powdrell of Albuquerque, N.M. Both were exciting basketball players who "could light it up," from anywhere on the court. While serving as the Texan coach, Travis was selected by the U.S. Olympic Committee to take a United States team into Red China as a result of the historic 1972 ping-pong and

---

[7] McClendon, an outstanding player in the Dallas area, was recruited away from SPC by Texas Christian University after his first season. Malaise said they "didn't give him a look until they saw him play for us at SPC; then they wanted him. He was an outstanding player."

Bill Powell coached the first SPC Texan basketball team. He was followed Dub Malaise *(left)*, a former Texas Tech University Red Raider. During his senior year in 1966, Malaise excited the Lubbock, Texas, crowd when he scored 40 points in a Southwest Conference contest against Texas A&M. He was assisted by SPC math instructor C.W. Dukes *(right)*. In the 1969-70 season, Malaise was assisted by Dennis Patton.

basketball team exchange arranged by the State Department in Washington, D.C. Travis represented the junior college coaches, while Gene Bartow and Bob Hopkins were chosen to represent the NJCAA Division I and NAIA schools. Travis' All-American George Pannell accompanied the Texan coach during a one month playing tour of the Chinese mainland.[8]

In addition to his international plaudits, Travis twice won the conference crown, 1970-1971 and 1972-1973, before accepting the head coaching job at Grayson County Community College in 1974. His coaching career spanned 33 years, 24 within the WJCAC at Clarendon College, Howard College and SPC.

After Travis' departure, the reins of the Texan basketball program were handed over to a former Hobbs, N.M., basketball star and former SPC Texan Dennis Patton. Patton's career as an SPC Texan has encompassed every facet of college life. He had played ball for the legendary Ralph Tasker at Hobbs High School. Coach Bill Powell recruited him to wear a Texan jersey in 1964, and he was named an All-WJCAC player his sophomore year. In 1972, he joined the faculty as director of the Natatorium and served as assistant coach to Dub Malaise and Buddy Travis before becoming head coach in 1974. After six seasons with the Texans, Patton entered private business and was elected to SPC's Board of Regents in May 1994.

Although Patton recruited players from throughout the Southwest, he and the SPC administrators focused on recruiting players from West Texas and Eastern New Mexico. At various times during the college's athletic history, proposals have been discussed in the conference meeting to limit recruiting to a radius of 300 miles from each college. Although always stirring a vigorous debate, the conference has never acted on the proposals. Every school in the conference has desired to compete on a national level. To do so, according to Patton, there is a "recruiting war" each season. Coaches in the WJCAC travel extensively recruiting the finest players who help to make the conference one of the nation's toughest in junior college competition.

Dennis Perryman and assistant coach Dennis Harp arrived at SPC in March of 1980. "Coach Dennis Patton was very helpful to me in the transition," said Perryman, now the athletic director at Garden City Community College in Kansas. "Although I wanted to bring in some of the players I had recruited, Dr. Baker

---

[8] Travis and the U.S. contingent traveled through eight major Chinese cities, demonstrating the game of basketball and staging coaching clinics for the Chinese sporting world. A select group of American players worked out in Memphis, Tenn., in preparation for the trip.

maintained the scholarship arrangements the college had made with Coach Patton's players," added Perryman. "I was from the north country and knew no one in the area, but I made some terrific friendships in Larry Roberts, Bill Clark, C.W. Dukes, W.A. Wise and many of the people in the Texan Booster Club. It was an enjoyable five years for Cheri (Cherilyn) and myself."[9] Perryman and Harp intensified the recruiting wars, relying on Harp's connections in basketball-rich Indiana. Perryman, with 12 years of experience at Dawson Community College in Glendive, Mont., and Harp, from LaGrange, Ind., worked the mid-west high schools, recruiting top players to wear the Texan blue and orange.

Harp, who played basketball at Mount Marty College in Yankton, S.D., was the first recruiting-assistant coach at SPC in several years. Harp said, "We recruited some great players in those days: Brad Blastick from Valparaiso, Ind., Chris Cooper from Akron, Ohio, and Scotty Ferrell from Ft. Wayne, Ind. They

---

[9] Perryman's two daughters, Wendy and Nikki, both graduated from South Plains College. His son, Brandon, completed his basketball playing career at the University of Texas in 1998, setting the Longhorns' all-time record for free-throw shooting percentage at 90%.

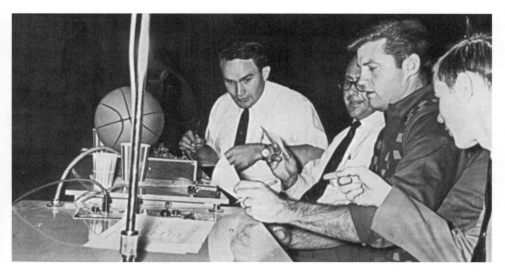

SPC faculty members have served as officials for a wide array of sporting events held on campus. During the 1969 Texan basketball season *(from left)* Travis Spears, Gary Wynn and Student Activities Director Donnie Roberts worked the scorekeeper's table at Texan Dome. In the early 1980s, the SPC Track Officials Association provided track and field event officials at numerous track meets across West Texas. The association officiated the NJCAA Track and Field Championships in San Angelo and the West Texas Indoor Track and Field Meet at Canyon, Texas.

really excited the fans with their aggressive style of play. Probably our best player, although he didn't start for us his freshman year, was Henry James," said Harp. James, a 6-foot-8 player who entered the professional ranks, has played for the Atlanta, Houston, Sacramento, Utah and Cleveland NBA franchises. "He wasn't that outstanding a player for us when we brought him down to Levelland, but he really matured as a player, and he has had a million-dollar contract at Cleveland," said Harp.[10] Perryman added that the WJCAC is one of the finest college conferences in the nation. "Up here in Kansas in the Jayhawk Conference, we will have two or three good teams. Down there in your league, they're tough from top to bottom," said Perryman. The veteran coach then added, "The Texan Dome is the finest facility in the nation, bar none; there's no question about it."

The Texans encountered serious competition in coach Jerry Stone's Midland College Chaparrals. NBA Atlanta Hawk and slam dunk champion Spud Webb dealt the Texans misery both in Texan Dome and at Chaparral Center. Webb, 5-foot-4, wowed the Texan Dome crowd with his leaping ability.[11] Several years later, NBA

---

[10] In 1998, James was diagnosed with diabetes and spent the end of the season on the injured list for the Cleveland Cavaliers.

[11] Webb, a Dallas native recruited by Jerry Stone to Midland College, now lives in DeSoto, Texas.

In 1965, Hockley County voters approved a $1,750,000 bond issue for the construction of additional college buildings. Passage of the issue was a first for county voters as no bond issue exceeding $1,000,000 had ever been approved in Hockley County history. Bond funds were used for construction of the Technical Arts Center, the Library, the Biological Sciences Building, Texan Dome and additions to the Student Union Building and the Fine Arts Building. The Dome, a premier basketball facility on the South Plains, is located on the south end of the campus and seats about 3,300.

player Larry Johnson, Odessa College's phenom, had an outstanding night at the expense of the Texans and was later named MVP of the WJCAC. Numerous players in the league have made their mark on the NBA. Henry James of the Cleveland Cavaliers, Spud Webb of the Atlanta Hawks, Craig Ehlo of the Seattle Supersonics, Larry Johnson of the New York Knicks, Mookie Blaylock of the Atlanta Hawks, and the Texan's own Charles "Bo" Outlaw of the Orlando Magic testify to the strength of the WJCAC during the 1980s and 1990s.

According to Harp, "We turned things around that first year (1981-82) with an 18-12 season record and the Texans' first regional tournament appearance in nine years. The next year disappointed us because we had some great players in Dickie Winter, Keith Gilbert, Jim Gross and Darrel Lyons." The Texans rebounded into the season's win column the next year with a 22 -10 record. "Chris Cooper and Dickie Winter played out front and could light 'em up from outside. Our big man was John Ludke, and George Kohelem was the play maker," said Harp. The 1983-84 season, with most of their previous year's starters returning to Texan

The 1965-66 season was a victorious one for the Texans. The team went 12-0 in conference action to lay claim to the WJCAC crown. Team members included *(kneeling left to right)* Roy Neff, Charles Ledbetter, Pat Risinger, Ronnie Phillips, Vic Hines, Dennis Patton, David Pape, *(standing left to right)* Jerry Mooney, Tom Hollen, Charlie Whitt, Elmo Vickers, Melvin Davis, Dwight Haley and Rickie Booker. Bill Powell was the coach. Patton and Haley were named All-WJCAC. Patton *(#10 in the photo)* joined the faculty as director of the Natatorium in 1972, served as assistant basketball coach to Dub Malaise and Buddy Travis and became head basketball coach of the SPC Texans in 1974. Patton left SPC in 1980 to enter private business.

Dome, resulted in another 22-victory season. The Texans added height under the basket with Larry Reed, a top player from Milwaukee, Wisc., who later completed his playing career at Ball State University in Indiana. According to Harp, the next year was our "disaster year, we just couldn't get anything to go right."

Head coach Dennis Perryman departed from SPC for a short stint of coaching European professional basketball. Perryman returned to Garden City Community College to assume the athletic director's position.[12] A decade later Perryman remembered Dickie Winter as his best all-round player during his five-year coaching era at SPC. "Winter could hit it from outside and post-up inside and was a great kid," added Perryman.

Finally, Perryman also remembered his most momentous basketball road trip to Plainview for a scrimmage with Wayland Baptist University. "Outside of Plainview the van caught on fire and burned completely to the ground. We got all the players out of the bus safely, and I'll never forget that trip," added Perryman.

Thirteen years after leaving SPC, Harp, now head basketball coach at Hardin-Simmons University in Abilene, fondly recalled his years in Levelland. "We had some great fans, and it was one of the best coaching experiences I've ever had."

The Perryman-Harp era concluded in 1985 when new athletic director Joe Tubb hired Ron Mayberry as the Texan head coach.[13] Mayberry guided the SPC Texans into post-season play for eight consecutive years, and he compiled an SPC Texan record of 204-58. Mayberry, a lanky former Texas Christian University player, was known for his desire to win on the court and an affable sense of humor off the court. Mayberry spent four seasons as head coach of the Odessa College Wranglers and three years as coach and athletic director at Wayland Baptist University. He came to SPC after two successful seasons at Kilgore College where he took the Rangers to the NJCAA Basketball Championships.

Mayberry's Texan success on the basketball court began in 1985. He coached five junior college All-Americans while at SPC.[14] Following the 1992 season, the *Basketball Times* selected Mayberry as National Junior College Coach of the Year.

---

[12] Perryman's wife, Cherilyn, worked in the SPC Student Assistance Center while Perryman served as Texan head coach.

[13] Mayberry and Tubb had been coaching associates since 1970 when Tubb, a senior at West Texas State University, drew his student-teaching assignment in Coach Mayberry's Hereford High School classroom.

[14] During Mayberry's tenure as SPC coach, 38 sophomore Texans continued their college and basketball careers at four-year universities throughout the nation.

In 1990, Mayberry led the Texans to their first appearance at the NJCAA Men's Basketball Championships in Hutchinson, Kansas.

"We had a great season when we went 33 and 2, and we were number one in the nation in *Basketball Times* magazine for 15 straight weeks," said Mayberry. "We had an extremely talented player in Corey Beck, now an NBA player, and Charles "Bo" Outlaw with the Orlando Magic. I had several professional scouts tell us we were better than many Southwest Conference teams that season." Amazingly, the Texans averaged 99 points on offense while giving up 66 points to their opponents. "That was a 33-point differential and there was no other team in the nation that had that kind of record that season," said Mayberry

Mayberry consistently recruited outstanding players during his seven-year tenure at SPC. Especially noteworthy was Charles Outlaw. "I had watched him his junior year at San Antonio Jay High School. So I put our assistant Eddie Fields on him, and I heard through the coaching ranks that he was going to Temple Junior College, and that they had him hidden out so that no coach could talk with him. I drove to his house and his mother, upset that Coach Fields had taken another job, would not let me in the house," said Mayberry. The Texan coach was undaunted and found the Jay High School vo-tech teacher. "I talked with him for an hour, sold him on SPC, and he took me to see Bo at his grandmother's house. His mom got mad and chewed me out, but after she finished, I got a glass of water. Bo came into the room after listening to our conversation and we talked for another hour. Bo decided to come to SPC. You have to go through every channel you can," added Mayberry. On that occasion the recruitment of an SPC Texan star player and a future NBA standout occurred with the help of a vocational teacher.

Maybe the most memorable basketball event in Texan Dome involved Outlaw and fellow Texan Jeff Stern. Outlaw, standing 6-foot-9, went up for a rebound with Stern at 6-foot-10, and neither would be denied clearing the boards. The Texan basketball goals, probably original equipment dating to 1968 when the Dome opened, could not stand the trauma. The backboard shattered, sending glass shards almost to mid-court. The crowd, watching aghast in disbelief, sat in stunned silence as maintenance crews attempted to replace the basket with a portable goal. As crews moved the replacement goal into place, counterweights were removed and for a second time that night, slivers of the glass backboard littered the Texan Dome floor. Athletic Director Joe Tubb disappointed the crowd when he suspended the game. The Texans resumed the "broken backboard game" with Howard College the next week and could not recover the momentum, losing the contest to the Hawks.

After 31 years in the coaching ranks, Mayberry with health problems retired as Texan coach in 1993. The new Texan mentor was Larry Brown, previously an assistant coach at Clemson University. Brown, the seventh coach in SPC's history, experienced two lackluster seasons before departing for an assistant coaching position at Baylor University. The next Texan coach continued to build on the successful seasons established by the previous coaches.

Shawn Scanlan became the new head coach in the fall of 1995 and firmly established the SPC Texans as a top competitor in the league. Scanlan's teams won the WJCAC championship outright in 1995-96 and were co-champions with Odessa College in 1996-97.

Scanlan, from Fredonia, Kan., a graduate of the University of Kansas in 1978, became an assistant coach at Baylor University. As a graduate assistant, he completed his master's degree and began his coaching career with positions at Paris Junior College and Kilgore College. Scanlan's assistant, Roger Raper, a graduate of Central Oklahoma State University, assisted Billy Tubbs at Oklahoma University for two years before joining Scanlan at Kilgore.

Student assistant Chad Tubb cleans up broken glass after Texan forward Charles "Bo" Outlaw and post player Jeff Stern "cleared the boards," shattering the backboard before a standing-room only crowd in Texan Dome. The game, which was played Jan. 29, 1990, and featured the No. 1 team in the nation, Howard College, and the No. 2 team, South Plains, came to a stop with the Texans holding a seven-point lead with 9:00 remaining. After an attempt to repair the backboard failed, the game was suspended and resumed a week later with the Hawks getting the victory. Following his SPC playing career, Outlaw transferred to the University of Houston and later entered the NBA where he plays for the Orlando Magic. *(Photo courtesy of Joe Tubb.)*

Scanlan and Raper continued their winning combination into the 1997-98 season. "We had a young team that had a rocky start. We lost our first game of the season to Midland College by 20 points and midway through the schedule we were still rough with a 9-8 record. Then we won 10 of our next 12 games, were in first place at one time, but lost two games at the conclusion of the season that put us back in second place," said Scanlan.

"By the time of the regional tournament at Waco, Texas, we were playing well, but five minutes into the first game, Donte Wilson, our returning team leader, was elbowed in the eye, and we lost him for the rest of the tournament. Derek Waters came in for Wilson and did a good job. But in the semifinals, we weren't as mentally sharp and New Mexico Junior College beat us 82-73," Scanlan recounted.

Finally, all the Texan coaches "hold our athletes to a higher standard; we always tell them that the game is a means to an end. Our kids are here to graduate, and we have to keep them on a graduation track," said Scanlan. The Texans coaching staff stays on the road watching players almost every weekend during the spring semester. "We canvass the state, recruiting the best players," said Scanlan.[15] During the summer months both Scanlan and Raper watch countless summer league contests across the Southwest. "We try to start the season with 15 scholarship players and ideally we'll have about half the team made up of sophomores," said Scanlan.

In much the same manner as the 1998 Texan basketball team, those early SPC athletes arrived back in Levelland in the early morning just hours before

The SPC Texan Coaches

Bill Powell, 1958-1967

Dub Malaise, 1967-1970
  Assistants, C.W. Dukes,
  Dennis Patton

Buddy Travis, 1970-1974
  Assistant, Dennis Patton

Dennis Patton, 1974-1980

Dennis Perryman, 1980-1985
  Assistant, Dennis Harp

Ron Mayberry, 1985-1993
  Assistants, Jerry Lloyd, Eddie Fields,
  Mike Mayberry, Darrell Beasley

Larry Brown, 1993-1995
  Assistants, Billy Clyde Gillespie,
  Lane Norsworthy

Shawn Scanlan, 1995-1998
  Assistants, Lane Norsworthy,
  Roger Raper

---

[15] Scanlan's Texans work out each afternoon at 3:30 p.m., while Coach Lyndon Hardin's Lady Texans practice in Texan Dome at 1:30 p.m.

their academic classes were to begin. The teams of the late 1950s and early 1960s then faced an additional drive to their homes in the outlying communities. Dormitory accommodations for the SPC athletes would not be a part of their academic life until 1961.

Golf and Tennis

When the college began in 1958, only an intramural type of competition in golf and tennis could be held. Bill Powell coached the men's golfers until 1973 when the program was discontinued.[16] After Powell's retirement, and with renewed area interest in men's golf, Larry Roberts became the SPC coach when the sport was reinstated.[17]

Traditionally, SPC's golfers practiced each day at the Levelland Country Club, the Sundown Municipal Golf Course and at the Reese Air Force Base course.[18] Roberts, hired in 1967 to teach physical education, coached the men's golf team from 1981 until 1987 when, for the second time, the program was discontinued because of budgetary restraints. In addition, Roberts directed the men's tennis program from 1974 until 1981.[19] Jeanelle Spears (Permenter) coached the women's tennis team from 1975 to 1979. Karen Knight coached both men's and women's tennis until the arrival of Mel Carter. Carter coached the tennis teams until the college ended its competitive tennis endeavor in 1987. "Tennis happened to be the most expensive sport we had," Dr. Marvin Baker said of the decision to eliminate the program. "We tried to cut back to show that we weren't spending all of our money on athletics. We could have kept the programs going, but the state legislature was getting really tight with the money (state appropriations for community college instruction) back then. We tried to cut back with fewer sports and do a better job on the others, rather than do poorly in all of them. We never did

---

[16] SPC and the majority of WJCAC colleges have never fielded a women's golf team. A lack of interest in West Texas and Eastern New Mexico and travel distances to compete with the East Texas schools made the program unfeasible.

[17] After Powell's retirement, Roberts served as chairman of the Physical Education Department for three years. He retired in 1993.

[18] According to current Athletic Director Joe Tubb, the college paid reduced fees for the team to practice at the Levelland Country Club. "We paid what two fathers and a bunch of kids would have paid for the ability to practice on the course."

[19] Roberts credited long-time Levelland sports enthusiast Bill Clark with influencing his academic and athletic career. "Bill took care of the Levelland athletes and was like a second father to me."

anything in sports and academics that we didn't want to be the best at. We weren't always the best, but being the best was our aim," said Baker.[20]

Texan Dome

President Baker and the SPC Board of Regents in the mid-1960s envisioned a first-class basketball and indoor sporting facility on the college campus. Lubbock architect Laverne Kirby had designed all the SPC buildings from the college's inception, and he drew the plans for a 3,000 seat domed building that would be the envy of many community colleges across the nation.[21] Structurally, Laverne Kirby patterned Texan Dome after the Lubbock Municipal Coliseum. Just as they

---

[20] South Plains College's tax base, primarily from the area's oil industry, declined greatly during the mid-1980s when West Texas crude oil fell below $20 per barrel.

[21] An additional 2,000 seats can be added on the floor of the Texan Dome to increase the seating capacity as the event may require.

Women's tennis competition at SPC dates from the first years of the college's existence. Jeanelle Spears (Permenter) coached the women's team in 1974 until she was followed by Karen Knight in 1979. Mel Carter coached the team until the program was phased out in the spring of 1987. Spears' team in 1978 included *(standing from left)* Yvonne Berryhill of Amarillo, Robin Winstead of El Paso, Coach Spears, Mimi Finch of Vernon, Debbie Cole of Amarillo, *(kneeling from left)* Kami Whitten of Littlefield, Rhonda Newton of Odessa, Melody Edwards of Amarillo, and Bambi Rader of Vernon. *(Photo courtesy of Jeanelle Permenter.)*

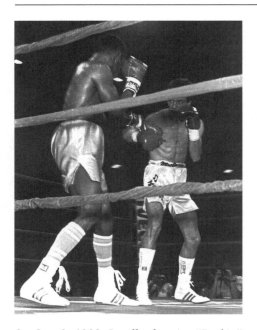

On Oct. 8, 1983, Levelland native "Rockin" Robin Blake boxed Tyrone "Butterfly" Crawley in Texan Dome. Boxing promoters set up the ring on the Dome floor for the bout.

had been called upon in the past, the college's student body was encouraged to submit an official name for the new $700,000 facility. The students responded with 10 names that were presented to the regents for final selection. The winning name, "Texan Dome," was submitted by a local radio station employee and an SPC student.[22]

Dr. Marvin Baker's original plans for the Dome included an Olympic-sized swimming pool on the south side of the Dome. According to Frank Wilson, an employee of the Haynes and Kirby architectural firm, the project ran over budget and the swimming facility was not included. Later in 1971, the Natatorium was built across John V. Morton Drive south of the Dome.[23]

When the facility opened in December 1967, the noise of a bouncing basketball was not the first sound to emanate from Texan Dome. Instead, the college administration and music department brought renowned musician Fred Waring and *The Pennsylvanians* to inaugurate the new facility. Since that first concert, a wide variety of events have been held in the Dome. Levelland High School's graduation ceremonies, awards programs, music events, gymnastics meets and summer camps and activities have been held

---

[22] Leland Martin, a journalism student from Slaton, Texas, and Del Kirby, an advertising salesman at the local radio station KLVT, both submitted the winning name.

[23] The SPC Natatorium serves a wide variety of individuals within the community. A popular feature at the "Nat" with physical fitness enthusiasts is the "Early Bird Swim." Natatorium Director DeeDee Ninemire opens the pool each Monday-Wednesday-Friday at 6:00 a.m. for lap and fitness swimming. Swimming lessons for the area's youngsters are taught by certified lifeguards year-round. Each summer the classes are filled to capacity with more than 200 children enrolled in the lessons. Additionally in 1997, the college introduced special swimming exercise lessons, held three days a week for persons with orthopedic problems and arthritis pain sufferers. The special education co-op students also use the Natatorium for physical fitness.

inside the Dome. The first basketball contest in the Dome was in January 1968 and involved the Texans and the Clarendon College Bulldogs. Since that time, indoor tennis matches and professional boxing have been held in the Dome.[24]

When Texan Dome opened, a new rubberized vinyl all-purpose surface covered the floor. The "tartan surface" provided an excellent basketball floor that could within minutes be transformed into an event center.[25] In 1984, as the tartan surface began to show the signs of age, a new removable hardwood basketball floor brought the familiar sounds of the bouncing basketball to the inside of the Dome. After each year's Texan and Lady Texan basketball schedules are completed, the hardwoods are taken up and the tartan floor serves to host the many visitors to Texan Dome. A 10-person crew can install or remove the floor in four hours. Later, four indoor racquetball courts and a suite of athletic offices were added on the west end of the Dome to accommodate an expanded physical education curriculum and staff. The Dome continues to be one of the premier basketball facilities on the South Plains.[26]

Physical Education Department Chairpersons

Bill Powell, 1958-1980

Larry Roberts, 1980-1984

W.A. Wise, 1984-1994

Judy Bryant, 1994-1998

The Physical Education Department

The Physical Education Department has trained students in a variety of sporting and recreational events since the college began classes in 1958. Initially, the college's physical education instructors taught archery, due to the lack of com-

---

[24] In December 1982, a large crowd watched Levelland native Robin Blake in a 10-round fight held in the Dome. Blake fought a second fight in Texan Dome, Oct. 8, 1983, against Tyrone "Butterfly" Crawley, with Blake losing a 10-round unanimous decision in the main event.

[25] At the time, the University of Tennessee and the University of Minnesota used the tartan surface on their basketball courts.

[26] Area basketball fans will recall great rivalries between such communities as Morton and Dimmitt. When the Indians and Bobcats met for a playoff game in Texan Dome, the facility was filled to capacity. More recently, Nazareth and Sudan usually meet for a Texan Dome playoff in their yearly quest for a state basketball championship.

pleted facilities. Traditional physical education classes in baseball, softball, soccer, tennis, golf, basketball, weight training and walk, jog, and run have been offered. Although the four bowling lanes in the Student Union Building were removed when the SUB was renovated in the early 1980s, bowling is an extremely popular sport with SPC students. College students enrolled in bowling use Lobo Lanes while students in golf classes practice at the Levelland Country Club. Another popular sports education class at SPC is racquetball. With the expansion of Texan Dome in the early 1980s, racquetball classes were added to the schedule.

The college's competitive sports coaching staff also teach within the Physical Education Department. A sport new to the SPC campus, "pickleball," is taught to men and women in physical education.[27] Chairman Judy Bryant and faculty members Pam Burnett, David Conder, Bart Bradshaw, Tina George, Ann Leach, Jon Marc Moore and DeeDee Ninemire welcome more than 2,572 students into the

---

[27] Pickleball is somewhat like tennis but uses a whiffle ball played over a net, in either singles or doubles competition. The court size is the outer boundary of the badminton court.

In 1992, the Athletic Department held a "birthday party" to commemorate the 25th anniversary of the opening of Texan Dome. The premier basketball and indoor sports facility has been host to a variety of sporting events during its three-decade history. At the 25th Texan Dome Birthday Bash, as the event was promoted, President Marvin Baker blew out the candles on the anniversary cake. Dr. Baker drew the original plans for the Dome.

"The World Turned Upside Down"

It was late April 1985. The annual SPC student awards ceremony neared its conclusion when Mark Lust, Muleshoe, received the "President's Award" from college President Marvin Baker. The congratulatory handshakes ensued from Vice President Bud Joyner and Arts and Sciences Dean Orlo Sundre. Lust exited the stage when, as the college's administrators returned to their seats, a crashing sound as had never been heard in Texan Dome enveloped the back of the stage. What transpired has been the subject of conjecture and discussion at "faculty coffee" since that memorable night. Apparently, throughout the two-hour event, the administrators' chairs had moved perilously close to the edge of the stage. As Dr. Baker returned to his seat to sit down, he tumbled off the stage, taking several administrators with him. Fortunately, no one was hurt; the crowd expressed their dismay; and faculty and administrators, when the smoke cleared, chuckled at the event. Regretfully, no video cameras recorded the event, and to avoid any such future occurrence, the size of the stage in Texan Dome was doubled.[28]

Physical Education Department each academic year.[29] Archery, the first sport taught in the Physical Education Department in 1958, has remained a part of the curriculum. Archery classes are still held in the Women's Gymnasium.

Athletic Scholarships

Since the days of Coach Bill Powell's effort to recruit a basketball team, SPC has offered a full scholarship program in all sports. The college's coaches actively recruit the finest players across West Texas and the nation. In addition, partial scholarships are offered to members of the Texan Cheerleaders and the athletic training program students. With the hiring of Mike Celli in 1982, SPC began an athletic training program in close association with local medical doctors and orthopedic surgeons. The curriculum offered by Celli and his successors, David Adams, Mark Chisum, Bruce White and Steve Ward provides up-to-date training techniques in the field of sports medicine.[30]

[28] Academic Dean Bud Joyner said, "I remember it like it was last night. Although my memory may embellish this story, I looked at Earl and he said what do we do now, and I said we throw ourselves off here."

[29] Burnett, Bradshaw, George and Moore are SPC graduates.

[30] Local physicians Bill and Mike Balch work closely with the athletic program. The Balch brothers grew up in the SPC family. Their father, J.B. Balch, was a member of the Science Department for more than two decades.

South Plains College's athletic influence extended into the international sporting world when in 1984 W.A. Wise, chairman of the Department of Physical Education, was selected to officiate at the Los Angeles Olympic Games. Wise established, with track coach Clint Ramsey, the SPC Track Officials Association. The association officiated numerous indoor and outdoor track meets across the state including the Southwest Conference Meet, the National Junior College Meet at Angelo State University and the West Texas Indoor Meet in Canyon. In addition, Coach Wise's protegees officiate the UIL Region I-A Meet each spring at the SPC track. Wise's legacy in promoting track and field officiating continued after his death. The "Wiseman," as he was affectionately known by those in the SPC association, trained Clyde Neff, David Conder, Bart Bradshaw and Bobby James. They represented South Plains College in Atlanta and officiated at the 1996 Summer Olympic Games. Coach Wise was posthumously inducted into the Texan Hall of Fame by the Athletic Department in 1996. A scholarship fund has also been established in his honor.

Women's Athletics

Women's intercollegiate athletics at SPC began with Coach Myrtle Lucke's volleyball team. The college competed in the sport from 1958 until 1966 when interest waned. Initially, the team posted a 19-9 record its second season, highlighted by two first-place tournament finishes. In fact, interest in women's athletics "wasn't really big back then," said Lyndon Hardin, women's basketball coach.

A women's gymnastic team, under the direction of Jeanelle Spears, was added for women in 1968 with the team hosting its first meet in April 1968 in the newly constructed Texan Dome. A year later, the team placed third at the Texas Collegiate Gymnastic Championships. In 1970, the team placed second in the Texas Collegiate Meet with Laquita Hargrove and Shirley Sowell selected for All-Around Performer honors.[31] The women's team continued to compete until 1976. However, the highlight of SPC's gymnastics competition occurred in 1971 when the women's team won the national junior college championship.

Women's intercollegiate basketball competition at South Plains College

---

[31] A men's gymnastic team, coached by W.A. Wise with Clint Ramsey as assistant, placed second in the state meet its first year of competition.

began somewhat tardily in 1974 when compared with the other colleges in the Western Junior College Athletic Conference. Initially, women's physical education instructor Judy Bryant accepted the task of starting a women's basketball program. "When they called me and asked me to coach, I just died laughing," Bryant said. "I said, 'No, I would not.' I had no exposure to basketball except for a

methods class in college. Basically, all I knew was the figure-eight drill. They called me back and said, 'You *will*' be the women's basketball coach." Bryant reluctantly agreed to her new assignment, but she quickly convinced Athletic Director Bill Powell that a basketball coach should be enlisted to get the program off to a proper start. "That first season turned out to be a nightmare," said Bryant. "We played Western Texas College in Loop, Texas,

Jeanelle Spears coached the first South Plains College women's gymnastics team in the fall of 1967. The SPC team won the national junior college title in 1971-72 but during the 1970s, the team was forced to travel increasingly greater distances for competitions. Most women's gymnastic teams were located in the Dallas area and the program was discontinued in 1974. In this 1972 photograph *(top left)*, Jeanelle Spears and College President Marvin Baker join with the team to celebrate their national championship. Team members *(above)* were Ginger Inman, Pam Hulsey, Laquita Hargrove, Glenda Tillman, Toni Brown, Kate Carson, Vicki Glass, Rissie Phillips, Shirley Sowell and Cathey Hafley. *(Photos courtesy of Jeanelle Permenter.)*

for our first game. They had a brand new gym and invited two college teams to play there to show it off. Western Texas had a real coach, and they were giving full scholarships. Later that season, Bryant's Texanettes would win their first game against Clarendon College 40-39. The first season's record was 5-9.

Bryant was relieved of her coaching duties and Powell coached the team with assistant Sheri Moore during the spring semester of 1975. Moore, an Eastern New Mexico University graduate, had been hired to supervise the Natatorium on the south end of the college campus.

In any event, as spring arrived and the college recruiting wars began, Powell offered the women's basketball job to Gayle Nicholas, an Olton, Texas, native, who recruited and coached the Texanettes to a 12-game winning streak during

In the fall of 1974, South Plains College began women's competition in the Western Junior College Athletic Conference. The first Texanettes team was coached by women's physical education instructor Judy Bryant. Bryant's team was recruited in the same manner as the first men's team in 1958, with signs and posters placed around campus inviting interested women to attend tryouts. The 11 team members and two managers received no scholarships or financial aid for their participation. In this 1974 photograph, team members are *(standing from left)* Kathy Robinson of Smyer, Kitty Brown of Smyer, Kathy Wood of Sundown, Roni Caswell of Meadow, Gail Berry of Smyer; Susan Luton of Lubbock, Kena Arthur of Ralls, co-captain DeAnn Bingham of Meadow, co-captain Paula King of Meadow, Jan Hall of Post, Miki Demel of Pep, *(kneeling from left)* Sally Fierro, manager from El Paso, Coach Judy Bryant, and Vanessa Word, player-manager from Wolfforth. During the spring 1975 semester, four players and a manager were added to the squad. They were Ceci Bandy of Sudan, Gloria Cuevas of Abernathy, Elaine Freeman of Loop, Rosemary Bailey of Petersburg, and Susan Moody of Lamesa. At the conclusion of the first season, the Texanettes had a season record of 5 wins and 9 losses. In conference play, the Texanettes were 4-4. Gail Berry scored 183 points during the Texanettes' first season. *(Photo courtesy of Judy Bryant)*

the 1975-76 season. The Texanettes placed second in the conference with a 4-2 record and advanced to the semifinals of the regional tournament before ending the season at 18-6. The team was paced by Lisa Risinger of Bula and Donnette Marble of Floydada. The next season SPC won the conference championship with a season record of 27 wins and 4 losses followed by a victory in the NJCAA Region V Championship. Marble was named Most Valuable Player of the regional tournament as the team advanced to the NJCAA Women's Basketball Championships for the first time ever. The Texanettes finished fifth in the nation.

Moreover, Texanette star forward Lisa Risinger was named SPC's first All-American athlete in women's basketball at the end of the season. Risinger hit 876 points and grabbed 389 rebounds during her 1975-77 SPC career. She averaged 17 points and eight rebounds a game for the Texanettes. At the conclusion of Risinger's playing career, the team captain had been twice named all-conference and all-region. Risinger continued her playing days at North Texas State University and ranked fourth in career points with 1,101, fourth in field goals with 457 and third in career free throws with 187. In 1979, Risinger was a second round draft choice of the Women's Professional Basketball League.

In 1994, SPC celebrated two decades of women's intercollegiate basketball competition. SPC women's physical education instructor and former women's basketball coach Judy Bryant welcomed two former players back to Texan Dome. Paula King Martin, co-captain of the first women's team, Bryant and DeAnn Bingham Seaton, also a co-captain, joined more than 30 former Lady Texans at the reunion. Both Martin and Seaton are now from Brownfield, Texas. Bryant is chairperson of the Physical Education Department. *(Photo courtesy of Judy Bryant)*

In 1992, Risinger was inducted into the University of North Texas Athletic Hall of Fame, the first female athlete to receive the honor. In November 1994, the college inducted Risinger into the Texan Hall of Fame in celebration of the 20th anniversary of women's basketball at SPC.

At some point during the first two seasons, the name Texanettes, having been chosen in a contest staged by Levelland State Bank, fell out of favor with SPC students, faculty and administration. Gradually, the name Texanettes disappeared, and the team became the Lady Texans in 1981. Womens' Coach Gayle Nicholas said, "We had a little discussion about it" and gradually adopted a new name. The Texanettes became Lady Texans with little fanfare.

Nicholas coached the Lady Texans until the 1983 season when Lyndon Hardin became the women's mentor. Hardin would become the winningest basketball coach in Texan history. He began his coaching career in 1974 at Tulia High School. He then coached at Canyon, Texas, for five years prior to his arrival at SPC. While at Canyon, Hardin took the Class 4A Eaglettes to the state championship in 1981 and to a regional finals contest in 1983.

"Making the transition from high school to college coaching was a big step," Hardin said. "It was a learning experience. It was challenging." To Hardin, coaching women's basketball is more than drawing up plays on a chalkboard or blowing a whistle during a practice session. It's counseling, consoling, cheering and cajoling. It's mediating, molding, motivating, and most of all, teaching. His teaching is not limited to the 94-foot-by-50-foot hardwood classroom on the floor of Texan Dome. The scope of his lessons, he hopes, is far-reaching and long-lasting.

"My philosophy has always been that success isn't always measured on the scoreboard or in the win-loss column," Hardin said. "We've always prided ourselves on the success of our players off the floor as well as on the floor and as they go on from here. That's what it's all about."

He has felt as much pride in the number of former players who have gone on to become successful dental assistants, teachers, coaches and homemakers as he has in his All-Americans. "Wins and losses go by the wayside," Hardin said, "but what you are able to carry with you throughout life is the most important part. We try to tie it all together, to teach them to work hard and be intent on the floor, and they can do it in life as well."

During the 1992-93 season, Hardin reached his 200th victory at South Plains. He recorded his 300th career victory with the Lady Texans as South Plains posted a 73-67 victory against Odessa College on Feb. 16, 1998, in Odessa.

WIN $100
NAME OUR SOUTH PLAINS COLLEGE GIRLS' BASKETBALL TEAM

RULES AND REGULATIONS:

1. The "Name our South Plains College Girls' Basketball Team" Contest is open to all residents of Hockley County, Texas, except employees, officers and stockholders of the Levelland State Bank and their respective families. It is not necessary for the contestant to have an account with the Levelland State Bank to be eligible to enter the contest.

2. Entry blanks may be obtained from any employee of the bank. The blanks contain a place for the contestant's name, address and telephone number and his or her choice of a name for the South Plains College Girls' Basketball Team.

3. All entries must be in the box in the lobby of the bank by 3:00 P. M., Friday, October 25, 1974.

4. The best three names will be selected by a group of South Plains College judges. Upon selection of the three names, a second contest will be held and South Plains College students will vote on the name of their choice (from the three previously selected names). The First Prize of $100 will be awarded to the person who submitted the winning name. The Second Prize will be $50 and the Third Prize $25. In the event of two or more persons submitting the winning names, the prize will be divided equally.

The following names should not be submitted since they are being used by existing S. P. C. organizations: TexAnns, Texans, or Texettes.

5. This Contest is subject to all federal, state, and local regulations. No purchase or account is required to enter.

6. The entries will be tabulated and certified by a local CPA concern.

7. The winners of the contest will be notified on November 12, 1974.

When South Plains College entered women's intercollegiate basketball competition in 1974, a team name was the subject of much discussion on campus. A "Name the South Plains College Girls' Basketball Team" contest was held by Levelland State Bank. The contest resulted in the Texanettes under coach Judy Bryant. Athletic Director Bill Powell became the coach in January 1975 and Sheri Moore, Natatorium director, was his assistant. In the fall of 1975, Gayle Nicholas became the Texanettes' coach. Lyndon Hardin has coached the Lady Texans since 1983.

SPC Lady Texan Coaches

Judy Bryant, 1974

Bill Powell, 1975
  Assistant, Sheri Moore

Gayle Nicholas, 1975-1983

Lyndon Hardin, 1983-1998
  Assistants, Cathy Booth, Roger
  Reding, Cheryl Watson, Joy Muller,
  Kim Pruitt

In 1997, Hardin was named Coach of the Year in the Western Junior College Athletic Conference and received the honor for a second consecutive year in 1998. He also was selected as the Junior College Coach of the Year by the Texas Association of Basketball Coaches in 1992, the NJCAA Region V Coach of the Year in 1990 and the Coach of the Year in the WJCAC in 1987.

An Olympic Champion

As Sheryl Swoopes and her teammates on the United States Olympic Basketball Team stood on the awards stand to receive their gold medals at the 1996 Summer Olympics in Atlanta, South Plains College fans felt more than a twinge of pride. After all, they knew her way back when ... long before the national championship, "Air Swoopes," and *The Late Show with David Letterman*. They knew her when she was just the unassuming girl from nearby Brownfield with a world of potential who had spurned the University of Texas in favor of becoming a Lady Texan.

Swoopes' decision to leave the Austin campus after only four days, when homesickness got the best of her, and enroll at South Plains College would ultimately change the face of women's basketball in the state of Texas and across the nation. At a time when the sport was coming of age, the young woman with the surname tailor-made for the game – Swoopes, which rhymes with hoops in an eerie coincidental way – would go on to become one of its marquee players.

"I signed with Texas (out of high school) because I thought it was perfect for me," Swoopes recalled. "I could be away from home, be away from my brothers, be away from my mother. It was my opportunity to get out of the house, but after I got there, I realized how much I missed my family. They told me that if I left the University of Texas, I wouldn't become an All-American; I would never make anything out of myself, and I'd never win a championship."

Swoopes' older brothers Earl and James knocked the spokes out of an old bicycle wheel and attached it to a post next to the house, then introduced their seven-year-old sister to the game. "I started playing with my two older brothers.

They told me I couldn't do it because I was a girl. The more they told me I couldn't do it, the harder I worked at it and the more it motivated me."

She quickly made herself at home when she arrived on the South Plains campus in August 1989. When she phoned Hardin to ask if she could play for the Lady Texans, after she had left Texas, he thought it was part of a practical joke Swoopes was in on with Debra Williams, one of her best friends and a high school teammate, who already had signed with the Lady Texans.

"We had recruited her (Swoopes) all year long until she signed with Texas," said Hardin. The Lady Texans' coach remembered the conversation. "We had continued to watch her play. The day before the last day of registration, she called me and told me she wanted to play at South Plains. First, I didn't believe it was her. Then I thought she was playing a joke. I told her if she was serious to be here at 8 a.m. the next day. She was there early."

Sheryl Swoopes from Brownfield, Texas, literally rewrote the Lady Texan record books during her two years at SPC. Swoopes set 15 school records in 64 games. She transferred to Texas Tech where she was named NCAA Player of the Year in 1993.

Swoopes, who became the first SPC basketball player to have a uniform number retired during a ceremony held at Texan Dome on Feb. 25, 1993, was selected as the National Junior College Player of the Year by the Women's Basketball Coaches Association in 1991.

She helped the Lady Texans to 52 victories in two seasons, the National Junior College Athletic Association Region V championship in 1990 and a sixth-place finish at the NJCAA Women's Basketball Championship in 1990, only the second time that South Plains had advanced to the national tournament. Swoopes twice earned NJCAA All-American recognition, the only two-time NJCAA All-American that SPC has ever had in basketball. She also is the only two-time Kodak All-American for the Lady Texans.

The all-time leading scorer at SPC, Swoopes shared Most Valuable Player honors in the Western Junior College Athletic Conference (WJCAC) in 1990 and held the conference MVP honor alone in 1991. In 64 games at South Plains, she established 15 school records.

Swoopes completed her education and a stellar two-year career at Texas Tech University, helping the Lady Raiders to a 58-8 record, two Southwest Conference championships and the 1993 NCAA title during that span. She was named as the MVP of the 1993 Final Four after setting an NCAA record with 47 points in an 84-82 victory against Ohio State University in the championship game. The accomplishments earned her National Player of the Year honors in 1993.

South Plains College basketball fans and the world watched Swoopes as she joined America's best women's basketball players when they showcased their tal-

The 1989-90 Lady Texans give the No. 1 sign in jubilation, following their 58-57 victory over Odessa College, giving them their first NJCAA Region V championship in 14 seasons. SPC went on to the NJCAA Women's Basketball Championships in Tyler where the Lady Texans finished sixth in the nation. Members of that history-making team included *(kneeling left to right)* Rachel Huseman of Nazareth, Kim Brown of Plano, Carol Bailey of Levelland, Rosie Llanas of Wolfforth, Charlotte Benford of Snook, Cassandra Smith of Hale Center, *(standing in back)* Deeadra Brown of Lubbock, Assistant Coach Roger Reding, Stephanie McColloch of Levelland, Missy Brockman of Nazareth, Vickie Rolen of Stratford, Jennifer Fritz of Amarillo, Sheryl Swoopes of Brownfield, Deborah Williams of Brownfield. Jeree Blakemore of Levelland, Joy Mueller of Olton, Sheena Anderson of Oklahoma City, Aimee Gill of Lamesa and Head Coach Lyndon Hardin.

ents and introduced millions to the game of women's basketball. The zenith was reached on Aug. 4, 1996, as the 6-foot guard scored 16 points in a 111-87 victory for the United States against Brazil in the gold-medal game, culminating a 60-0 record over two seasons in Olympic competition and exhibition contests. "The first thing that came to my mind was that this was something I've been working for my entire life," Swoopes said of the gold-medal moment. "It's something I'd always dreamed of."

While Swoopes helped the U.S. Olympic Team plow up new soil for the future growth of women's basketball at all levels nationwide, the seeds she planted at Texas Tech and South Plains College are still bearing fruit. Swoopes also enabled South Plains to garner national recognition, an achievement which continues to be a factor in the recruiting process. "It put our program on the map," said Hardin. "It gave us an opportunity to recruit a more high-profile athlete."

This success helped the Lady Texans attract such standout athletes as Angie Braziel, a 6-foot-3 post from Permian High School in Odessa and Aleah Johnson, a 6-foot-2 forward-post from Newman Smith High School in Carrollton, who both followed in Swoopes' footsteps by signing scholarship pacts with Texas Tech.

A two-time all-WJCAC selection, Braziel played for the Lady Texans during the 1995-96 and the 1996-97 seasons, leading South Plains to a 42-19 record during that span. Braziel, who led the Lady Texans in scoring and rebounding as a freshman and a sophomore, received first team All-NJCAA Region 5 and NJCAA All-American honors as a sophomore. She also was only the second South Plains player (after Swoopes) to be named a Kodak All-American.

Johnson, who played for the Lady Texans during the 1996-97 and 1997-98 seasons, also was a two-time All-WJCAC selection. She won the Most Valuable Player Award in the WJCAC as a sophomore in 1998 and was named to the NJCAA All-Region 5 first team for two consecutive years. Johnson led the Lady Texans in both scoring and rebounding as a sophomore and she averaged 23.4 points per game offensively, leading the WJCAC and ranking third in the nation in scoring. She also led the conference in individual field-goal shooting proficiency, hitting 58.8 percent of her shots from the field.

Johnson, who helped South Plains to a 48-13 record in two seasons, became the fourth Lady Texan to receive All-American honors from the NJCAA in 1998, following Lisa (Risinger) Suttle, now a junior high coach in Denver City, Swoopes and Braziel. In 1998, Johnson also became the third Lady Texan to be selected as a Kodak All-American.

South Plains advanced to post-season play eight out of nine years from 1990 through 1998, reaching the regional finals or semifinals during seven of those nine years and averaging 20 or more victories during seven of the nine years as well. With Braziel as a sophomore, the Lady Texans climbed to No. 7 in the final NJCAA poll (their highest ranking ever) and posted a 26-5 record overall, just one victory shy of tying the school record of 27 victories held by the 1976-77 team (27-4) and the 1989-90 squad (a 27-9 mark with Swoopes as a freshman).

While Swoopes and her teammates advanced to the national tournament, it was the 1997-98 squad, led by Johnson, that accomplished a feat which had been unattainable for 22 years - a conference championship. After a near-miss the year before, the Lady Texans finished WJCAC play tied with Howard College and Midland College for first place, after posting a 12-2 league mark. They forged a 22-8 overall record before the season ended abruptly with a loss in the regional quarterfinals.

The growth and development of women's athletics, in general, and women's basketball, in particular, at South Plains College and in West Texas during the last 24 years have practically paralleled the growth of women's sports across the nation. "It has developed from nothing to a very high-profile program simply because of the interest across the nation," Hardin said of the growing interest in women's basketball. "Women want to participate. There's more emphasis on it, there's more money being spent on the college level and coaches are better qualified," said Hardin.

Hardin continued, "The level of talent has grown by leaps and bounds because of so many opportunities to play and develop skills at an early age in programs such as Little Dribblers, and the players coming out of high school programs are better."[31]

South Plains College contributed to this national growth in its own way during the two-year nurturing and development of Swoopes, while the continued success of the college's women's athletic teams has facilitated the spread of its reputation throughout the state and across the nation.

---

[32] Levelland businessmen Harold Phelan, Hulon Moreland, Chester Bridges and Frank Burnett began the Little Dribblers program in 1969, and the first National Tournament was held in Texan Dome in 1970. Noted broadcaster Paul Harvey was the guest of honor and spoke to the 16 teams who competed for the national title.

Fingerball Farquhar and Soft Mushy Baseballs

South Plains College's entry into intercollegiate athletic competition began slowly. The Texan basketball and baseball teams did not enjoy a victory the first season. The second year of competition proved to be more positive. Texan baseball team pitcher Rufus George, now a resident of Portales, N.M., chalked up the first Texan baseball win against Cisco Junior College 10-9. George, who graduated from Eastern New Mexico, later became a coach and athletic director in the Portales, N.M., school system. George married Barbara Edwards, a Levelland High School graduate who was a member of the first Texan cheerleader squad and first volleyball team. Their daughter, Tina George, also a Texan cheerleader, 1982-1984, continues the SPC family tradition as a faculty member in the SPC Physical Education Department.

South Plains College's entry into intercollegiate baseball in 1959 began with a group of 13 young men, many of whom were rather inexperienced at America's game. Coach Arthur Dawson's team came primarily from Ropesville and Plains, Texas. "We didn't really have a pitcher, except for Troy Witherspoon, so all of us tried the duties on the mound," said Leslie Lewis, another Ropesville High School graduate who played on the Texans that first year. At each game, Lewis found himself behind the plate catching a variety of hurlers who found the strike zone quite elusive. The most interesting player was Royce Farquhar of Plains who shortstop Troy Witherspoon "tagged with an unusual nickname, Fingerball Farquhar, because of a pitch he threw with only one finger wrapped around the ball," said Lewis. Needless to say, their hitting, fielding and pitching skills were not up to par with Odessa College, Frank Phillips College, Howard College and Amarillo College's players. Said Lewis, after losing numerous games, "It was a humbling experience. After the first few games, we just went out there to have fun." The Texans were winless that first season; Lewis' batting average was .100, but they did make several of the games interesting. "We played a double-header in Amarillo when the temperature was 104 degrees and in both games we almost won," remembered Lewis. The Texans were given a baseball lesson that first season by the Texas Tech freshman squad when the Tech frosh beat the Texans 22 - 2. Moreover, insult was added to injury when the Levelland High School team beat the Texans in two practice games. The Texans' baseball fortunes were bound to improve.

During the second season, behind the arm of Rufus George, the Texans would win their first baseball game. George pitched a winning effort against Cisco Junior College and the Texans got into the win column. Royce Waltrip replaced Arthur Dawson for the 1961 spring season when Dawson moved to South Texas. Waltrip coached the team for three seasons until John Yates took the helm in 1964.[33] Stories of Yates' often questionable coaching techniques bear repeating. It seems that Yates would find an excuse to visit the mound and give his pitcher a soft mushy baseball to serve up to the opposing team. However, when the Texans were at the plate and a foul ball would be hit out of play, a hard "lively" baseball would

---

[33] Despite their winless season, Dawson did provide the team members with ample levity. According to Leslie Lewis, now the cardiac care chaplain at Methodist Hospital in Lubbock, "Dawson told the team we could smoke cigarettes, but if they start to hurt you, I'll take you off 'em."

A Texan baseball team was first organized in the spring of 1959 with Arthur Dawson as coach. By the 1964 season, the team was coached by John Yates and the Texans had become a competitive team in the WJCAC. Members of the 1963-64 squad included *(kneeling left to right)* Tommy Zachery, Don Green, Johnny West, Walt McAlexander, Ronnie Baker, Maurice Smith, Ronnie Jones, Gary Hudgins, *(standing left to right)* Coach Yates, Oran Hamilton, Eddie Patterson, Robert Simpson, Paul Dobbs, Riley Lamm, Jerry Sarchet, Larry Cates, Alcarie Baiza, Casey Wiley and manager Donald McCulloch.

Robert's Rules of Order

When Robert Pearce became SPC's baseball coach in 1967 he instituted 14 team "General Rules" for the Texan team. It has been said that the game of baseball reflects American society. If that axiom is true, Pearce's rules certainly reflected his attitudes toward not only the game of baseball, but also toward the game of life. The last three precepts are particularly noteworthy.[34]

1. 10 minutes of exercise before throwing.

2. Loosen up throwing easy.

3. During hitting practice never cross infield while coming in to take your turn at bat. Always go to the foul line and come in.

4. When in the field during hitting practice always play the hitter under game conditions and learn to read each hitter.

5. During a game always hustle all the way in after the third out.

6. Baseball is very individual, so always concentrate on improving yourself whether at practice or in a game. Profit by your mistakes and the miscues of others. If you reach a point where you can't improve or take constructive criticism, you're through as a player.

7. Extra work is a must to becoming better than average.

8. Confidence, poise, hustle and mental alertness are major factors in a winning effort.

9. When a situation gets tight and pressure mounts, always try to be the man under the gun and don't let a failure on one occasion stop this attitude. If in the field in such a situation, let everyone know, particularly the pitcher, that you want the chance to make the play. Eventually it becomes routine. If at bat, go to the plate with confidence, poise and aggressiveness. Remember, the pitcher is in the hole, not the batter.

10. Always call for any ball in the air and be able to recognize voices of your team-mates. Keep chatter going regardless of situation.

11. Always know the situation--possible plays on balls hit to different areas of your position.

12. Mental errors lose more games than physical errors.

13. The code of conduct is an important element in any champion.

14. Never let likes and dislikes interfere with a winning effort -- it's the easiest excuse for losing.

---

[34] Robert Pearce's rules were found among copies of original Texan baseball scorebooks.

237

The SPC Athletic Directors

Bill Powell, 1958-1978

William "Hi" Walker, 1978-1979,
Acting Athletic Director

Clint Ramsey, 1979-1982

Earl Gerstenberger, 1982-1983,
Acting Athletic Director

Joe Tubb, 1983-1998

be thrown to the umpire for introduction into the game. Yates sought every advantage to put his team into the win column.

Yates coached the Texans until C.W. Dukes took over the team in 1966, and then in 1967, Robert Pearce accepted the position as baseball coach. Pearce, having played baseball at West Texas State College, coached the team with his no-nonsense serious attitude. Pearce jokingly said Social Science Department member Gary Wynn was my "assistant;" he attended all the games and "was our biggest fan." The baseball field, due east of Frazier Hall, was the focus of lively contests during the middle and late 1960s. Earlier Texan baseball games were held at the Levelland City Park baseball field.

Finally, as other teams in the Western Junior College Athletic Conference moved to discontinue their baseball programs, SPC followed suit. Conference rules required at least half the conference members to compete in a sport for sanctioning by the WJCAC.[35] Moreover, travel to the distant locations strained the college budgets and required team members' absence from the classroom.[36] Nevertheless, Pearce completed the 1967, 1968 and 1969 years with winning seasons. One of his outstanding pitchers, Newell Squyres, continued his pitching career at Oklahoma State University after graduation from SPC. Squyres, named all-conference his freshman year, first met Pearce at the Andrews, Texas, baseball camp.[37] Although SPC's participation in America's game only lasted a dozen years, it was a successful experience. SPC's baseball Texans carried with them the memories of competing on the baseball fields of West Texas and Eastern New Mexico.

---

[35] Amarillo College discontinued its baseball program after the 1969 season.

[36] At the time of the cancellation of the baseball program, Pearce awarded 12 scholarships to those selected to the Texan team.

[37] Squyres, an agronomy major, completed his degree at Oklahoma State University with 130 college hours. "That was exactly the number of college hours I had. They even accepted from SPC one hour in orientation toward my degree plan."

Texan Track and Field

Although a track and field program was a part of President Spencer's overall plan, the college did not compete in the sport until the second year of operation. In 1960, the SPC Track, one of the few West Texas tracks laid out on an east-west axis, was constructed due east of the Administration Building. First mention of the track's construction appeared in the Oct. 13, 1959, edition of *The Plainsman.* Earl Gerstenberger did the site survey for the track and supervised the dirt work. College workers used an Army surplus scraper and grader to prepare the site. The base material of rock tailings was brought in from the Yellowhouse Ranch and red cinders were obtained from Strawn, Texas.

The inaugural track meet was an invitational event, maybe the largest ever held on the SPC campus, with more than 600 competitors from the schools of West Texas.[38] State UIL Director Dr. Ray Williams attended the meet and later was instrumental in SPC's hosting of the regional UIL events.[39] In 1983, the red cinders were replaced with an all-weather track installed by the Vibrawhirl Corporation of Panhandle, Texas. Local rancher James Lattimore donated the trees for landscaping, and the college's welding program constructed the spectator stands.[40]

Tommy Hinson coached the first SPC track team in the spring of 1960, while the SPC Track was still under construction. Hinson, a member of the faculty at Levelland High School, coached the team on a part-time basis. According to the 1960 *Caprock* yearbook, the Texans fielded a team of five runners which included Clyde Brownlow, Jim Pyburn, Melvin Poeck, Eddie Barton and Newlon Rowland. With the exception of Barton, the team members had been members of Bill Powell's

---

[38] Whiteface coaches Emmett Broderson and Charles Booz organized the meet with SPC faculty serving as meet officials.

[39] The UIL regional track meet had previously been held at Canyon, Texas.

[40] The college's track, running east-west, was necessitated by the playa lake just northeast of the college. Later, on the east end of the track, an oil well was drilled and pump jack set, prompting some to speculate about the east-west orientation of the track because of future oil well locations. Heavy spring rains still flood the playa lake, now named Breshear Lake, onto the edges of the SPC Track. Evening events became possible in 1980 after Buddy Moore, Larry McVay, district superintendent of the Amoco Slaughter District, and other members of the South Plains Chapter of the American Petroleum Institute erected poles and artificial lighting. McVay, a Levelland High School graduate, completed his SPC studies in 1967 and graduated with an engineering degree from Texas Tech University. Bob Bailey, district foreman for the Amoco East Slaughter District, arranged for the donation of the flagpole, signs and timer stands at the track.

The SPC Track and Field Coaches

Tommy Hinson, 1960-1961

Frank Hunt, 1961-1964

A.C. Halsell, 1964-1967

Richard James, 1968-1969

Clint Ramsey, 1969-1982

James Morris, 1982-1998

Texan basketball squad. The next season the team expanded to eight competitors: Noel Carter, team captain, James Carter, Jerry Vorheis, Sidney Worthen, Joy Lea Brazell, James Collins, Alton Robertson and Bill Butts. Neither the 1960 or 1961 squads enjoyed much success their first two seasons.

The Texans began to lay the foundation for the program's winning tradition in the spring of 1962 when Evening School Director Frank Hunt became track coach. SPC's sprint medley relay team qualified for the NJCAA Outdoor Track and Field Championships with the fifth best time in the nation at 3:49.9. Team members included Deryl Lavender, Mike Plumlee, Noel Carter and Delbert Spencer. Carter also qualified for national competition in the 440-yard dash with a time of 49.1, the fifth best in the NJCAA. At the national meet, Hunt's relay team finished third with a time of 3:46.6. Carter finished fourth in the 440 with a personal best of 48.4.

The next season Spencer set a new Western Junior Athletic Conference record in the mile run with a time of 4:29.5. He garnered first place in the mile at the conference meet held in Amarillo that year.

Hunt continued to coach the Texan track team until he was named dean of the newly created Technical, Vocational and Occupational Division in 1964. A.C. Halsell became track coach and guided the team through three seasons. During his tenure, the team continued to grow in numbers and records. Richard James, instructor in the Mathematics Department, coached the team for the 1968-69 season.

In 1969, Clint Ramsey joined the SPC Athletic Department as track and field coach. Previously he had served as head track coach at Portales (N.M.) High School. Ramsey served not only as a highly successful student motivator, but encouraged many faculty members to join the SPC Track Officials Association.

"Clint could get more work and performance out of his student-athletes than even the students knew they had in them," said colleague and U.S. Olympic track and field official Bobby James. "Clint was a verbal motivator of students who could convince the student to give every ounce of effort."

Ramsey's coaching skills had an immediate effect on the success of the track program. He expanded the program to include competition in cross country upon his arrival in the fall of 1969. The following spring, the Texan mile relay team set a new school record of 3:20.9. Kenneth McCabe became the first SPC track athlete to earn All-American honors in the 440-yard dash. The next year, Eddie Eberhart became the college's first national track champion, winning the 440-yard intermediate hurdles at the 1971 NJCAA Outdoor Track and Field Championships and setting a new junior college record of 51.8 in the hurdles. Eberhart returned to the national championships in 1972 to defend successfully his championship title in the hurdles and for a second time set a new national record of 51.6. That same spring, SPC's mile relay team won the regional championship and advanced to the national meet as well.

Ramsey's 1972-73 cross country team went undefeated in junior college competition and advanced for the first time to the NJCAA Cross Country Championships held in Pensacola, Fla., that year. Team members Darrell Williams, Abel Villarreal, David Williams, Dennis Smith, George Beltran and Gary Harter finished 11th out of a field of 32 teams. That spring, sprinter Ron Penny was ranked No. 1 in the nation in the 440-yard dash with a time of 48.4.

The Texans continued to build a reputation in track and field competition, and in 1977 the cross country team finished second at the NJCAA Region 5 meet

In 1993, six former SPC Texan coaches, two former college administrators and Dr. Marvin Baker were feted at Texan Dome. Pictured *(from left)* are former Texanettes basketball coach Judy Bryant, College Regent Johnnie Keen, golf and tennis coach Larry Roberts, tennis and gymnastic coach Jeanelle Permenter, baseball coach Robert Pearce, SPC's first basketball coach and athletic director Bill Powell, Administrative Dean W.L. Walker, Physical Education Department Chairman W.A. Wise, and President Baker.

to advance to the national championships. Larry Sims became the first SPC Texan to earn All-American honors in cross country at the national meet. In outdoor competition, the Texans track team captured its first WJCAC championship in 1978, scoring 96 points to edge out conference favorite New Mexico Junior College with 85 points.

Ramsey led his team to a fourth place team finish at the 1979 NJCAA Outdoor Track and Field Championships with Ralph Rose taking national championship honors in the discus with a toss of 165-8. It was the team's highest national finish at the time, and Ramsey was named NJCAA Track Coach of the Year for his team's efforts.

While Ramsey had clearly set a goal to achieve a national track championship for the SPC Texans, the title eluded his track teams. The Texans came close in 1981 when they finished national runners-up at the NJCAA Track and Field Championships, the highest national finish of any SPC athletic team in the school's history at the time. The Texans were paced by three national junior college champions: Carl Young in the 400 meter hurdles, Wilson Kiegen in the 5,000 meter run and 10,000 meter run and Sam Sitonik in the 3,000 meter steeplechase. Eight SPC Texans received All-American honors at that meet.

The following spring, Young repeated his national championship in the 400 meter hurdles, and Greg Gonsalves won the national high jump championship with a leap of 7-2. Decathletes Lance Bingham and Alan Moore finished second and fifth respectively to pace the SPC track team to a fifth place national finish. At the meet hosted by Angelo State University, Ramsey announced he would leave SPC to become head track coach at Angelo State.

Clint Ramsey became track and field coach in 1969. During his 13-year tenure he brought the SPC track program to national prominence.

During his 13-year tenure at SPC, Ramsey coached 11 national junior college championship performances achieved by eight athletes and

44 All-American performances earned by 31 track athletes. He served three years as president of the NJCAA Track and Field Coaches Association from 1973-76. In 1974, he was selected by the U.S. State Department to be a lecturer for a series of coaching clinics for Olympic coaches in Africa. He served as a delegate to the U.S. Collegiate Sports Council and was named to the U.S. Games Committee for track and field for the World University Games in Rome, Italy, in 1975, helping pick U.S. team members for the games. In August 1976, a plaque recognizing Ramsey's contributions to furthering the interests of U.S. track and field was unveiled in the National Track and Field Hall of Fame of the U.S.A. in Charleston, W. Va. A

One of Many West Texas Tracksters

In 1982, coaches Clint Ramsey and James Morris recruited Ropesville High School track competitor Alex Torrez. A half-miler and cross country runner, Torrez had finished fourth in the 800 meters at the state UIL meet his senior year. He received a one-quarter scholarship his first semester which was increased to a full scholarship his sophomore year. New SPC track coach James Morris convinced Torrez to compete in the mile. Torrez, who roomed at Forrest Hall with fellow trackster and shot putter, Mike Williams, graduated from SPC in 1984, continued his athletic endeavors under scholarship for Coach David Conder at Lubbock Christian University and completed his bachelor's degree in 1986. After coaching stints in Denver City and Seminole, Torrez returned to the college

classroom to complete his administrative certifications. He currently is the associate principal at Lubbock High School. Torrez and wife Wresha Rhoderick, a counselor at Irons Junior High in Lubbock, have two sons, Braden (SPC Class of 2011) and Max, (SPC Class of 2013). They will continue the Torrez family SPC tradition. Alex, his brother Tony and sisters Elva and Leticia all attended SPC.

Alex Torrez served as co-captain of the Texan Track and Field Team as a freshman in 1983 and a sophomore in 1984. He was a national qualifier in cross country, the indoor 1000 yard run and the outdoor 800 meter run.

Southwest Conference football coach, Ramsey joined the Texas Tech University Athletic Department as academic-athletic counselor in 1984.

The track and field legacy built by Ramsey was handed over in June 1982 to James Morris, a highly successful track and field coach from Brownfield, Texas. Morris had served as head cross country coach the year before at Texas Tech University. He quickly found his niche in guiding the Texans to their first national championship in the sport and in establishing a coaching legacy that will stand for many years at SPC. In his first season as head coach, Morris was accorded NJCAA Track Coach of the Year honors after his athletes swept the decathlon and shot put at the 1983 outdoor championships in San Angelo. Moore and Bingham

In 1986, the track and field team accomplished what no other SPC athletic team had ever accomplished – a national championship. The 14-member squad won the 1986 NJCAA Indoor Track and Field Championship scoring 119 points. Members of the squad included *(seated left to right)*, Mike Okot, Junior James, Leodgard Martin, *(kneeling left to right)* Chris Sims, Abel Almendariz, Zak Tullah, *(standing left to right)* Peter Biwott, Jim Braunstein, Brian Sheriff, Zach Gwandu, Brad Avants, Chris Edwards, Craig Stone and Ike Mbadugah. After leaving SPC, Okot, Martin, Tullah and Gwandu became Olympic athletes for their respective countries.

finished first and second in the decathlon and Ken Matney, Glen Calvert and Mike Williams finished first, second and third, respectively, in the shot put. SPC finished fifth as a team and brought home eight All-American performances.

That fall, Morris coached a freshman from Lamesa, Texas, Carlos Ybarra, to a sixth place individual finish at the NJCAA Cross Country Championships, the highest national finish for any SPC cross country runner. In his second year of competition, Ybarra won the NJCAA Region V cross country title and finished fourth at the national meet in 1984.

Morris built his track teams around the distance events, and in the fall of 1985 recruited a stellar distance runner to his fold. Leodgard Martin, a diminutive Tanzanian, transferred to SPC from Ranger Junior College where he had won the 1985 outdoor championship in the 5000 meter run and 10,000 meter run the previous spring. Martin also finished fourth in the 3000 meter steeplechase and fifth in the 1500 meter run at the same meet. He immediately sailed to a first place finish at the 1985 NJCAA Cross Country Championships.

Buoyed by Martin and six other returning All-American performers from the 1984-85 squad, South Plains College saw its first national championship trophy when the Texans laid claim to the 1986 NJCAA Indoor Track and Field Championship. The team set 10 new school records and three national records. Martin, who

South Plains College won its first NJCAA Cross Country Championship Nov. 16, 1991, placing first among 30 teams at the event. Coach James Morris was selected NJCAA Cross Country Coach of the Year. Members of the history-making squad included *(kneeling left to right)* Diego Cordoba, Phillimon Hanneck, Jose Mondragon, *(standing left to right)* Joseph Tengelei, Reuben Njau, Shaun Walsh, Coach Morris, and Abukar Adani.

turned in six All-American performances at the meet, set a new record in the indoor 3-mile run with 13:49.59; Brian Sheriff set a new national mark in the 10,000 meters with 28.54.46; and SPC's distance medley team set a new mark with 9:53. Team members included Chris Sims, George Bullard, Mike Okot and Sheriff. At the NJCAA outdoor meet which followed three months later, the same Texan squad finished third as a team. It was the highest team finish for Morris.

Martin continued to fuel the Texan team. At the 1986 NJCAA Cross Country Championships, he led the SPC squad to a fifth place finish, the highest team finish at the time. Martin finished runner-up at the meet in a photo finish which saw the meet officials award him the same time as the first place finisher. In his final appearance at an NJCAA track meet, Martin ran away with first place in the one-mile, two-mile and three-mile runs at the 1987 indoor championships. He was named High Point Man at the meet as well as Outstanding Meet Performer. When Martin ended his junior college career in the spring of 1987, he had collected 15 All-American awards and nine national championships, an unprecedented

Leogard Martin won nine national championships and accomplished 15 All-American performances while at SPC.

performance record at the time. He was twice named Academic All-American in cross country. Martin transferred to Wayland Baptist University in Plainview, Texas.

"Leodgard Martin was a world-class runner," said Morris. "He was one of the most dedicated and intense athletes I have had the privilege to coach. He was a phenomenal athlete, a great runner."

The success of the 1985, 1986 and 1987 seasons catapulted the SPC Texans into national prominence on the junior college track and field circuit. The Texans finished third at the 1988 NJCAA Cross Country Championships with Mbarak Hussein and Bernardo Barrios finishing first and second, respectively, at the meet. Morris would have the opportunity to coach one more exceptional runner who would lead the Texans to another national championship and who would equal the standard set by Leodgard Martin.

Phillimon Hanneck, a middle-distance runner from Zimbabwe, joined the Texans squad in January 1990. Like Martin, his impact was immediate. Hanneck, in his first collegiate competition, earned high point individual honors at the 1990 NJCAA Indoor Track and Field Championship by winning the mile run and the 1000-yard run and finishing second in the 880-yard run. He led the Texans to a third place team finish at the meet. At the national outdoor meet that year, he claimed the national championship in the 1500 meter run. That fall, Hanneck cruised to a first place individual finish at the 1990 NJCAA Cross Country Championships, shattering the course record, and the Texans finished fourth as a team at the meet. As a sophomore, Hanneck continued to set a championship pace, winning the national championship in six middle-distance events in indoor and outdoor competition. The Texans qualified an unprecedented 19 competitors for the 1991 outdoor championships who scored a school-record 119 team points to finish runners-up at the meet. When the dust had cleared, the Texans had placed in every running event at the meet, the best outdoor season since Ramsey's 1981 runners-up finish.

At the 1991 NJCAA Cross Country Championships, Hanneck won the individual championship for the second consecutive year and led the Texans to their first NJCAA cross country team championship. SPC placed four runners among the top 10 finishers. Following Hanneck, SPC runners Abukar Adani finished third, Joseph Tengelei finished ninth, Shaun Walsh was 10th, and Reuben Njau placed 24th. "Our 45 points was among the lowest ever scored," said Morris. "It was something we had been working on for six years. It was really a satisfying moment for us."

Four years after Leodgard Martin left SPC, another track phenomenon named Phillimon Hanneck joined the Texan fold. Hanneck set new SPC records on his way to earning nine NJCAA individual championships and 15 All-American performances.

When Hanneck left SPC at the conclusion of the 1991 cross country season to transfer to the University of Texas-El Paso, he had matched Martin's record of 15 All-American performances and nine individual championships.

Under Morris' tutelage, the Texans continued to dominate cross country and distance events at NJCAA national meets. In a bid for back-to-back national championships, SPC finished second at the 1992 national cross country meet with Tengelei taking second individually in a close race. But Texan distance runners won the 1993 national marathon championship in their first-ever showing at the event. SPC placed three runners among the top 10 finishers and Morris was named Coach of the Meet at the 20th Annual NJCAA Marathon Championship. The Texans captured a second national marathon championship in 1995, again placing three runners among the top 10 finishers. None of the South Plains College runners had ever competed in a marathon before.

On the cross country scene, SPC finished national runner-up at the 1994 and 1995 NJCAA Cross Country Championships but brought back the coveted national championship trophy from the 1996 outing. David Kemei covered the 8,000 meter course on the campus of Johnson County Community College in Overland Park, Kan., a full minute ahead of the course record to place second.

SPC's Tim James was the national champion in the pole vault at the 1990 NJCAA indoor and outdoor national meets and he repeated his championship status at the 1991 indoor and outdoor meets. Additionally, James set a new meet record in the pole vault at each of the four meets, and in 1998, still held the national indoor meet record. He set the all-time junior college record in the vault at 17-10 in April 1991 and was inducted into the NJCAA Track and Cross Country Hall of Fame in May 1997. A Levelland High School graduate, James transferred to Texas Tech University where he was the Southwest Conference pole vault champion in both indoor and outdoor competition his senior year in 1994. James, an Academic All-American at SPC and at Tech, graduated magna cum laude with a civil engineering degree. He is the son of Richard and Michael James. Richard joined the SPC math faculty in 1968.

SPC hosted the 39th annual NJCAA Cross Country Championships in 1997, and led by Salem Messaoui, the Texans captured their second consecutive national championship, the first-ever, back-to-back national championship for the college in any sport. Messaoui, who had placed eighth at the 1996 meet, covered the Levelland City Park course in 24:41.5 to become the fifth Texan to capture top individual honors at the national cross country meet. The Texans placed three runners among the top 10 to best meet favorite Dine College of New Mexico by 22 points. Morris was named Coach of the Meet and NJCAA Cross Country Coach of the Year.

In his 16 years at SPC, James Morris has earned the reputation of being the Texans' winningest coach.

The SPC track program expanded in the fall of 1995 with the addition of a women's cross country and track team. With Morris' expertise and success in distance events, the SPC Athletic Department decided to drop competition in men's sprint events and field events in order to concentrate on training for middle distance and distance events. The move allowed for scholarships to support the women's program.

In their first appearance at the NJCAA Cross Country Championships in November 1995, the Lady Texans finished in sixth place as a team. El Paso freshman Freda Valdez became the first female cross country All-American for SPC, finishing fifth individually at the meet. Valdez finished third in both the women's 5000 and 10,000 meter runs at the 1996 national outdoor championships to take All-American honors and lead the Lady Texans to a 10th place showing at the meet.

The next season, the Lady Texans finished ninth at the national cross country meet hosted by SPC and 14th at the NJCAA outdoor meet. But Morris would take four of his runners to the 1997 NJCAA Marathon Championships in Lansing, Mich., where the Lady Texans would win their first national championship. Freshmen Aivilli Marquez, Yadira Marquez, Freda Valdez and Leslea Vardy captured the team's first national championship in their first-ever appearance at the meet. Aivilli Marquez placed third overall, while Yadira finished fifth and Valdez placed seventh. Vardy was 13th. The Marquez sisters, from Ropesville, received All-American honors for their performances.

In his 16 years of coaching college track and field, James Morris' name has become synonymous with success and championships. During his tenure, a total of 167 Texans and Lady Texans have turned in 360 All-American performances. Among those performances are 51 individual national champions and 13 national relay championships. He also has coached nine Olympians. His teams have earned seven national championship team trophies in track and field events. Morris' coaching success has also been recognized by his peers. He was named National Outdoor Track Coach of the Year in 1983 and 1991, National Indoor Track Coach of the Year in 1986, 1991, and 1995, National Cross Country Coach of the Year in 1991, 1994, 1996 and 1997, and Coach of the Meet at the NJCAA Marathon Championships in 1993 and 1995. With the exception of the 400 meter intermediate hurdles record set by Carl Young in 1981, every school racing event record has been broken by Morris' athletes since 1982. New field event records have been set in the pole vault, shot put, long jump and hammer throw. A new steeplechase record was set in 1995.

"When you get to work with outstanding athletes," Morris said, "it makes it easy to get these kinds of awards. The awards are a reflection of your athletes, maybe more than a reflection of your coaching knowledge." His coaching legacy will carry on well into the college's next decade.

UIL Athletic Competition

In the spring of 1971, Dr. Baker submitted SPC's bid to host the Region 1-A UIL literary and athletic contests. The college was successful in its bid and since then has hosted the Region I-A literary contest and track and field meet. SPC faculty serve as judges for the literary events and constitute the track officials association. The two-day literary meet is held in mid-April followed by the track meet the last weekend in April or the first weekend in May as the school calendar dictates. Top athletes from more than 70 schools compete for qualifying positions at the Texas State Track and Field Meet held two weeks later in Austin. More than 500 student athletes, their parents and coaches attend the two-day event.

The top two finishers in each event and the two best relay teams are certified by the UIL meet coordinator David Conder.

Overall UIL Region I-A Contest Director-General Jerry Barton and his staff coordinate the event from the track press box. Since the first regional meet in 1971, Math and Engineering Department Chairman Robert Pearce has served as meet starter. In 1983, the college purchased an Acutrack timing system for complete accuracy in event timing. The system uses a Polaroid film process, with imprinted competitors' times calculated to the 100th of a second as runners cross the finish line.

The next chapter in the history of track and field competition at SPC will be completed in 1999. The Board of Regents implemented major renovations to the SPC Track in 1998 by approving the expansion of the running surface to eight all-weather lanes, increased spectator seating and the addition of new long jump, high jump and pole vault areas. Improvements to the SPC Track will enhance the college's ability to host the regional high school meet each spring and provide improved facilities for additional meets held at the college.

The Texan Club and Texan Hall of Fame

The Texan Club, founded in November 1968 by "Doc" Ellis Wilkins, Ray Parsons, Warren G. Tabor, Sr., James Harder, Dr. G.W. Payne and Gene Rush, was instituted to "aid, assist, supplement and complement the athletic programs of South Plains College." The six Levelland businessmen formed the original Texan Club board of directors. Today the club is directed by three officers and three directors, serving three-year terms, with an average attendance of over 70 at the weekly meetings.[41]

In 1981, South Plains College began recognizing an individual who, during the past four decades, has continually supported the Texan athletic programs. The recipient is named each year at the SPC Athletic Awards Banquet. The hon-

---

[41] In the late 1950s, the Texan Club had its origin in a combined "Lobo-Texan Basketball Booster Club." At that time, Bill Powell coached the Texans, and Gano Tubb coached the Lobos. With long-time Levelland businessman Bill Clark and other interested individuals, the club met weekly to support the athletic teams at the college and high school. Tubb coached the Levelland Lobos for 36 years and compiled a record of 647 wins and 248 losses. His teams won 16 district championships and three regional titles.

oree is presented with the traditional Texan blue blazer and his or her portrait is displayed in the Hall of Fame gallery in the T-Club Lounge. The T-Club, at the west end of Texan Dome, is the site of the weekly Texan Club luncheons. The meetings, held during the basketball and cross country seasons, are attended by sports fans, business leaders and college personnel. The Texan coaching staff provides an update of their respective team's performance, previews upcoming contests and introduces players to the gathered sports fans.

Texan Hall of Fame Honorees

South Plains College's Texan Hall of Fame was established in 1980 to recognize a select group of people who have had a special impact on the college and its athletic programs. Inductees to the Hall of Fame are selected annually by a committee of the Texan Club. Since its establishment in 1981, 19 individuals have received the honor.

1981
Bill Clark
Levelland businessman

1982
W.L. Walker
Retired SPC Administrative Dean

1983
Bob Reid
Levelland banking executive

1984
Marvin L. Baker
President Emeritus of South Plains College

1985
Burnett Roberts
Levelland businessman

1986
Nathan Tubb
Retired Academic Vice President, SPC

1987
James Harder
Levelland insurance businessman

1988
Jim Montgomery
Owner of Hockley Co. Abstract and Title Co.

1989
O.R. "Ott" Roberts
Levelland businessman

1990
Earl Gerstenberger
Retired Vice President for Administrative Affairs, SPC

1991
Bill Powell
Former head men's basketball coach

1992
Frank Hunt
Retired Technical Division Dean, former Texan track coach

1993
Dennis Patton
Former SPC Texan and head men's basketball coach.

1994
Larry Roberts
Retired SPC men's tennis and men's golf coach

1995
Lisa Risinger Suttle
First Lady Texan All-American

1996
W.A. Wise
Former chairperson of the Physical Education Dept.

1997
Bill and Gayle Smith
Owners and managers of Walt Smith Production Service, Inc.

1998
Walter Reed
Former Levelland High School Principal

The Presidential Hostesses were organized in 1972 and for more than 22 years a select group of SPC coeds served as campus ambassadors at official functions. The first group of six freshmen and six sophomores chosen for the honor included *(front row from left)* Phyllis Blair, Kathie Trull, Dusty Hensley, Janice Robertson, Debbie Hammerle, Kathy Kirkpatrick, *(back row from left)* Ruth Anne Blankenship, Kathy Newsom, Cindy Gann, Cheri Butler, Terri Gerik and Janet Setliff.

Adapting to the times, the Presidential Hostesses gave way to a Campus Ambassador program in 1995. SPC's Campus Ambassadors for 1997-98 included *(front row from left)* Amanda Slape, Shannon Blume, Leslea Vardy, Joy Stanaland, Amy Hicks, Mario Layne, Tera Isaacs, Stephanie Stanley, *(back row from left)* Joseph Castle, Robbie Stansifer, Joe David Lehmberg and Michael Swain.

CHAPTER 15

Toward the Fifth Decade

As South Plains College enters its fifth decade of education, the Board of Regents continues to devote its efforts to maintaining the institution in its premier role among Texas community colleges. Just as when the original college Board of Regents began their regular meetings in 1957, the board continues to meet monthly to conduct the college's business. Originally, President Spencer's board met in the evenings. However, President Baker, during the early 1960s, established the Regents' traditional noon meeting time on the second Thursday of each month.

While successive boards have dealt with many challenges during the college's history, Regents faced the important task of selecting the college's third president in February 1994 when Dr. Marvin L. Baker announced his retirement. Dr. Baker had served as president of the college for 33 years and his leadership had guided and influenced the development of the college in a monumental way. The board unanimously chose Gary D. McDaniel, Ph.D., to fill the vacancy which was to be created by the departing Baker.

Dr. McDaniel had joined the college's administration in August 1992 as vice president and coordinator of academic affairs. He previously had served four years as president of Frank Phillips College in nearby Borger, Texas, and 11 years as president of Panola College in Carthage, Texas. A native of Brownsboro, Texas, Dr. McDaniel was the first in his family to attend college and he graduated from Tyler Junior College with an associate of arts degree in 1960. He went on to receive his bachelor of science and master of science degrees from Stephen F. Austin State University and his doctorate from East Texas State University.

Dr. McDaniel took office as president March 1, 1994. At the same time, Regents named Dr. Baker chancellor of South Plains College, an interim title he held until his official retirement July 4, 1994. On the eve of a community-wide retirement reception for Marvin Baker and his wife, Mildred, Regents accorded Baker the title of President Emeritus.

In an administrative restructuring brought about by the new presidency, James Taylor, Ph.D., was named vice president for academic and student affairs. Dr. Taylor had joined the college in August 1993 as vice president for administrative affairs, succeeding Earl Gerstenberger who had retired after 35 years service with the college. Taylor came to SPC from Temple Junior College where he had served as vice president for student services and institutional research and planning.

Anthony Riley, C.P.A., M.B.A., who was selected business manager in May 1993 upon the retirement of John Dickson, was named vice president for administration and finance. Riley had previously taught accounting classes part-time at the Reese extension center for nine years and became a full-time faculty member on the Levelland campus from 1990-92. He left the college for a year to enter private business.

Dr. Gary McDaniel joined SPC's administrative team in 1992 as vice president and coordinator of academic affairs. He became the college's third president in 1994. He had previously served as president of Frank Phillips College and Panola College. McDaniel and wife Kay, a graduate of St. Mary's University, have three children. Gary is a social science teacher in Carthage, Texas, while Greg is a math teacher with Texas State Technical College in Marshall, Texas. Joanna is a systems engineer with Compaq Computer Corp. in Austin, Texas. The McDaniel family has an established educational tradition in the community college system. Sons Gary and Greg graduated from Panola College during McDaniel's 11-year tenure as president of the Carthage college and Joanna graduated from SPC in 1994. President McDaniel and Kay have four grandchildren.

Dr. McDaniel's executive team was completed with Dick Walsh, Ed.D. who had joined the college as provost of the Lubbock Campus in January 1993. Walsh came to SPC from Eastern New Mexico University in Portales, N.M.

Dr. McDaniel's four-year tenure as president has been characterized by a renewed willingness to collaborate with business, industry and other educational entities in order to expand educational opportunities within the college's district and service area. Dr. McDaniel and his staff have worked to lay the groundwork for the establishment of viable educational partnerships. The work has resulted in numerous dynamic changes in the college's educational focus.

South Plains College established a unique relationship in 1996 with the Lubbock Independent School District and seven other community partners to create the Byron Martin Advanced Technology Center in Lubbock. The ATC is a $5.5 million state-of-the-art technical training center designed to deliver technical education and workforce training programs for high school and college students and working adults. What makes the ATC unique is the approach which was used to create the center. Recognizing the opportunities for pooling collective instructional programs, faculty, financial resources, and physical facilities, SPC and Lubbock ISD secured the support of Lubbock's economic development corporation, the State Legislature through special appropriations, and a federal economic development grant to fund the project. The ATC served more than 1,200 high school and college students with technical training programs its inaugural year and provided the area's businesses and industry a training center for work force development. The ATC has

Chairman of the Board

L.C. Kearney served on the South Plains College Board of Regents for 27 years and holds the distinction of serving longest as board chairman. Initially, the college's founders sought community leaders from every part of the county to serve on the college's governing board. Two Levelland agribusinessmen interested in the college's success encouraged Kearney to serve on the Hockley County Junior College Board of Regents in 1957. "Artie Forehand and Harry Mann came to see me about serving on the board, and it was a very rewarding experience," said Kearney. As the owner of L.C. Kearney Trucking Service, the Sundown native worked closely with Presidents Spencer and Baker. "Both Spencer and Baker would explain the legal angles and then line out our possible choices so we could make the best decision," said Kearney. He moved to Hockley County in 1927, one year before the City of Sundown was organized and the first Sundown School Building was constructed. Kearney's service on the Board of Regents continued until 1984 when he was replaced by Marshall Cooper. Kearney and wife Lois have one daughter, Etta Lou Anderson, of Tularosa, N.M.

been viewed as a model educational program by other college, university and school district officials in the state who have examined the program.

South Plains College received notice in January 1998 that the Lubbock Reese Redevelopment Authority had granted approval to seek public conveyance of four educational buildings on the former Reese Air Force Base. Under McDaniel's guidance, SPC had presented a proposal for the use of educational facilities at Reese in order to continue the college's long-standing evening college program at the base. The facilities and contents, valued at $5 million, will allow the college to expand its evening college offerings as well as technical and workforce development programs to meet the needs of business and industry.

In addition, the college has responded to numerous local high schools to assist in offering high school juniors and seniors access to early admissions enrollment and dual credit courses. Educational partnerships between SPC and 14

In 1998, members of the SPC Board of Regents included *(seated in front)* Chairman Mike Box of Levelland, Vice Chairman Bobby Neal of Whiteface, Secretary Charles Miller of Levelland, and *(standing in back)* members Alton "Pete" Pettiet of Ropesville, William Clements of Sundown, Dennis Patton of Levelland, and Jim Montgomery of Levelland. Regents serve six-year terms and are selected in a district-wide election.

area high schools have been established. SPC piloted the dual credit program with the Levelland Public Schools in the spring of 1996. Moreover, the college has become a partner in two area distance learning consortia and has begun the process for the delivery of interactive television classes to remote sites within the college's service area. This new technology enables consortia participants the opportunity to share faculty and deliver courses which might not otherwise be available within participating schools.

During President McDaniel's tenure, South Plains College has hosted the West Texas Rural School Superintendents' Association's monthly meetings. McDaniel has made meeting facilities available to this group in an effort to bring these educational leaders to Levelland and SPC on a regular basis.

A Keen Sense of Service

When the South Plains College Regents appointed a well-respected Pettit farmer, Johnnie Keen, to the Board of Regents in 1967, the college had just expanded its Technical, Vocational and Occupational Division, construction personnel were completing Texan Dome, and an enrollment surge had begun that would continue for the next three decades.

Keen served with the SPC Board of Regents for 27 years. During his tenure, SPC's enrollment grew from 1,441 to 5,923 when he retired in 1994. Keen, a cotton farmer born and reared in the Pettit community northwest of Levelland, had made SPC a part of his life since the college's founding. Although Keen did not become a member of the Regents until 1967 when original Board member C.M. "Charley" Sanders died, Keen and his family have been avid SPC supporters from the beginning. Fellow Regents elected Keen chairman of the board in 1987.

Three of Keen's children graduated from SPC and completed their education at Texas Tech University. Twin daughters, Jeanne, now an elementary school teacher in Midland, Texas, and Donna, now teaching school in Amarillo, Texas, followed their older sister, Margaret Boggs, in attending SPC. After graduation from Texas Tech, Margaret became a loan review officer at South Plains Bank. Keen's son, Terry, elected not to attend college and farms the Keen land located in Hockley County.

After almost three decades on the SPC Board of Regents, Johnnie Keen continues his steadfast support of SPC. He can be seen at numerous college functions, always with a broad smile and healthy handshake, supporting the institution that he helped mold. Johnnie's broad smile reveals a "gentleman farmer" who believes in education. SPC's growth during his 27-year tenure is a lasting legacy to the SPC Keen era.

Working with the South Plains College Board of Regents, Dr. McDaniel has dedicated fiscal resources to the upgrading of the college's technology infrastructure. The project began in 1995 and by fall 1997, SPC's fiber optic telecommunications backbone, linking all campus facilities and remote sites, became fully operational. The communications systems allows the college full access to the Internet and the World Wide Web for the purpose of communications, information retrieval and research. As a result, SPC faculty now offer college courses via the Internet and through interactive television to remote sites. Faculty have also incorporated multimedia technology using computers and instructional software to enhance the educational process at the college. The college has come a long way in upgrading its technological capabilities as it approaches the second millennium.

Dr. McDaniel, Texas Tech Chancellor John Montford and Tech President Dr. Donald Haragan have entered into an educational partnership for SPC and Texas Tech University students. The program will allow the college to offer selected freshman and sophomore college courses to serve the needs of currently enrolled Texas Tech students. While this has been taking place informally at the Reese Educational Center for several years, the concurrent enrollment program initiated by the two institutions will formalize SPC's relationship with Tech and result in increased enrollment for the college.

In a bold move, Dr. McDaniel and the Board of Directors of the South Plains College Foundation formally announced on April 18, 1998, the establishment of the Founders Challenge Campaign, a $3 million fund drive to provide scholarships for college students. The Founders Challenge Campaign is the first and largest such endowed scholarship campaign ever launched by the college. Its goal is to provide a scholarship base which will allow any deserving high school graduate in the college district and beyond scholarship assistance to attend SPC.

Under President McDaniel's leadership, these initiatives and projects have raised the stature of South Plains College within the educational community of Texas. Dr. McDaniel's credo, working together to "improve each student's life," has characterized his leadership goal. This strategic vision has brought recognition to South Plains College and the Levelland community, has ensured the continued growth and success of the college, and has established a model for other educational leaders to follow.

Under the leadership of three presidents, the growth of South Plains College has been staggering. Spencer and his team directed the establishment, operation and accreditation of a fledgling college. Dr. Baker and his administrative team set the course for the college and guided it through three decades of growth and expansion which clearly established South Plains College as an institution of excellence. Dr. McDaniel's leadership in directing a vastly different institution will no doubt take the college into the next millennium.

From the first enrollment of 574 students in five partially-completed buildings in September 1958, the college has expanded to more than 6,300 students enrolled in more than 100 educational programs offered through a multi-campus system. The obstacles Dr. Spencer faced in 1958 undoubtedly seemed insurmountable at the time. Similar financial and expansion difficulties have been successfully overcome by the Baker and McDaniel administrations. The common threads of an educational plan, state funding, local tax revenues, programs, facilities and expansion are woven through the four decades of SPC's existence. During the Spencer, Baker and McDaniel administrations, more than 252,953 students have walked the halls of South Plains College and their lives have been changed

As the college observes its 40th anniversary, Joe David Lehmberg became the 14,000th graduate of South Plains College on May 15, 1998. Joe David majored in agriculture and graduated from Mason High School, Mason, Texas. Joe David was a member of the SPC Livestock Judging Team, served as a Campus Ambassador and was a member of the Phi Theta Kappa Honor Society. His parents are Randy and Brenda Lehmberg. Dr. Gary McDaniel, SPC president, *(right)* joins the Lehmbergs in congratulating Joe David following the graduation ceremony.

by their experiences at SPC. South Plains College has educated and trained students in a variety of educational programs and endeavors. Medical and legal professionals, engineers, teachers, scientists, technicians, business leaders and athletes began their educations at South Plains College.

Dr. Anthony (Tony) Hunt's message to the Levelland Rotary Club in 1957 was indeed prophetic. His wise counsel, coupled with the community leadership of Weldon Marcom, Forrest Weimhold, John Potts, J.G. Stacy, Walter Reed, O.R. Watkins and Levelland's educational leaders, did indeed result in the "biggest thing Hockley County could ever do."

The positive wisdom of 1,577 voters in 1957 and the tax dollars of about 22,000 Hockley County residents changed the western South Plains. When the college was founded, of the 517 major tax-paying entities on the first college tax roll, only 179 were listed with Hockley County addresses. Similar circumstances existed in 1997. Almost 51 percent of South Plains College taxpayers live outside the college district. That 51 percent provides about 80 percent of the college tax revenues.[1] Hockley County was indeed the logical location in the central South Plains area with an oil and natural gas tax base that could support an institution of higher learning.

What had been a part of the C.W. Post estate, a field of grain sorghum on the edge of a small West Texas town, was transformed into an educational institution now known throughout the Southwest. South Plains College maintains its connections to the past. Its traditions are rooted in the individuals who founded, organized and charted the course of a new community college. Founding committee member J.G. Stacy's proposal for the SPC motto could not have been more appropriate: "Dreams Precede Realities." Indeed, as the college enters its fifth decade, the idea expressed by Stacy will continue to serve as a premise for the college's vision and mission.

---

[1] In 1997, 74 percent of South Plains College's funding was derived from the taxes levied on oil and natural gas reserves in the district. Eight percent of the total college tax revenue was obtained from homeowners, 9.0 percent from Levelland and district businesses, and 6.7 percent from agriculture.

By tradition, faculty members with the longest tenure lead the graduation line at each year's commencement. At the first graduation in 1959, President Tom Spencer led the procession of 20 faculty members and two graduates, Billy Alexander and Betty Rowell. In 1998, Robert Pearce *(left)*, chairman of the Math Department with 33 years service, and Gwen Wynn *(right)*, professor of history and government with 32 years, led the procession of 249 faculty and 707 graduates.

Lee Weldon Stephenson *(below left)* has been teaching English and philosophy at South Plains College since 1969. Prior to his teaching career, Stephenson, an ordained Methodist minister, pastored the Polk Street Methodist church in Amarillo. From 1976-78, Stephenson sponsored the SPC yearbook, *Caprock*. After Academic Dean Nathan Tubb relinquished the duty of announcing the names of graduates at commencement in 1981, Stephenson willingly became the announcer. Since then he has introduced, in his distinctive manner, thousands of graduates as they receive their diploma or certificate from the chairman of the SPC Board of Regents.

SPC President Marvin Baker, wife Mildred, and the SPC Board of Regents and their wives toured the nation's capital in 1969. Congressman George Mahon, long a friend of South Plains College and the community college system, hosted the group in Washington. The group posed for this photo on the steps of the Capitol Building. Regents included *(standing at top from left)* Gordon Martin, Vern Beebe, L.C. Kearney, Johnnie Keen, E.D. Barnes, M.D. and Hank Matthews. Also pictured are *(from left)* Mrs. Mahon, Myra Beebe, Cleo Martin, Lois Kearney, Avis Keen, Gracie Matthews, Mildred Baker, Congressman Mahon and Dr. Baker.

APPENDIX

MEMBERS OF THE
SOUTH PLAINS COLLEGE BOARD OF REGENTS

Since its official organization April 9, 1957, the Board of Regents has been the governing body of South Plains College. In the past 40 years, 33 individuals have served as elected or appointed members of the board. They are listed as follows with the years they served on the board.

1998 Board of Regents

Mike Box, Chairman, Levelland. Elected April 1986. Elected chairman of the board May 1994.

Bobby Neal, Vice Chairman, Whiteface. Elected April 1992. Elected vice chairman May 1994.

Charles Miller, Secretary, Levelland. Appointed May 1988 to fill unexpired term of Gary Stacy who died in office April 5, 1988. Elected secretary by the board May 1990.

Alton "Pete" Pettiet, Ropesville. Appointed March 1989 to fill unexpired term of C.E. Bradshaw who died in office Nov. 19, 1988.

William Clements, Sundown. Appointed Aug. 27, 1992, to fill unexpired term of G.F. "Buz" Poage who resigned from the board May 7, 1992.

Dennis Patton, Levelland. Elected April 1994.

James "Jim" Montgomery, Levelland. Elected April 1996.

First Board of Regents

Organized April 9, 1957

Lamar G. West, Chairman, Levelland. Elected to 6-year term. Served from 1957 until his death June 15, 1963.

E.M. Barnes, Vice Chairman, Levelland. Elected to 6-year term. Served from 1957 to April 1963. Died March 1976.

L.C. Kearney, Jr., Secretary, Sundown. Elected to 2-year term. Served from 1957 to April 1984.

C.M. Sanders, Pettit. Elected to 6-year term. Served from 1957 until his death July 1967.

Harry Matthews, Levelland. Elected to 2-year term. Resigned April 25, 1957. (Deceased)

N.J. Green, Ropesville. Elected to 4-year term. Resigned May 1957.

Emmett Kerr, Anton. Elected to 4-year term. Served from 1957 until his resignation November 1959. (Deceased)

Subsequent Board Members

John V. Morton, Levelland. Appointed April 25, 1957, to replace Harry Matthews. Served from 1957 to April 1978. Died November, 1989.

Haskell O. Grant, Ropesville. Appointed May 9, 1957, to fill unexpired term of N.J. Green. Served until his resignation April 4, 1958. (Deceased)

Vern C. Beebe, Whiteface. Appointed April 4, 1958, to fill unexpired term of Haskell O. Grant. Served from 1958 until his death April 1979.

Clarence "Hank" Matthews, Anton. Appointed Nov. 12, 1959, to fill unexpired term of Emmett Kerr. Served from 1959 to April 1976. Died May 30, 1983.

E.D. Barnes, M.D., Levelland. Served April 1963 to April 1978.

C.E. Bradshaw, Ropesville. Elected April 1982. Served from 1982 until his death Nov. 19, 1988.

Larry Beseda, Whiteface. Appointed October 1987 to fill unexpired term of Marshall Cooper who resigned September 1987. Served from 1987 to April 1990.

Marshall Cooper, Whiteface. Elected 1984. Resigned September 1987.

E.E. Jennings, Whiteface. Appointed June 1979 to fill unexpired term of Vern C. Beebe who died in office April 1979. Served from June 1979 to April 1980.

Johnnie Keen, Pettit. Appointed in August 1967 to fill unexpired term of C.M. Sanders. Served from 1967 to April 1994.

Gordon Martin, Levelland. Appointed June 13, 1963. Served from 1963 until his death June 1986.

*Pat McCutchin, Levelland. Elected 1980. Served from 1980 until his resignation August 1985.

*Buddy Moore, Levelland. Elected April, 1980. Served from 1980 to April 1982.

G.F. "Buz" Poage, Levelland. Appointed August 1986 to fill unexpired term of Gordon Martin who died June 1986. Resigned May 7, 1992.

Gary Stacy, Levelland. Elected April 1976. Served from 1976 until his death April 5, 1988.

Don Stroud, Levelland. Elected April 1990. Served from 1990 until his death Oct. 2, 1991.

Nathan Tubb, Levelland. Elected 1988. Served from 1988 to April 1996.

Mark Wyatt, Levelland. Elected May 1980. Served from 1980 until his resignation December 1987.

Board Officers**

Chairman
Lamar G. West, 1957-1963
John V. Morton, 1963-1978
L.C. Kearney Jr., 1978-1984
Gary Stacy, 1984-1988
Johnnie Keen, 1988-1994
Mike Box, 1994-1998

Vice Chairman
E.M. Barnes, 1957-1963
L.C. Kearney Jr., 1963-1978
Vern C. Beebe, 1978-1979
Gordon Martin, 1980-1982
Gary Stacy, 1982-1984
Gordon Martin, 1984-1986
Mark Wyatt, 1986-1987
Mike Box, 1988-1994
Bobby Neal, 1994-1998

Secretary
L.C. Kearney Jr., 1957-1963
E.D. Barnes, 1963-1978
Johnnie Keen, 1978-1988
Larry Beseda, 1988-1990
Charles Miller, 1990-1998

---

* Pat McCutchin and Buddy Moore share the distinction of having served as faculty, in an administrative capacity and as a member of the SPC Board of Regents.

** During the early 1960s, the chairman and vice chairman of the board were sometimes referred to as president and vice president of the board in the Board Minutes.

SPC EMPLOYEES, 1997-98

The following list includes all SPC personnel employed during the college's 40th year of operation (1997-1998) and the date they joined the college.

Abbe, Allene 1996
Anderson, Christi 1994
Anderson, Terry Ann 1994
Anglin, Thad 1996
Arnold, Roger 1988
Baldwin, Reva 1990
Banks, Cary 1993
Barfield, Sally 1980
Barham-Hoey, Elizabeth 1995
Barnes, Densial 1981
Barnett, Stacy 1995
Barnhill, Sandra, Ph.D. 1992
Barton, Jerry 1969
Batenhorst, Jimmie Ann 1990
Bayer, Kim 1989 - 1994, 1995
Benz, Nancy 1983
Berryhill, Korbi 1992
Berset, Jill 1996
Biggers, Jamie 1980
Bilodeau, Robert 1992
Blair, Nanette 1990 - 1994, 1997
Blair, Robbie 1995
Bly, Frances 1974 - 90, 1994
Bogener, Sharon, Ph.D. 1997
Boles, Carolyn 1993
Bollinger, Irma 1979
Bollinger, Joe 1981
Boucher, Brenda 1990
Bowman, Teresa 1996
Boyd, Donald 1989
Brackens, Georgia 1980
Brackens, Ruby 1978
Bradshaw, Bart 1991
Bridges, Dianne 1971
Brown, Cindy 1974
Browne, Elise 1985
Brunner, Judy 1989
Bryant, Glenda 1993
Bryant, Judy 1968
Bryant, Natalie 1992
Bryant, Steven 1997
Bunye, Daniel 1991
Burnett, Pam 1980

Burns, Kenny 1997
Caddell, Deborrah, Ed.D. 1994
Caddell, Sherri 1995
Campbell, Linda 1984
Carden, Ron, Ph.D. 1969
Carr, Joe 1984
Cartwright, Nina 1989
Cearley, Pat, Ed.D. 1983
Chavez, Patricia 1996
Cheek, Jaunez 1982
Clark, Wanda, Ph.D. 1998
Cleavinger, Dave 1991
Coats, Frances 1982
Cobb, George 1997
Cole, Eugene O. 1996
Collier, Shonni 1988
Conder, David 1994
Cottenoir, Marla 1984
Cox, Eddie 1985
Cox, Lee 1994
Crowell, Donneva 1991
Cruz, Juanita 1989
Damron, Mark 1995
Daniel, Kay 1990
Daniel, Philip 1994
Daniels, Winnifer 1995
Darr, Leannah 1983
Davidson, Paul 1995
Davis, Karen 1993
Dennis, Patricia 1982
Densford, Stacey 1996
Dewbre, Carla 1984
Dewbre, Dane 1996
Dewbre, Jeri Ann 1996
Diaz, Patsy 1988
Doak, Daniel 1984
Dodd, Will 1996
Doshier, Stacia 1982 - 1986, 1992
Dozier, Calvin 1989
Dozier, Sue 1986
Driver, Jay 1995
Dulin, Minnie 1996
Dunlap, Brenda 1989

Dubberly, Susan 1990
Elizondo, Raymund 1991
Elliott, Stacy 1988
Ellis, Leann, Ph.D. 1982
Ellis, Randy 1980
Ellison, Lou Ann 1993
Endsley, Emalie 1992
English, Dan 1994
Escarcega, Pauline 1979
Esch, Wendy 1994
Etheredge, David 1988
Etheredge, Debra 1998
Evans, Allyn 1994-95, 1998
Featherston, Jayson 1997
Featherston, Jim 1981
Felker, Michael, Ph.D. 1988
Ferguson, Betsy 1990
Fesperman, Randall 1990
Fincannon, Juanita 1993
Findley, Deanna 1995
Fly, Joseph 1994
Fry, Ellen 1993
Foard, Patricia 1984
Forcum, Pamela 1990
Foster, Lynda 1994
Foster, Virginia 1995
Fox, Orville 1996
Franklin, Elizabeth 1996
Galbadon, Antonia 1989
Gardner, Albutt 1990
Gardner, Stephen 1992
Garner, Patsy 1997
Garrett, Brenda 1981
Geisler, Betty 1981
George, Tina 1992
Gilmer, Jerry 1985
Gilmer, Kay 1986
Glass, Beth 1984
Gober, Linda 1989
Golden, Tamara 1997
Gomez, Drake 1993
Gomez, Martin 1998
Graf, Rachel 1988

Graves, Laura Ph.D. 1993
Graves, Mylinda 1991
Green, Bette 1989
Gregg, William 1978
Gregory, Sycily Ann 1979
Griffin, Suzanne 1986
Grimes, Darrell 1975
Grisby, Jennette 1976
Gross, Roxanne 1995
Guerra, Jody 1996
Gunn, Nancy 1998
Hagood, Joel 1990
Hall, Linda 1981
Ham, Billy 1988
Hamrich, David 1997
Harbin, Paul 1997
Hardin, Lyndon 1983
Hardy, Dave 1991
Harrell, J. D. 1986
Hartin, John 1975
Haynes, Bob 1979
Heard, René 1985
Henager, Jeanie 1988
Hendrickson, Betsy 1979
Henry, Billy 1994
Hensley, Glenda 1992
Hernandez, Romana 1984
Hines, Deanna 1982
Hoard, Andrea 1994
Hobbs, David 1992
Hogue, Charlene 1990
Holley, Helen 1989
Holt-Day, Janna 1994
Homan, Jacqueline, Ph.D. 1993
Horney, Jo Beth 1988
Hudelson, Rusty 1990
Hudson, Rick 1998
Hudson, Rodney 1992
Husen, Dale 1990
Isaacs, Terry 1980
Israel, Sherry 1995
Jackson, Eddie 1993
Jacquez, Cayetano 1996
James, Billy 1986
James, Bobby 1973
James, Richard 1968
Jantzen, Amy 1997
Jenkins, Jim 1968
Jenkins, Rosemary 1997
Jock, Jerome 1997
John, Stephen 1981
Johnson, Jon 1984
Johnson, Julie 1991
Jones, David 1995
Jones, Martha 1993
Jordan, Karen, J.D. 1990

Jourden, Lee 1992
Junker, Barbara 1990
Keeling, Bruce, D.M.A. 1984
Keeling, Iris 1992
Keller, Jerry 1988
King, Edward, Ph.D. 1989
Kopf, Nora 1989
Lack, Betty 1996
LaGrone, James 1997
Lamb, Irene 1989
Lamprecht, Debra 1991
Lavigne, Donald 1992
Lawler, Vicki 1990
Lawless, George 1973
Leach, Ann 1993
Leal, Alfred 1980
Leiker, Ronnie 1981
Lemon, Jay 1991
Lewallen, Kathy 1991
Lewis, Suzanne 1989
Long, Carole 1967
Long, Jackie 1992
Looney, Debbie 1997
Lopez, Alma 1993
Lopez, Sam 1992
Lopez, Sue Ann 1994
Lozano, Olga 1995
Mahan, Virginia (Ginny), Ed.D. 1991
Marlar, Tammy 1994
Marrow, Cary 1996
Marsh, Edwin (Ed) 1978
Martin, Joseph 1980
Martinez, Anacleta 1975
Martinez, Candelario 1995
Martinez, Mike 1981
Matthews, Sue 1990
McCallister Rudy 1976
McCasland, Tim 1977
McClellan, Kay 1990
McCook, Molly 1980 - 1981, 1988
McCulloch, Linda 1988
McCutchin, Pat 1978 - 1980, 1985
McDaniel, Gary, Ph.D. 1992
McDonald, Blaine 1980
McGee, Jimmie 1992
McGowen, Carolyn 1997
McKinney, Joel 1990
McClure, Victoria 1992
McNabb, Teresa 1990 - 1993, 1996
McWilliams, Betty 1983
Medina, Molly 1977
Melcher, Quita 1991
Melchor, Elisa 1994
Mendoza, Abe 1980
Mendoza, Norma 1975

Menges, Janna 1996
Mersiovsky, Connie 1994
Mills, Marlin 1991
Mills, Susan 1993
Millsap, David 1991
Moody, Stuart 1989
Moore, Jill 1990
Moore, Jon Marc 1993
Moore, Lee 1985
Moore, Vivian 1991
Moreira, Roland 1995
Moreno, Vickey 1994
Morin, Yolanda 1988
Morris, James 1982
Moultrie, Ruby 1989
Mulloy, Ginger 1995
Munde, Alan 1986
Muniz, Anita 1982
Murillo, Gloria 1974
Murphey, Jimidene 1988
Neff, Clyde 1988
Neher, Sue 1979
Newkirk, Carolyn 1987
Nichols, Larry 1975
Nicholson, Kim 1997
Ninemire, Dee Anna 1996
Noel, Billie 1992
Norris, Larry 1987
Nowell, Deanna 1983
Nowell, Kevin 1994
Oakley, Gary 1980
Oliver, Claudine 1981
Ortiz, Juanita 1995
Ortiz, Tony 1993
Osornio, Bertha 1985
Owens, Whitney 1990
Patton, Denise 1998
Pearce, Robert 1965
Peerenboom, Terri 1997
Pequeño, Gina 1996
Perez, Charlene 1997
Perez, Connie 1992
Peterson, Carol 1983
Phillips, Kevin 1998
Pierce, Denna 1994
Pineda, Tracey 1988
Pitcock, Jim 1994
Pitts, Bette 1976
Pitts, Jill 1996
Platt, Gail, Ph.D. 1979
Poffenbarger, Gary 1989
Ponto, Jennifer 1993
Poole, Rebecca 1995
Presley, Ron 1989
Price, Paul 1992
Prince, Linda 1987

Previous Contracted Employees of SPC

The following list was compiled from the personnel records at South Plains College. It includes individuals who were contracted to work full-time at SPC and their dates of employment from 1958 until their resignation and/or retirement. During the administration of SPC's first president, Dr. Thomas Spencer, numerous individuals worked at the college without a contract. In fact, no contract exists in the SPC archives for the first president. Many of the early faculty were "hired on a handshake" by Spencer. Undoubtedly, many individuals worked at SPC during the college's history for whom no personnel file exists.

Aaron, Jerry 1966 - 1972
Abernathy, Angela 1987 - 1989
Adair, Henry 1964 - 1969
Adams, David 1986 - 1991
Adams, Jerri 1982 - 1988
Aguilar, Manuel 1982
Ahlenius, Richard 1981
Ahrens, Mike 1992 - 1995
Aldredge, Stormy 1979
Amis, Joe 1968 - 1980
Anaya, Eddie 1977 - 1979
Anderson, Dianne 1984
Anderson, Jeff 1982 - 1986
Anderson, Sam 1995 - 1996
Appling, Don 1958 - 1966
Armstrong, G. C. 1959 - 1960
Aulbach, George F. 1992 - 1995
Baker, Marvin L., Ph.D. 1961 - 1994
Baker, Mary Gale 1967
Balch, J. B. 1965 - 1982
Baldwin, Catherine 1993 - 1995
Barkowsky, Edward 1967 - 1969
Barnes, James 1986 - 1993
Barnhart, Mary Ann 1966 - 1974
Barrientes, Jose 1994 - 1996
Bartley, Floyd 1983
Barton, Beverly Sue 1977 - 1980
Baulch, Joe R. Ph.D. 1966 - 1976
Bazzell, Teddy 1983 - 1984
Beard, Jerry V. 1993 - 1994
Beasley, Darryl 1991 - 1993
Beck, Robert E. 1959 - 1996
Beck, Jean 1959 - 1964, 1975 - 1996

Beck, Kim 1982 - 1983
Beck, Steven 1981 - 1989
Beesinger, Joe 1982 - 1992
Bell, Paula 1960 - 1994
Benham, Dale 1982 - 1985
Bennett, Arvel 1975 - 1985
Bennett, Barbara 1995 - 1996
Benos, Kay 1982 - 1991
Berry, Christina 1991 - 1994
Bessent, Billy R. 1985 - 1991
Bigham, William 1983 - 1988
Billingsley, William C. 1968 - 1997
Bitsche, Cathy 1985 - 1988
Black, William 1983 - 1984
Blackstone, Joseph 1976
Blassingame, Jim 1967 - 1996
Blassingame, Roy 1965 - 1966
Bledsoe, Darrell 1980 - 1982
Boedeker, E. W. 1959
Boggs, Norma 1967 - 1987
Bond, Eleanor 1960
Booth, Kathy 1985 - 1987
Bowen, Marcie 1958 - 1966
Bowen, Von 1968 - 1969
Bowman, Jean 1959 - 1988
Bradley, Zoe 1993 - 1997
Bratton, Keith 1979 - 1986
Bray, Vera Sue 1984
Brewton, Fred 1958
Broome, Rick 1987
Brown, Brian 1970 - 1973
Brown, Helen 1971 - 1983
Brown, Jack 1973 - 1977
Brown, Jay 1991 - 1995

Brown, Larry 1993 - 1995
Brown, Mary Lynn 1971 - 1972
Brown, Mickey 1994 - 1996
Brown, Terry 1993 - 1996
Brown, Wes 1986 - 1987
Bruni, Rose Mary 1980 - 1981
Bryant, Charlotte 1982 - 1985
Buckner, Tommy 1965 - 1968
Bulls, Anne 1958 - 1984
Bulls, Harley 1959 - 1979
Burkhart, Lori Ann 1990 - 1991
Burks, Deane 1959 - 1961
Burks, Robert S. 1958 - 1961
Burrier, Wanda Gail 1966 - 1977
Burton, Eddie 1982 - 1983
Bush, Joyce 1978 - 1982
Carmargo, Janice 1991 - 1996
Campbell, Judy 1982 - 1983
Capps, Robert 1973 - 1975
Carley, Cynthia 1986 - 1987
Caroland, Michael 1980 - 1991
Carpenter, Brian 1992 - 1994
Carroll, James 1968 - 1983
Carter, Lorrie 1991 - 1992
Carter, Mel 1985 - 1987
Cash, Bryan 1991 - 1992
Cash, Evelyn 1982 - 1983
Cearley, J. B. 1962 - 1966
Celli, Michael 1978 - 1986
Chambers, Dewayne 1992 - 1994
Chapman, Brenda 1982 - 1993
Chase, Gary 1986 - 1987
Chisum, Mark 1991 - 1996
Christoffel, Joan 1994 - 1995

Christmas, John 1958 - 1963
Clayborn, Jerrell 1984 - 1986
Clardy, Terry 1977 - 1978
Cloud, Robert, Ph.D. 1986 - 1988
Copeland, Mary Nell 1958 - 1959
Curran, Terry 1992 - 1997
Coats, Linda 1984 - 1987
Cochran, Douglas 1982 - 1983
Cocke, James 1987 - 1989
Cockrell, Kathleen 1990 - 1993
Cogdell, Jim 1992 - 1996
Cole, Burl 1968 - 1976
Cole, Linda 1992 - 1994
Cook, Lynn 1988 - 1989
Cooper, Glenna 1969 - 1990
Cooper, Jim, Ph.D. 1970 - 1987
Coplin, Jess 1958 - 1959
Cormack, George 1994 - 1996
Coronado, Herlinda 1991 - 1996
Couch, Scott 1967 - 1993
Courtney, James 1981 - 1988
Cowart, Elmo 1982 - 1983
Crowell, Odis 1969 - 1970
Dailey, Teresa 1991 - 1993
Dale, Leona, Ph.D. 1968 - 1983
Dawson, Arthur 1958 - 1960
Daniel, Lynn 1980 - 1983
Danner, Nevelle 1964 - 1974
Daughtrey, Glenda 1980
Davis, Doyle 1973 - 1980
Davis, Vivian 1991 - 1993
Deardorf, Ann 1980 - 1984
Dickens, Faye 1980 - 1986
Dickson, Lunette 1969 - 1993
Dickson, John 1962 - 1993
Dillingham, Diann 1987 - 1989
Dodge, Betty 1974 - 1976
Dominguez, Katherine 1968 - 1977
Douglas, Linda 1988 - 1992
Dreith, Ron 1968 - 1969
Duesterhaus, Katherine 1993 - 1994
Dukes, C. W. 1965 - 1984
Dunlay, Dennis 1984 - 1989
Dunn, Tommy 1973 - 1993
Durham, David 1969 - 1972
Durham, Jane 1991 - 1993
Dwyer, Jon Ann 1967 - 1969
Dye, Roger 1975 - 1979
Dyer, Stan, Ph.D. 1988 - 1992
Dyer, Lorene 1980 - 1987
Edwards, Vicki 1981 - 1983
Errico, DeZane 1991 - 1993
Ervin, Bill 1991 - 1994
Evans, Marsha 1994 - 1995
Fallon, Robert 1975 - 1980

Farrar, Cydney 1979 - 1980
Feola, Arlene 1984 - 1992
Ferrel, James 1966 - 1967
Fields, Eddie 1986 - 1989
Flagg, Laura 1979 - 1984
Flanagan, David 1983 - 1986
Forehand, Artie 1958
Forman, Mary Ruth 1980 - 1982
Foster, Cynthia 1985
Foster, Jewell 1991 - 1993
Foster, Sherley 1970 - 1993
Fox, Orville 1973 - 1974
Franklin, Don 1988 - 1990
Funderburke, Arlano 1973 - 1998
Garcia, Albert 1992 - 1995
Garcia, Salvador 1985 - 1990
Geer, Donald 1970 - 1972
Geffken, Jack 1959 - 1967
George, Jesse T. 1964 - 1965
Gerstenberger, Earl 1958 - 1993
Gill, Eugene 1977 - 1978
Gill, Linda 1994 - 1995
Gilley, Barbara 1978 - 1989
Gillispie, Billy 1993 - 1994
Glasscock, Ronnie, Ed.D. 1981 - 1992
Glaze, David 1978 - 1982
Godley, Sharyn 1972 - 1974
Goen, James 1994 - 1995
Goheen, Dennis 1983 - 1986
Golden, Patsy 1979 - 1980
Gomez, Demencio 1981 - 1983
Gonzalez, Adam 1975 - 1979
Gonzalez, Paul Franklin 1967 - 1975
Goodman, Marion 1988 - 1990
Graham, Jan (J.J.) 1995 - 1997
Graham, Marvin 1977 - 1979
Grant, Inez 1958 - 1972
Gravitt, John 1985 - 1986
Greaves, Lola 1967 - 1968
Griffith, Janet 1979 - 1980
Griffith, Ruth 1969 - 1971
Gross, Sherene 1992 - 1994
Guajardo, Robert 1973 - 1975
Haggerton, Loretta Sue 1988
Hall, Kathleen 1978 - 1980
Halsell, A. C. 1964 - 1966
Hamilton, Robert 1966 - 1970
Hanson, Dan 1977 - 1982
Haralson, Tommy 1978 - 1982
Hardcastle, Donald 1961 - 1963
Hardin, James 1994 - 1996
Harp, Dennis 1980 - 1985
Harman, Pamela 1993 - 1995
Harnar, James 1972 - 1973

Harris, Dan 1993 - 1995
Harris, Fred 1984 - 1996
Harris, Leon 1971 - 1979
Hart, Kenneth 1969 - 1970
Hawkins, Odus 1971 - 1993
Haynie, James 1963 - 1966
Hays, Charles 1966 - 1969
Head, John (Jack) 1967 - 1969
Headley, Pauline 1989 - 1992
Headrick, Troy 1991 - 1993
Healy, Therman 1959 - 1960
Heflin, Donna M. 1991 - 1992
Helbert, Aubrey 1966 - 1968
Helsel, Deloris 1988 - 1989
Henderson, Billie 1982 - 1983
Henderson, John Howard 1984 - 1986
Henegar, C. Anthony (Tony) 1975 - 1983
Henegar, Edward 1976 - 1980
Hermesmeyer, Paul 1987 - 1988
Hernandez, Louis 1969 - 1978
Herring, (Champion) Cathy 1981 - 1984
Hester, Renee 1988 - 1994
Hicks, Mattie 1988 - 1995
Higginbotham, Judy 1992
Hill, Catherine 1991 - 1995
Hillin, Greta 1981 - 1985
Hill, Sam, Ph.D. 1986 - 1990
Hinton, Billy 1962 - 1967
Hinz, Mittie 1990
Hittson, Jesse 1972 - 1978
Holcomb, Sharon 1995
Holland, Ruth 1973 - 1995
Hopson, Don 1984 - 1986
Houchin, Sam 1989 - 1994
Hudson, Rick 1980 - 1983
Hudelson, Schahara 1991 - 1997
Hudson, Robert 1985 - 1988
Huffman, Jo Anne 1992 - 1993
Huggins, Mar-Jo 1981 - 1993
Humphreys, Ronnie 1989 - 1990
Hunt, J. Frank 1961 - 1995
Hutchinson, Kathy 1979 - 1984
Ingraham, Margaret 1972 - 1988
Ison, James Don 1974 - 1996
Ivie, Rachel 1992 - 1996
Jackson, Ross 1992 - 1993
Jacques, Shirley 1991 - 1992
Jacques, Mary A. (Pinny) 1982 - 1988
Jarrett, James 1981 - 1985
James, Michael 1980 - 1981
Jessup, Jan 1982 - 1984
Johnston, Robert 1990 - 1991

Johnson, Gerald 1964 - 1966
Jones, Barbara 1979 - 1987
Jones, Stephen 1991 - 1992
Jordon, Paul 1994 - 1995
Joyner, Luther (Bud), Ed.D. 1978 - 1986
Joyner, Janice 1980 - 1986
Kantor, Scott 1982 - 1986
Kelsay, Kenneth 1980 - 1985
Kennedy, Shirley 1958 - 1965
Kennedy, Marti 1992 - 1994
Kennedy, Weston 1984 - 1991
Kerr, Lynn 1992
Key, Carolyn 1967 - 1969
King, Edward 1989 - 1998
King, Steve 1982 - 1986
Kinney, Della 1997
Kinnison, Fred 1995
Kirchhoff, Albert 1986 - 1987
Kirkpatrick, Claude 1969 - 1984
Kirkpatrick, Larry 1976 - 1977
Knight, Karen 1979 - 1985
Knowles, Betty 1958 - 1965
Knowles, Michael J. 1958 - 1965
Kolb, Basil 1962 - 1966
Kroeker, Richard 1978 - 1982
Kuhl, Sherri 1989 - 1990
Kunz, Russell 1982 - 1985
La Mar, James 1960
Larsen, Lana 1977 - 1979
Lattimore, Sycily 1958 - 1979
Leahy, Robert, Ph.D. 1984 - 1997
Leggitt, Jim 1967 - 1996
Leland, Cyrus 1967 - 1968
Lewis, Danny 1978 - 1980
Lewis, Hobert 1968 - 1969
Lewis, Wynona 1980 - 1982
Lindell, Steven 1977
Littlefield, Donnie 1994 - 1996
Livingston, Travis 1963 - 1966
Llanes, Cynthia 1992 - 1993
Lloyd, Jan 1989 - 1992
Lloyd, Jerry 1985 - 1986
Long, Johnny 1982 - 1986
Long, Frieda 1960 - 1966
Lough, Jeulia 1984 - 1986
Loveless, Steve 1981 - 1989
Lucke, Henry 1958 - 1967
Lucke, Myrtle 1958 - 1967
Mackey, Paul 1969 - 1971
Maddox, Ann 1981 - 1988
Martin, Lance 1988 - 1989
Malaise, John (Dub) 1967 - 1970
Martinez, Ruben 1978 - 1979
Masters, Mitchell 1966 - 1976
Mauzey, Addie Belle 1964 - 1972

Mayberry, Mike 1989 - 1991
Mayberry, Ron 1985 - 1995
Mayo, David 1967 - 1973
McCarroll, John 1977 - 1979
McCasland, Jennifer 1985 - 1994
McCown, Don 1985 - 1989
McCown, Palmer 1970
McDaniel, Gordon 1974 - 1976
McDonald, Russell 1972 - 1978
McLean, Homer 1965 - 1992
McMasters, Dennis 1983 - 1985
McMillan, Barbara (Bobbi) 1981 - 1987
McMillan, Walter 1970 - 1971
McMullan, Scott 1996 - 1997
McNutt, Janie 1994 - 1997
McRae, Bonnie 1993 - 1994
Meek, Keith 1993 - 1994
Melcher, Verna Kathy 1986 - 1991
Melton, Donald 1967 - 1977
Melvin, Robert 1978 - 1990
Mercado, Lolo 1988 - 1994
Meriwether, Allan 1993 - 1995
Merrill, Marilyn 1974 - 1976
Messall, Anne 1980 - 1990
Meyers, Jeff 1993
Miller, Harry 1991 - 1994
Miller, Linda 1994 - 1996
Miller, Patricia 1996 - 1997
Miller, Sue Ann 1995 - 1996
Mills, Thomas 1958
Mixon, Kieth 1966 - 1993
Moore, Buddy 1973 - 1978
Moore, Florence 1994 - 1995
Moore, Kenneth 1969 - 1978
Moore, Michael 1992 - 1995
Moore, Nita 1966 - 1970
Moore, Sheri 1974 - 1981
Moorhead, Michael 1968 - 1969
Morgan, Clyde 1968 - 1972
Morgan, Debra 1993 - 1995
Morris, Nancy 1965 - 1967
Morris, Sharon 1978 - 1984
Moss, Theresa 1994
Mott, Barbara 1980 - 1981
Mullen, Mike 1977 - 1981
Muller, Joy 1993 - 1996
Murray, Mark 1988 - 1997
Neill, Randy 1978 - 1988
Newsom, Cecyle 1989 - 1995
Newth, Laura 1993 - 1995
Nicholas, Gayle 1975 - 1983
Nielson, Roger 1980 - 1987
Nobles, Brian 1992
Nolte, Harold 1980 - 1982
Norsworthy, Lane 1994 - 1997

Nowlin, Miles Jackson (Jack) 1968 - 1978
Nutt, Lee Ann 1990 - 1993
O'Bannon, L.C. 1972 - 1981
O'Connor, Helen 1985 - 1988
O'Connor, Lynn 1975 - 1980
O'Dea John 1995 - 1996
Oakley, Gary 1980 - 1998
Oates, Micki 1990 - 1995
O'Mohundro, Janice 1997
Palma, Eugenia 1958
Parker, Barbara 1978 - 1983
Parker, Sam 1977 - 1982
Parmer, Jerold, Ph.D. 1970 - 1973
Parmer Polly 1966 - 1993
Pasewark, Marion 1991 - 1994
Patrick, John 1991 - 1994
Patton, Dennis 1969 - 1980
Payne, Karla 1989 - 1990
Payne, Patsy Jo 1966 - 1968
Pedigo, Glenda 1980 - 1991
Permenter, Jeanelle 1967 - 1993
Perryman, Cherilyn 1980 - 1985
Perryman, Dennis 1980 - 1985
Pieraerts, Jean Henri 1969 - 1972
Pierce, Elizabeth 1984 - 1985
Pierce, Paul 1996
Pierce, William Clay 1983
Pilcher, Rose Marie 1959 - 1960
Pohl, Donna 1969 - 1977
Pohl, William 1969 - 1982
Polley, Arja 1980 - 1989
Pounds, Glenn 1967 - 1997
Pounds, Shirley 1968 - 1994
Powell, Bill 1958 - 1980
Price, Paul 1992 - 1998
Puente, James 1992 - 1995
Pults, Carolyn 1970
Prestwood, Clyde 1958 - 1961
Raines, Jo 1984 - 1995
Ramos, Elizabeth 1966 - 1967
Ramsey, Clint 1969 - 1982
Ray, Billy Joe 1981 - 1984
Reding, Roger 1987 - 1990
Reeder, Clayton Wayne 1992 - 1997
Reichle, Helen 1986 - 1987
Reid, Melanie 1982 - 1986
Rice, Larry 1978 - 1985
Rice, Tonie D. 1992 - 1994
Rich, William 1978 - 1980
Richards, Bill 1968 - 1991
Risley, Charles 1997
Roach, Glenn 1977 - 1983
Roberdeau, George 1962 - 1965
Roberts, Don 1967 - 1970
Roberts, Gerald (Jerry) 1976 - 1996

Roberts, Helen 1967 - 1994
Roberts, Larry 1967 - 1993
Robertson, Linda 1993 - 1995
Robinson, Bobby Ray 1969 - 1972
Robinson, Burett Presley (B. P. - Robbie) 1968 - 1986
Robinson, Mary 1968-1978
Robinson, William 1960 - 1970
Rocha, Michael 1984 - 1985
Rogers, Robert Mark 1978 - 1985
Rodgers, Jimmie 1984 - 1995
Rodriguez, Danny 1975 - 1977
Roe, Frances Sue 1991 - 1994
Rooker, Mary 1978 - 1989
Rose, Martha 1994
Rosson, Kyle 1986 - 1989
Rowe, Sharon Kay 1977 - 1978
Roysden, Robert 1981 - 1982
Rucker, Howard 1979 - 1980
Rush, Sandra 1983 - 1987
St. Clair, Robert 1989 - 1993
Sanders, Melissa 1987 - 1988
Sanders, Wendell 1977 - 1981
Sappington, Thomas 1958
Scarborough, Annette 1990 - 1994
Schaffer, Stephen 1985 - 1987
Schneider, Carl 1987 - 1989
Schuknecht, David 1980
Schwantz, Gary 1989 - 1993
Seago, Barbara 1992 - 1993
Seidletz, Mark 1988 - 1989
Selman, Thomas 1969 - 1973
Sexton, Kelly, Ph.D. 1991 - 1993
Shea, Mary 1968 - 1979
Shewmake, Hollis 1972 - 1977
Shires, Wilma 1991 - 1992
Shockey, Marion D. (Dan) 1977 - 1981
Siers, Laura Kasischke 1987 - 1988
Simmons, Russell 1994 - 1995
Simmons, Willie 1976 - 1980
Skinner, Byron 1978 - 1981
Smith, Billy 1987 - 1990
Smith, Jean 1991 - 1993
Smith, Guy 1991 - 1992
Smith, Kelli 1990 - 1996
Smith, Roger Mae 1958 - 1968
Smothers, Vernon H. 1977
Snyder, Kimbal 1991 - 1992
Snodgrass, Bill 1973 - 1976
Southerland, Dennis 1983 - 1985
Spencer, Thomas, Ph.D. 1957 - 1961
Spurgeon, Kenneth 1990 - 1992
St. John, Shirley 1980 - 1989
Stanley, David 1965 - 1987

Stanley, Jackie 1988
Stephens, James 1978 - 1982
Stewart, John 1978
Stone, Wylodene 1981 - 1987
Stoughton, Fred 1958 - 1959
Stovall, Connie 1988 - 1989
Strange, Joe 1987 - 1994
Strickland, Jim 1978 - 1989
Stroud, Don 1958 - 1988
Stroud, Joan 1966 - 1968
Sturgess, Amber 1992 - 1994
Sullender, Rohlin 1979 - 1984
Sundre, Elizabeth (Beth) 1983 - 1995
Sundre, Orlo A., Ph.D. 1983 - 1995
Sweiven, Edris Ann 1966 - 1967
Sylvester, Charles, Ph.D. 1958 - 1974
Symons, Susan 1990 - 1994
Tallman, Jeffery 1994 - 1995
Taaffe, Thomas 1968 - 1969
Tabor, Fred 1988 - 1990
Tarr, Kent 1985
Taylor, Bob 1968 - 1969
Taylor, Leesa 1980 - 1988
Thacker, John 1989
Thomman, Connie 1988 - 1993
Tichenor, Annie 1992 - 1994
Tidwell, Billy 1989 - 1990
Tiger, Miller 1984 - 1988
Tipton, Emmitt 1976 - 1983
Todd, Lisa 1990 - 1992
Toomire, Mary Jo 1980 - 1982
Travis, D. E. (Buddy) 1970 - 1974
Treadway, Betty 1966 - 1993
Trice, Eddie 1975 - 1980
Tubb, Nathan 1958 - 1981
Tucker, Gary 1982 - 1985
Tunstall, Paul (Ken) 1986 - 1992
Turner, Karen 1986 - 1995
Turner, Kathleen 1980 - 1981
Turpen, Bernadyne 1966 - 1969
Van Burkleo, Robert 1964
Vandertuin, Chris 1992 - 1995
Vaughan, Jeanette 1990 - 1991
Velez, Roy 1988 - 1989
Vera, Otto 1991 - 1993
Walker, Richard 1985 - 1996
Walker, Timothy 1972 - 1973
Walker, W. L. (Hi) 1961 - 1981
Waltrip, Royce 1960 - 1981
Wamsley, Mary 1991
Wannamaker, Gordon 1978 - 1980
Warren, Ted 1978 - 1979
Warren, Troy 1976 - 1977
Watkins, Frances 1959 - 1979

Watson, Cheryl 1990 - 1993
Watson, Connie 1995 - 1997
Watson, Dawn 1991 - 1994
Webb, Frank 1988 - 1990
Webb, Wallace 1968 - 1975
Weems, Richard 1980 - 1983
Wheeler, Margaret 1982 - 1984
Wheeler, Wilburn 1958 - 1974
White, Bruce 1996 - 1997
White, Kelton 1985 - 1989
Whitley, Jeff 1989 - 1994
Wid, Larry 1989 - 1991
Wiley, Larry Don 1966 - 1977
Willis, Byron 1980 - 1981
Wilkerson, Martha 1967 - 1968
Williamson, Kim 1981 - 1993
Wilson, Charles 1984 - 1987
Wise, W. A. 1966 - 1994
Wiswall, Marlyn 1961 - 1967
Wood, Gwyneth 1967 - 1987
Wood, Marylea 1966 - 1967
Wood, Richard 1965 - 1967
Wyatt, Jimmy 1962 - 1967
Wyatt, Joan 1994 - 1995
Wynn, Gary 1966 - 1996
Yates, John 1963 - 1967
Yeary, James 1965 - 1970
Young, Mariluz 1992
Young, Wayne 1976 - 1980
Young, Raymond 1985 - 1986
Zeller, Julie 1981 - 1982

Student Organization Sponsors, 1959

From the college's beginning, student organizations have played an important part of the institution's history. The September 1959 Faculty Handbook listed the following active student organizations and faculty sponsors. Faculty were assigned by President Thomas Spencer to guide and advise the organizations. Faculty and students were instructed to consult the "Activity Calendar" in the Dean's Office for time and place of meetings.

Agriculture Club .... Earl Gerstenberger
Athletic Council .... Bill Powell
Baptist Student Union .... Inez Grant
Caprock Staff .... Robert Burks
Cheerleaders and Pep Club .... Myrtle Lucke
Circle K Club .... Henry Lucke
College Chorus .... Harley Bulls
Drama Club .... L.A. Kendrick
Freshman Class .... Arthur A. Dawson
Future Business Leaders of America .... M.J. Knowles
Future Teachers of America .... Roger Mae Smith
Koshare .... Myrtle Lucke
Lutheran Students Association .... John Christmas
Methodist Club .... Nathan Tubb
Newman Club .... Frances Watkins
Plainsman Band .... W.R. Wheeler
Plainsman Staff .... Deane Burks
Phi Rho Pi.. L.A. Kendrick
Phi Theta Kappa .... Rose Marie Pilcher
Rodeo Club .... Earl Gerstenberger, Clyde Prestwood
Science Club.. Robert Beck
Sophomore Class... Don Appling
Student Council .... Charles Sylvester, Clyde Prestwood
South Plains Music Club.. Harley Bulls
TexAnns .... Rose Marie Pilcher

South Plains College Enrollment
Semester-Hour Credit Students
Fall 1958 - Fall 1997

South Plains College's enrollment has expanded 12-fold in the past 40 years. This table presents fall enrollments based upon the unduplicated headcount of students enrolled in semester-hour credit courses as reported to the Texas Higher Education Coordinating Board. Missing from this enrollment data are students who were enrolled in certain clock-hour programs such as vocational nursing, cosmetology, surgical technology and welding. The Coordinating Board has traditionally counted these students separately for funding purposes.

Date	Enrollment	Date	Enrollment
1958	536	1978	2,731
1959	431	1979	2,760
1960	473	1980	2,840
1961	509	1981	2,955
1962	610	1982	3,200
1963	682	1983	3,451
1964	788	1984	3,532
1965	1,103	1985	3,405
1966	1,366	1986	3,517
1967	1,441	1987	4,044
1968	1,641	1988	4,302
1969	1,600	1989	4,667
1970	1,812	1990	5,009
1971	1,685	1991	5,416
1972	1,738	1992	5,861
1973	1,750	1993	5,763
1974	2,010	1994	5,760
1975	2,493	1995	5,652
1976	2,418	1996	5,701
1977	2,469	1997	6,217

Source: Reports to the Texas Higher Education Coordinating Board

Growth of the
South Plains College Physical Plant

As enrollment has grown, so has the college's physical plant. SPC's Levelland Campus has grown from five original buildings to a modern college campus comprised of 39 buildings valued at more than $55 million. The Lubbock Campus is valued at more than $4 million. This historic timeline charts the physical growth of SPC.

1957   Hockley County voters established South Plains College and elected a Board of Regents in April. A $900,000 bond issue to build a college campus in Levelland was approved in July. Construction of the campus began in December.

1958   Original campus opened with five new buildings: Administration Building, Auditorium, Agriculture Shop, Library Building and Gymnasium/Student Union Building. The President's Home was also completed.

1959   Work began on the SPC Track which was completed in early 1960.

1960   Three campus residence halls were constructed: Frazier Hall, Sue Spencer Hall and Stroud Hall. A residence for the administrative dean was also completed.

1961   Forrest Hall was completed.

1963   District voters approved a $690,000 bond issue for construction of the Physical Science Building and Agriculture Building and additions to the Student Union Building, Library, Auditorium and Gymnasium.

1964   The Physical Science and Agriculture Buildings were completed. Texan Hall was added to the Student Union Building. A wing to house music and art classes was added to the Auditorium and named the Fine Arts Building. A business office wing was added to the Administration Building. The original Agriculture Shop became the Maintenance Shop.

1965   District voters approved a $1,750,000 bond issue for construction of the Technical Arts Center, the Texan Dome, a new three-floor Library, Biological Sciences Building, and additions to the Student Union Building and Fine Arts Building.

1966   Three additional campus residence halls were completed: Lamar Hall, Magee Hall and Gillespie Hall. The Fine Arts Building was expanded to include a band hall and additional art studios and classrooms. The original Library Building was connected to the Student Union Building with new construction.

1967   Texan Dome and a new SPC Library were completed. The original gymnasium was renamed the Women's Gymnasium.

1968   Biological Science Building and Technical Arts Center were completed. The old Library was remodeled into expanded facilities for the Student Center, including the installation of a four-lane bowling alley. A Welding Shop was constructed south of the Agriculture Building.

1970   South Plains College established an extension program at Reese Air Force Base. A greenhouse facility was added to the Biological Science Building.

1971   The Automotive-Diesel Mechanics Building was completed. Tennis courts were constructed south of the Women's Gymnasium.

1972   The Natatorium and Animal Science Center were completed.

1973   South Plains College opened an extension center at Lubbock, leasing a small office at 2402 Ave. Q, and conducted classes in Lubbock high schools.

1974   South Plains College opened an extension center in Plainview. The Regional Occupational Training Center was opened on the campus of Wayland Baptist College.

1975   Marvin Baker Center was constructed, connecting all three women's residence halls into one complex. Additional tennis courts and handball courts were constructed south of the Library.

1977   South Plains College received a $2,000,000 federal economic development grant to convert the old West Texas Hospital building into a vocational branch campus. Renovation of the building began that year.

1978   South Plains College opened its Lubbock Campus building at 1302 Main Street.

1979   The Maintenance Building was constructed.

1980   The campus' original Maintenance Shop Building was renovated into the Country and Bluegrass Music Building. The Student Assistance Center opened on the third floor of the Library Building. The Auditorium was renovated and renamed the Theatre for the Performing Arts.

1981   District voters approved a $5,500,000 bond issue for modernization and renovation of all campus buildings. The proposal called for the construction of the Petroleum Technology/Law Enforcement Building, the Metals Technology Building and Welding Technology Building, extensive renovation of the Student Center, and remodeling and additions to nine other buildings. The Smallwood Apartment Complex was completed and opened on campus. The Metals Technology Building was completed.

1982   Remodeling and expansion of the Administration Building was completed.

1983   The Welding Technology Building was completed, and the old Welding Shop was converted into the Mass Communications Building. Renovation of the Student Center was completed. An annex to Texan Dome housing athletic offices and racquetball courts was completed. The fly-loft and a scenery shop was added to the Theatre for the Performing Arts and the resulting fine arts complex was named the Creative Arts Building. New construction joined the Physical and Biological Sciences Buildings to house the Mathematics Department and the science greenhouse facilities were expanded. The complex was named the Mathematics and Science Building. The Technical Arts Center was completely remodeled. The Petroleum Technology/Law Enforcement Technology Building was opened.

1984   The old band hall was converted into classroom and instructional facilities for a new cosmetology program. The Auto-Diesel Shop was expanded. The President's Home on campus was remodeled into the Visitors Center.

1986   The Country and Bluegrass Music Building was expanded with the construction of a video and sound studio, faculty offices, and classrooms.

1987   The Tom T. Hall Recording and Production Center in the Country and Bluegrass Music Building was dedicated.

1989   New construction joined the old Agriculture Building to the Mass Communications Building. The new facility was named the Communications-Mathematics Building. The Creative Arts Building housing theatre, art and music was renamed the Fine Arts Building, and the Country and Bluegrass Music Building was renamed the Creative Arts Building. The original Science Building was renamed the Agriculture and Science Building.

1991   The indoor firing range in the Petroleum Technology/Law Enforcement Building was expanded. A classroom-lab annex was added to the Agriculture and Science Building. Additional rehearsal classrooms were added to the Creative Arts Building and Fine Arts Building. New construction joined the Auto-Diesel Mechanics Building and the Welding Technology Building to house the electronics service technology program.

1992   The Mathematics and Engineering Building was constructed. South Plains College received a gift of property from the Dr. Clifford Payne Sr. estate. The former health clinic located at 2416 6th Street in Lubbock was converted into a workforce training center.

1997   South Plains College and the Lubbock Independent School District opened the Byron Martin Advanced Technology Center in Lubbock.

SOUTH PLAINS COLLEGE
Levelland Campus

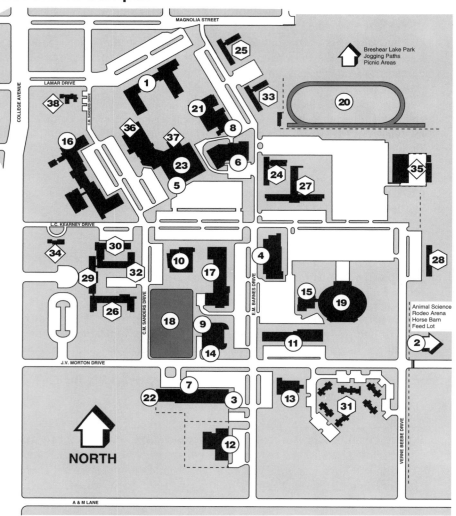

Key to Campus Buildings

● INSTRUCTIONAL BUILDINGS
1. Administration Building
2. Animal Science Building
3. Auto - Diesel Shop
4. Communications and English Building
5. Cosmetology
6. Creative Arts Building
7. Electronics Service Technology
8 Fine Arts Building
9. Law Enforcement Building
10. Library
11. Math and Engineering Building
12. Metals Technology Building
13. Natatorium
14. Petroleum Technology Building

15. Racquetball Courts
16. Science and Agriculture Building
17. Technical Arts Center
18. Tennis Courts
19. Texan Dome
20. Texan Track
21. Theater for the Performing Arts
22. Welding Technology Building
23. Women's Gym

● RESIDENCE HALLS
24. Forrest Hall
25. Frazier Hall
26. Gillespie Hall

27. Lamar Hall
28. Magee Hall
29. Marvin Baker Center
30. N. Sue Spencer Hall
31. Smallwood Apts.
32. S. Sue Spencer Hall
33. Stroud Hall

◆ NON-INSTRUCTIONAL FACILITIES
34. Dean's Residence
35. Maintenance Building
36. Student Center
37. Texan Hall
38. Visitors Center

280

Sources

Interviews

Interviews were conducted with the following individuals during the research for the SPC history. Video and audio tapes of the interviews are stored with the college's archival records.

Aguilar, Robert, November 20, 1998
Alexander, Bill, March 6, 1998
Appling, Don, February 13, 1998
Baker, Marvin, Ph.D., October 22, 1997
Beck, R.E. (Bob), May 15, 1998
Bell, Paula, February 11, 1998
Ballew, Guy, January 28, 1998
Blakeley, Hazel, May 6, 1998
Bollinger, Irma, February 4, 1998
Brown, Bob, April 19, 1998
Bryant, Judy, April 15, 1998
Bulls, Anne, February 28, 1998
Bulls, Harley, February 28, 1998
Burks, Bob, November 30, 1998
Burks-Espensen, Deanne, April 8, 1998
Carroll, James, May 8, 1998
Carr, Nancy, May 6, 1998
Costin, Davie Mac, February 6, 1998
Crossland, Don, February 15, 1998
Dawson, Arthur, January 13, 1998
Dickson, John, April 22, 1998
Durham, David, April 22, 1998
Edwards, Barbara, February 6, 1998
Floyd, "Lucky," Harold, April 22, 1998
Gardner, Albutt, March 25, 1998
George, Jesse T., February 18, 1998
Gerstenberger, Earl, October 10, 1998
Grant, Gary, February 10, 1998
Grimes, Darrell, March 25, 1998
Harp, Dennis, April 26, 1998

Hunt, Frank, December 5, 1997
Ingraham, Margaret, January 3, 1999
Jackson, Frederick, February 9, 1998
Joyner, Bud, Ed.D., April 3, 1998
Keeling, Bruce, D.M.A., March 25, 1998
Knight, Karen, March 6, 1998
Lowrie, Lavoid, February 25, 1998
Lucke, Henry, January 12, 1998
Lucke, Myrtle, January 12, 1998
Malaise, Dub, April 13, 1998
Marcom, O.W., Ph.D., October 3, 1998
Mayberry, Ron, April 27, 1998
McClellan, Danny, January 31, 1998
McCullough, Parker, J.D., February 4, 1998
McDaniel, Gary, Ph.D., October 24, 1997
Motheral, Mike, May 7, 1998
Nicholas, Gayle, March 2, 1998
Nowlin, Jack, March 11, 1998
O'Connor, Lynn, January 28, 1998
Patton, Dennis, February 2, 1998
Pearce, Robert, April 20, 1998
Permenter, Jeanelle, March 3, 1998
Perryman, Dennis, April 24, 1998
Petty, Olen, February 23, 1998
Pierce, Clay, April 3, 1998
Reid, Lynda, March 25, 1998
Roberts, Helen, February 11, 1998
Roberts, Larry, April 20, 1998
Rowell, Betty, April 17, 1998
Rowland, Newlon, April 8, 1998
Silhan, Rene, April 19, 1998
Spencer, Rachel, January 4, 1998
Spencer, Thomas, Jr., Ph.D., Feb. 16, 1998
Squyres, Newell, March 4, 1998
Stacy, J.G., December 17, 1998
Stephenson, Lee Weldon, April 15, 1998
Taylor, James, Ph.D., April 26, 1998

Torrez, Alex, March 25, 1998
Travis, Buddy, April 29, 1998
Tubb, Joe, January 28, 1998
Tubb, Nathan, October 24, 1998
Von Maszewski, Wolfram, January 4, 1998
Walker, William "Hi," February 4, 1998
Walsh, Dick, Ed.D., February 22, 1998
Watson-Nelson, Rachel, May 26, 1998
Wilkes, Jim, April 6, 1998
Wilson, Frank, March 6, 1998
Yarbrough, Donald, February 13, 1998

Contributors

Bridges, Dianne
Ehrenfeld, Charles
Foster, Sherley
Glass, Elizabeth
John, Stephen
Lawless, George
Platt, Gail, Ph.D.
Sparks, John
Wilhelm, Jim, Ed.D.

Letters to the author

Lewis, Barbara Bradford
Permenter, Jeanelle
Schlecten, Judy Hendrix
Spencer, Thomas Jr., Ph.D.

Documents

An Evaluation of South Plains College, (Self Study) 1962
Hockley County Clerk, Court Records
South Plains College, Board of Regents, Minutes
Sundown Independent School Board of Trustees, Minutes
Morals Committee Minutes

Newspapers

Levelland Daily Sun News
Lubbock Avalanche-Journal

Consultants, Reviewers and Proofreaders

Jamie Biggers
Harley and Anne Bulls
Jim Blassingame
Frances Bly
Dianne Bridges
Judy Bryant
Ron Carden, Ph.D.
Scott Couch
Mike Felker, Ph.D.
Earl and June Gerstenberger
Elizabeth Glass
Stephen John
Sycily Lattimore
Vicki Lawler
Glenn and Shirley Pounds
Shirley Prothro
Randy Rowan, Ph.D.
Lee Weldon Stephenson
Judy Stocks
Nathan Tubb
Dick Walsh, Ed.D.
Dianne Whisenand

INDEX

A number of individuals assisted with compiling the index for this publication. The author gratefully acknowledges the following individuals: Julie S. Baiza, Nanette Blair, Carolyn Boles, Sherri Caddell, Leannah Darr, Sue Dozier, Lou Ann Ellison, Dr. Mike Felker, Beth Franklin, Kaye Frazier, Robbie Gage, Betty Geisler, Jennette Grisby, Betty Hendrickson, Tammy Marlar, Linda McCulloch, Betty McWilliams, Ginger Mulloy, Billie Noel, Sherra Pruitt, Dorothy Riley, Carolyn Rollwitz, DeeLaine Ruiz, Elaine Stout and Linda Young.

During Dr. Marvin Baker's 33-year tenure as president, every Texas governor visited the SPC Levelland Campus at one time or another. Former Texas Gov. Ann Richards made a campaign stop at the campus in May 1994 and posed for this photo with Dr. Baker prior to his retirement in July.

The South Plains College Faculty Women's Club was an active organization on campus. In 1973, club officers were *(left to right)* Jo Raines, Shirley Pounds, Jean Bowman and Donna Pohl.

L

From South Plains College's inception, the SPC Cheerleaders have been an active spirit organization on campus. They were a separate organization from the dance group known as the Tex-Anns. In 1979, the two groups were merged into the dance and tumbling group that is known as the Texan Cheerleaders. In this fall semester 1968 photograph, members of the Cheerleaders included *(front row from left)* Lynda Packard of Springlake, Lynda Streiff of Levelland, Donna Hoffman of Morton, Kathie Barton of Brownfield, *(back row from left)* Karen Phillips of Sundown, Gayla Olson of Levelland and Jeanette Childs of Morton.

Following his highly successful teaching career at Brownfield High School, Burl Cole joined the SPC Art Department in 1968. Cole and fellow art instructor Don Stroud left a lasting legacy in Levelland with their mosaic artwork that decorates numerous buildings in the city. Their most visible mosaic adorns the Hockley County Library building and depicts the education of Hockley County school children and the agriculture and oil industries of the county. Cole was a devotee of the artistry of the Mogollon and Anasazi Indian cultures of the Southwestern United States. Cole retired from the SPC faculty in 1976.

Jim Cooper, Ph.D. began his association with the South Plains College English Department in 1970. He taught grammar, rhetoric, literature and philosophy until his death in 1987. In addition, Cooper sponsored the *Plainsman Press* for several years during his teaching career. His wife, Glenna Cooper, taught anatomy and physiology in the Science Department from 1969 to 1990. A scholar on the works of Jack London, his friendly smile and compassionate demeanor endeared him to students and faculty.

SPC's instructional strength has been attributed to the dedication and longevity of master teachers and staff who established distinguished careers in education. In 1993, eight long-time employees retired from service at the college. Their combined service records encompassed 211 years at SPC. The largest group of employees to retire at any one time, they included *(from left)* Polly Parmer, botany; Sherley Foster, counseling; June Gerstenberger, business office; Betty Treadway, English; Jeanelle Permenter, physical education; Larry Roberts, physical education; Lunette Dickson, business administration; and John Dickson, business office.

Dianne Bridges began her educational career at South Plains College in 1970, teaching courses in business machines, typing and business mathematics. In 1993, she became chairperson of the Business Administration Department after the retirement of Lunette Dickson. Bridges, a West Texas State University graduate, jointly sponsored the Office Education Association with Dickson during much of the 1970s and 1980s.